BREAKING THE BOWLS

Contemporary Societies Series

Jeffrey C. Alexander, Series Editor

Andrew Abbott   *Methods of Discovery: Heuristics for the Social Sciences*

Judith Lorber   *Breaking the Bowls: Degendering and Feminist Change*

Douglas Massey   *Strangers in a Strange Land: Humans in an Urbanizing World*

Michael Schudson   *The Sociology of News*

Steven Seidman   *The Social Construction of Sexuality*

Bryan Turner   *The New Medical Sociology: Social Forms of Health and Illness*

Forthcoming

Craig Calhoun   *The Public Sphere*

Arne Kalleberg   *The Mismatched Worker*

Saskia Sassen   *A Sociology of Globalization*

Mike Shanahan   *The Life Course*

David Snow and Sarah Soule   *A Primer on Social Movements*

BREAKING THE BOWLS

Degendering and Feminist Change

Judith Lorber

GRADUATE SCHOOL AND BROOKLYN COLLEGE,
CITY UNIVERSITY OF NEW YORK

CONTEMPORARY SOCIETIES
Jeffrey C. Alexander
SERIES EDITOR

 W. W. NORTON & COMPANY ☉ NEW YORK LONDON

W. W. Norton & Company has been independent since its founding in 1923, when William Warder Norton and Mary D. Herter Norton first published lectures delivered at the People's Institute, the adult education division of New York City's Cooper Union. The Nortons soon expanded their program beyond the Institute, publishing books by celebrated academics from America and abroad. By mid-century, the two major pillars of Norton's publishing program—trade books and college texts—were firmly established. In the 1950s, the Norton family transferred control of the company to its employees, and today—with a staff of four hundred and a comparable number of trade, college, and professional titles published each year—W. W. Norton & Company stands as the largest and oldest publishing house owned wholly by its employees.

Composition by PennSet, Inc.
Manufacturing by Quebecor World—Fairfield Division.
Production manager: Benjamin Reynolds.
Series design by Beth Tondreau Design.

Library of Congress Cataloging-in-Publication Data
Lorber, Judith.
    Breaking the bowls : degendering and feminist change / Judith Lorber.
    p. cm. — (Contemporary societies)
    Includes bibliographical references and index.

ISBN 0-393-97325-5 (pbk.)

    1. Sex role. 2. Sex discrimination against women. 3. Social structure.
4. Social status. 5. Equality. 6. Feminism. I. Title. II. Series.

HQ1075.L666 2005
305.3—dc22

                                                        2005040528

W. W. Norton & Company, Inc., 500 Fifth Avenue, New York, NY 10110-0017
www.wwnorton.com

W. W. Norton & Company Ltd., Castle House,
75/76 Wells Street, London W1T 3QT

1 2 3 4 5 6 7 8 9 0

In Memory of Dafna Nundi Izraeli, *z˝l*
(September 9, 1937–February 21, 2003)
*My dear friend and colleague who dared
to think the impossible*

CONTENTS

ACKNOWLEDGMENTS   ix

INTRODUCTION   xi

CHAPTER ONE   Framing the Issues:
                   Gender Theory and Degendering   3

CHAPTER TWO   No More Mothers and Fathers:
                   Degendering Parenting   39

CHAPTER THREE   Workers Have Families:
                   Degendering the Workplace   69

CHAPTER FOUR   Heroes, Warriors, and Burqas:
                   Gender after September 11   102

CHAPTER FIVE   Paradoxes of Gender Identity:
                   Strategies of Feminist Politics   130

CHAPTER SIX   A World without Gender:
                   Making the Revolution   151

EPILOGUE: What Degendering Does to the
                   Components of Gender   171

NOTES   177

INDEX   213

ACKNOWLEDGMENTS

My THANKS GO to Stephen Dunn for suggesting my inclusion in the Contemporary Societies series and to Melea Seward for her supportive and astute editorial critique. In the course of numerous presentations and publications, much of the material in this book has benefited from the critical input of listeners and reviewers in Israel and Germany, as well as at international conferences in other parts of the world and numerous venues in the United States. Maren Carden, Carolle Charles, Susan A. Farrell, Eileen Moran, and Barbara Katz Rothman deserve particular thanks for reading the early versions of these presentations and publications. I thank Rachel Burr and Barbara Katz Rothman for their critiques of the parenting chapter and Patricia Yancey Martin for her critique of the work chapter. Salvador Vidal-Ortiz generously provided many articles on transgendering. I also thank Phyllis Holman Weisbard, Women's Studies Librarian at the University of Wisconsin, Madison, for tracking down the source of the Stanislaw Lem story.

An early reader of *Paradoxes of Gender* told me that she thought that by the end of that book, I would lay out solutions to the detrimental effects of gendering I had described. After many years of thinking about how to answer her, I offer in this book my ideas of how to degender parenting, workplaces, and politics.

Dafna Izraeli, z'l, to whose memory this book is dedicated, was for over twenty-five years a sounding board for and challenger of my ideas and theories about women, men, and gender. I wish she could have lived to critique this book.

New York City, September 2004

PARTS OF THIS BOOK have been adapted from my recently published papers and professional presentations: "Heroes, Warriors, and Burqas: A Feminist Sociologist's Reflections on September 11," *Sociological Forum* 17 (2002): 377–96 (presidential address, Eastern Sociological Society, Boston, March 2002); "Gender Regimes and Gender Politics: Reflections on September 11 and After," *Kvinder, køn, & forskning* [Women, Gender, & Research] 3 (2003): 51–62; "Paradoxes of Gender Identity and Feminist Politics" (keynote address, "Women's Worlds 2002," Eighth International Interdisciplinary Congress on Women, Kampala, Uganda, July 2002); "It's the 21st Century—Do You Know What Gender You Are?" in *International Feminist Challenges to Theory,* Advances in Gender Research, vol. 5, ed. Vasilikie Demos and Marcia Texler Segal (Greenwich, Conn.: JAI Press, 2001); "Using Gender to Undo Gender: A Feminist Degendering Movement," *Feminist Theory* 1 (2000): 101–18; review of *Halving It All: How Equally Shared Parenting Works,* by Francine M. Deutsch, *Society* 37 (September–October 2000): 92–94; "Crossing Borders and Erasing Boundaries: Paradoxes of Identity Politics," *Sociological Focus* 32 (1999): 355–69; "Beyond the Binaries: Depolarizing the Categories of Sex, Sexuality, and Gender," *Sociological Inquiry* 66 (1996): 143–59.

INTRODUCTION

. . . to create a new way of looking at life
—Doris Lessing[1]

FOR THE PAST TEN YEARS, I have had a bifurcated vision of gender. One eye sees gender everywhere, organizing personal lives, emotions, intimate relationships and friendships, sexuality, procreation, bodies, families, workplaces, the global economy, politics—the whole social world. This vision of how gender constructs the social world was laid out in *Paradoxes of Gender,* where I argued that gender's power and ubiquity make it a social institution—a structure produced and maintained by widespread, deeply embedded practices, legitimated by rarely questioned beliefs and values.[2] As a social institution, gender makes one category of people subordinate to the other. I concluded that if we are to do away with gender inequality, either the genders must be made scrupulously equal, or gender must no longer be a major social category for the allocation of social status. But both visions—perfect gender equality and worlds without gender—seemed to be science fiction.

Since the publication of *Paradoxes* in 1994, I have, in a series of papers, looked at the world with an eye that fragments gender, seeing gender statuses and identities cut up by other important social statuses—national, racial ethnic, religious, so-

cial class, economic, and by personal differences of body, sexual
orientation, coupling, parenting, occupation.[3]

As multicultural and postmodern feminists of the 1990s
have discussed, gender cannot be a unitary theoretical concept,
and the oppression of women cannot be a homogeneous political rallying cry.[4] Feminist studies of men have examined the
nuances of patriarchal privilege and dominance.[5] The concepts
of *matrices of domination* and *complex inequality* have laid out the
multiple, intertwined sources of structural inequality, each
subordinate social status feeding on the other, exploitation in
public arenas spilling over into private life.[6] At the top of
Western societies is the heterosexual, married (sometimes
much-married) White man, owner of capital, inheritor of property, graduate of the best schools, father of several children,
monopolizing most of the positions of world power, and at the
bottom, the woman of color, single mother, poorly educated,
unemployed, immigrant, from a family with no capital or
property, often with no home, living on welfare, scavenging,
begging, or engaging in sex work, infected with HIV. And in
between? The rest of us, privileged and disadvantaged to varying degrees.

Where is *gender* in this web of dominance and subordination? Paradoxically, it still exerts an enormous organizing, socializing, and discriminatory power. Rather than disappearing,
gender intersects with all the other social processes of family,
work, culture, and political power. The person at the top of the
social ladder is a man; the person at the bottom is a woman.
Gender may be fragmenting, but it still permeates the structure of the social order.[7] Part of the reason for its stability is
that it is codified by laws, like the economy and the family,

Western society's other main institutions (both of which are gendered). Since the advent of the second wave of feminism, many laws have degendered workplaces. Currently, degendering is the source of the battle over gay marriage. But gender is still a legal and bureaucratic identity for life. Changing gender as a personal status must be done legally.

In personal terms, gender still asserts its effects throughout life—prenatally, if fetuses are aborted because they are female, and after death, if women's corpses are buried differently from men's. Psychologically, gender permeates our individual sense of self. Socially, gender organizes almost every aspect of our daily lives. Its legal and bureaucratic status is a powerful source of social control, determining where and how people are educated and trained for occupations and professions, how jobs and salaries are allocated, who can participate in the political process and wield power, how child care and other family responsibilities are distributed, and many other aspects of life determined by state gender regimes.

Feminists have long called for an end to gendered practices that maintain gender inequality. These countermeasures to the effects of gender are now termed undoing gender. I am saying that it is gender itself that has to be dismantled. It is the bureaucratic, structural, and allocational aspects of gender that I am attacking in this book. I am arguing for a degendering movement that acknowledges the continuing power of gender but looks for ways of dismantling it in the family and the workplace, the areas most significant for our daily lives. Politically, gender is already sliced up by so many other social statuses that a unitary politics of gender identity is virtually impossible. During times of disaster and war, when traditional gender roles seem comforting, people still exhibit unconventional gender behavior. These complexities and multiplicities of gender, I argue, are wedges to weaken gender's power over our lives and challenges to gender as a social institution. Ultimately, gender as a social status may become irrelevant. If it is no longer a mandatory legal status, its power as a social institution will fade.

Degendering is not gender neutrality—ignoring the discriminatory processes and effects of differential treatment of women and men. It goes further than "mainstreaming" or countering the effects of gendering. Degendering is heading off those effects by not gendering in the first place. I am arguing that by treating people as a conglomeration of status positions, characteristics, attitudes, and behavior, we can undermine gendering, which is creating two opposing groups out of diverse people and treating them as if each group were all the same on status positions, characteristics, attitudes, and behavior. It is not enough to say that each group is as good as the other; nor, once the distinction has been made, can each group be treated the same as the other. The very effort of dividing and discriminating between them invites comparisons of good or bad. Cultural devaluation, long-standing stereotypes, the power to bias judgments, and the insidious effects of putting these unexplored assumptions into practice in the family, the workplace, the media, and politics systematically diminish one of the groups. If the goal is equality among diverse humans, why separate them into differentiated legal statuses in the first place?

Degendering is not a prescription for utopia. It will not right most of the wrongs of the world. Indeed, it might seem like a foolish fantasy to pursue when there are people starving in a world of plentiful food, working in globalized sweatshops, dying of preventable diseases, and being killed in wars and by terrorists. But if developed and undeveloped countries alike can buy arms, build nuclear weapons, and send expensive equipment and highly trained astronauts to Mars and the moon while their citizens are starving and dying, then feminists can consider a degendering movement. If we have to wait for world peace and prosperity to create the conditions for true gender equality, we'll be waiting until the sun implodes.

PLAN OF THE BOOK

Chapter 1, "Framing the Issues: Gender Theory and Degendering," lays out the premises of degendering and its place in uses of gender. I argue for a focus on degendering family, work, and politics rather than individual rebellion because gender is primarily an organizing principle of social practices and processes. These gender practices divide people into two and only two categories or social statuses ("woman," "man") despite their bodily, sexual, and racial ethnic heterogeneity. Gendered processes of allocation and training parcel out to women and men different educational opportunities, jobs, family responsibilities, and authority. It is this legal, bureaucratic, and socially institutionalized binary gender system that I am challenging with a call for a degendering movement.

The chapter discusses heterogeneity in sex and sexuality, laying out the reasons why they are not barriers to degendering and why transgendering does not do away with gender. It takes up the question of research on gender, suggesting that it is more accurate to use multiple gender categories than to use just two. The chapter ends by laying out the goals of degendering family and work and building on multiplicities in gender regimes and identity politics.

Chapter 2, "No More Mothers and Fathers: Degendering Parenting," shows we can degender a major source of the continuation of the gendered social structure. The supposed biological base of gender locks women into the prime responsibility for child rearing and, by extension, household labor. This gendering is the bedrock of gender as a social institution in modern Western societies, as the gendering of the family justifies the gendering of the paid workplace. Thus, work and family are the arenas that must be structurally degendered for real change to take place in gendered societies.

Degendering parenting is not impossible. In fact, shared parenting between fathers and mothers as well as among women kin—"alloparents"—has been a common survival pattern for much of human history and in many parts of the world. In contemporary U.S. society, studies of egalitarian households show that shared parenting is feasible and that men can parent competently. Other sources of support for the parenting abilities of men are households headed by single men and by homosexual partners. Degendered parenting encourages children to put less emphasis on conforming to the norms of gender they are bombarded with in schools and by peers and the media.

If parenting is to be degendered, then workplaces must be structured to encourage, or at least allow, all parents to devote time to their families without penalizing them as workers. Chapter 3, "Workers Have Families: Degendering the Workplace," argues that paid work and family work are a unit. In much of the postindustrial world, paid workplaces and family residences are separate, but some governments have institutionalized policies that make it possible for both women and men to do paid work and to share family responsibilities as caring citizens.

Where domestic responsibilities are primarily the burden of women, as they are in the United States, workplace practices of inclusion and exclusion discriminate against women trying to combine careers and attention to their families, because they are the workers most unlike full-time, career-oriented men workers. The discourse, practices, and structuring of work organizations and families assume that men's prime family responsibility is to provide economic support and women's to take care of home and children. Without degendering family and work commitments, mothers will continue to make less money, be more likely to be fired, and achieve fewer positions of authority and prestige. Working-class single mothers frequently end up on welfare.

In this chapter, I will explore what is needed to degender the workplace to make degendered parenting possible. First, how we talk about work and workers—the discourse that reflects assumptions and values—needs to change. Second, work practices need to recognize that workers are caretakers, too. Third, work organizations need to structure into their schedules technologically flexible ways of using place and time. Finally, all governments need to recognize the concept of "caring citizenship" that "includes the right to have time to care, to make, on a daily basis, a place for care."[8]

Experimentation with new gender norms requires social stability. Degendering families and workplaces needs time and attention from policy makers and governments. Unfortunately, in periods of upheaval, such as the present, there is little official inclination to support changes in the gender order in much of the Western world. Chapter 4, "Heroes, Warriors, and Burqas: Gender after September 11," describes the way the media depicted gender in the events of September 11, 2001, in the aftermath of the destruction of the World Trade Center, and in the subsequent wars in Afghanistan and Iraq. Cultural representations of gender reflect and shape social values and attitudes. There is a large body of feminist research and criticism on long-term cultural changes and continuities in representations of women and men in art, literature, music, and the mass media.[9] This chapter focuses on a small but dramatic recent period—September 11, 2001 (iconically referred to as "September 11"), the date of the terrorist attack on the World Trade Center, to September 11, 2004, the third anniversary of the event. Its focus is the way gender was symbolically implicated in terrorist acts, the U.S. military, and the Afghan and Iraqi wars.

In the media, blue-collar American men were depicted as heroes and comrades; Middle Eastern men, as religious fundamentalists and suicide bombers. American women were depicted as widows; Middle Eastern women, as oppressed wives veiled in head-to-toe burqas. In actuality, American women were rescuers and brave soldiers, and a few were sexual torturers of prisoners; Middle Eastern women were resisters and feminists, and a few were suicide bombers. For the most part, mainstream media depicted American and Middle Eastern women and men as "good" or "bad" national symbols in response to political ups and downs, military successes and failures, and the violence of terrorism and torture.

I argue that the valorization of conventional gender behavior and the scope of gender diversity through cultural representations and state policies depend on national vulnerability or power. When a nation feels threatened, it reverts to conventional gendering. Degendering, a form of civil disorder, needs a time of political strength or order to form a base from which to make changes. In the meantime, and in preparation for a time of gender change, feminist political action has to work internationally with women and men who have diverse social identifications.

Chapter 5, "Paradoxes of Gender Identity: Strategies of Feminist Politics," discusses the effect on feminist politics of intersecting identities throughout the world. Feminists have despaired as women's movements have broken up over identity politics. But intersecting identities can be a way of degendering, of undercutting the power of gender to structure women's and men's lives. The "borderlands" view offers the possibility of new perspectives and new politics based on panethnic, cross-racial, and transgendered affiliations and coalitions.[10]

Politically, I argue that the best way to use gender to undo gender is through feminist networks in which coalitions of diverse women and men join in knowledge sharing and political action. Grassroots activism tends to be gender-focused and local, but transnational nongovernmental organizations (NGOs) and national and international governing bodies and agencies are loci for degendered and diversity-based political action.

Chapter 6, "A World without Gender: Making the Revolution," addresses the feminist theoretical implications of degendering. Feminists focusing on difference have critiqued the concept of gender for neglecting bodies, sexualities, procreation, and emotions. Standpoint feminism has shown how women's perspectives arise from the gendered division of family work and paid work. Postmodern and multicultural feminists and feminists studying men have attacked the unity of gender as a theoretical concept. Feminist theories of justice have called for attention to gender as a form of inequality different from class or racial ethnic disadvantage.

Degendering is in many ways a logical outcome of the major feminist theories. I am arguing that feminism has to go beyond critiquing the processes of gender inequality and challenge the ubiquitous division of people into two unequally valued categories that undergirds the continual reappearance of gender inequality.

Envisaging a world without gender is thinking about what may be impossible. But the vision itself helps to break the binds of binary thinking. A world completely without gender may be unattainable, but a world without gender all the time is revolutionary. That, to me, is the goal of degendering.

The Epilogue, "What Degendering Does to the Components of Gender," revisits the construction of gender for the society and for the individual as described in *Paradoxes of Gender* and shows the ways they would be changed by degendering.

BREAKING THE BOWLS

Chapter One
FRAMING THE ISSUES: GENDER THEORY AND DEGENDERING

Use what is dominant in a culture to change it quickly.

—Jenny Holzer[1]

I KEEP A FILE of newspaper clippings and articles that I entitle, ironically, "plus ça change." In this file are pieces twenty-five years apart that say the same thing: women are absent from the boards of large corporations and unequally represented in political governing bodies; occupations resegregate when dominant men leave because of worsening work conditions; married women with children at all levels of the workforce have prime responsibility for their family; prostitution pays better than other work for poor women and girls in many countries; abortion may be legal, but access is often blocked or ringed with restrictions.[2]

I also have a file for "progress"—descriptions of women prime ministers of several large countries, the new women CEOs of major corporations, women winners of the Nobel science prizes, women's sports achievements. Most recently, there have been what I call degendering pieces—women athletes playing on men's teams, women astronauts, women in the military on the front lines and flying fighter planes, and even women suicide bombers.

3

Then there are the ambivalent cases—more women with children in the labor force and subsidized parental leave but without equal sharing of child care and housework between women and men household members.[3] There has been some desegregation of occupations, accompanied by a continued glass ceiling on promotions for women in occupations normatively identified as men's work and a glass escalator for men in occupations gender-typed as women's work. Work done mostly by women continues to be devalued in pay and prestige.

In the past 150 years, women's status in the Western world has improved enormously, but the revolution that would make women and men truly equal has not yet occurred. The question that puzzles me is, Why, with regard to gender inequality, the more things change, the more they stay the same? The answer, I suggest, is that gender divisions still deeply bifurcate the structure of modern society, and it is this ubiquitous division of people into two unequally valued categories that undergirds the continually reappearing instances of gender inequality. It is this gendering that needs to be challenged for lasting social change, with the long-term goal of not just minimizing but doing away with binary gender divisions completely.

I argue in this book that it is time to rebel against gender as a social institution—to challenge its categorizations and ascriptive practices. I'm calling for a rebellion against the division of everyone into "women" and "men" and all that is built on that division—gendered work organizations, families, political power, and culture. Feminists have tried to restructure and change the dynamics of interaction between women and men, to redress gender imbalances in politics and control of valued resources, to alter gender-discriminatory social practices, and to challenge the invisibility and "naturalness" of what is taken for granted about women and men. But they have not pushed these agendas to the point of calling for the abolition of gender boundaries and categories, with the goal of doing away with them altogether. I am arguing here that if the gendered structures of social orders are to be dismantled, degendering—legally and bureaucratically, in practices and processes—must be the ultimate feminist goal.

To create a true revolution, you have to confront the dominant discourse. The title of this book, *Breaking the Bowls*, is rooted in kabbalah and is based on a translation of a colloquial Israeli Hebrew phrase, *lo nishbor et hakelim,* a warning against "breaking the dishes," or making an irreparable breach by challenging accepted ideas and ways of doing things. I am saying, "Break the bowls!" To me, *breaking the bowls* is a metaphor for new thinking about gender. I would like to see the genders unified (degendered) as a way of repairing the world.[4]

Breaking the Bowls, although it can be read completely on its own as twenty-first-century gender theory and feminist politics, is a sequel to *Paradoxes of Gender. Paradoxes* laid out the weight of gender as a social institution, arguing that gender is one of the major ways by which human beings organize their lives. *Breaking the Bowls* will show the cracks, anomalies, resistances, and multiplicities that are breaking down the gendered social order in Western postindustrial societies and how we can take the process further by deliberate degendering. My dream is a multiplex society, not a two-sizes-fit-all society—and not a unisex society, either. In that sense, this book takes up where my 1986 paper, "Dismantling Noah's Ark," began and where *Paradoxes* left off:

When we no longer ask "boy or girl?" in order to start gendering an infant, when the information about genitalia is as irrelevant as the color of the child's eyes (but not yet the color of
skin), then and only then will women and men be socially interchangeable and really equal. And when that happens, there
will no longer be any need for gender at all. . . . Free of gender,
race, and class inequality, what might we all be? Perhaps culturally identified women, men, heterosexuals, homosexuals,
citizens of different countries, adherents of different religions,
members of different occupations and professions, birth and social parents, and so on.[5]

How do we get to that point? I suggest that it is by *deliberate
degendering.*

In gendered societies, work, family, and other major areas of
a society are organized by dividing people into two categories,
"men" and "women," and socializing people to fit into those
categories. The categorization of infants into "boys" and "girls"
may originally be based on genitalia, but the systematic allocation of people into gendered positions and the positions themselves are based on socially produced statuses, not bodies. Body
characteristics, including procreative functions, are used by
gendered societies; body characteristics do not create gender
differences. Inequalities emerge through the distribution of
privileges and rewards based on the allocation of social positions by gender, so that men's work is more prestigious and
better paid than work done by women. Child care and domestic work are women's unpaid work, a form of exploitation because they are not rewarded as workers. Unpaid work puts
women into a condition of economic dependency by cutting

out or cutting down on their ability to support themselves and their children. People in gendered societies are persuaded to accept the inequalities by a belief that they emerge from natural differences and divisions, beliefs that are reinforced by culture, the mass media, religions, and knowledge systems. Questioning the status quo and rebellions against gender norms and expectations are suppressed through power, politics, and violence.

Degendering doesn't mean not thinking about gender; rather, it starts with the recognition that gender is a binary system of social organization that creates inequality. Therefore, degendering attacks the structure and process of gender—the division of people into two social statuses and the social construction of what we call the opposites. In methodological terms, degendering is a counterfactual heuristic, posing the challenge of *what if?*[26] I ask, What if we did not divide people by gender? (What would and would not change in a society?) What if we did not divide household tasks and child care by gender? (How do same-gender couples structure family duties?) What if we did not allocate positions in the workforce by gender? (How do organizations of all women or all men allocate their jobs?) What if we did not form personal and group identities by gender? (Don't we all have individualized characteristics and multiple group memberships?)

An easy place to start degendering is to recognize that the two genders are not at all homogeneous categories since they are intersected by other major social statuses—racial ethnic group, social class, national identity, religious affiliation—and by individual variations—such as age, sexual orientation, relational and parental statuses, and physical status. All of these social statuses may or may not be major identities, but when they are, they create multiplicities of gender. Recognizing the complexity of social hierarchies and statuses helps to undercut the strength of the constant gendering that maintains the two-gender structure.

The other important process of degendering—in addition to recognizing gender complexity—is recognizing and building on the similarities of women and men in behavior and thinking and emotions—*blurring the gender boundaries*. We already have women combat pilots, astronauts, and firefighters and men nurses, secretaries, and nursery-school teachers. Such melding of women's and men's work can be expanded into many more workplaces and into the family as well.

In sum, degendering recognizes that any grouping of women and men will be intersected by other major social statuses and that there will be significant overlaps in behavior and attitudes among the women and men of any particular group. Look closely at people and social interaction in modern industrial societies, and you will see that gender is receding. Look closely at social structuring and organizational practices, and gender reappears. For deep-seated change to take place, degendering has to occur at the structural and organizational level as well as at the personal and interactive levels.

TRYING TO UNDO GENDER

In recent years, there have been various attempts to "undo gender," that is, to counteract the insidious effects of gendering. One movement is *mainstreaming*—including an analysis of the potential impact of policy decisions on women and men. Mainstreaming gender may end up ignoring what the policy will do to women and men of different social classes or racial ethnic groups. Another movement is *parity*—ensuring equal numbers of women and men in a group. Parity is usually a goal for political bodies, but its shortcomings can be illustrated by an example from the Israeli army.[7]

In May 2003, students in short-term officer training courses were gender-integrated—equal numbers of women and men were assigned to each unit. They were diverse in academic, marital, and parental status, ethnicity, physical characteristics (height, weight), but these characteristics did not factor into the goal of balance, nor into subsequent evaluations of the students. Despite all the various factors that could affect outcomes on written and physical tests and evaluations of command capabilities, the one comparison factor used over and over—in prescribed tests, evaluations, and informal comments by teachers and the students themselves—was gender, with an idealized masculine model as the comparative touchstone.

The characteristics attributed to the "boys" and "girls" by men and women staff members were, as the outside assessors of the program say, a chaos of gender differences. The staff claimed that the girl students cried, whined, were shoddy, swore constantly, chewed gum, were orderly and organized in their studying but didn't speak up or argue in class the way they did in the women-only courses. The boy students were cleaner, more disciplined, learned better but relied on the girls' note taking, volunteered more, were physically more capable. When the women and men were in separate units and went on marches, each soldier carried an equal load an equal distance. When they were together, the men insisted on carrying heavier loads, and when the women took on some of those loads, the men soon took them back—and then complained bitterly about the women getting away with less strenuous physical tasks. In short, mixing men and women created the conditions for greater gendering than had existed when the students were gender-segregated.

When I was asked by one of the assessors to suggest ways the program could really be gender-integrated, I suggested several degendering practices.[8] The first was to make a rule that on a march everyone carries the same load the same distance and that in the classroom everyone talks at least once and not again until everyone else has had a say. The second was to set up the formal evaluations (written and physical) for comparisons, first by level of education, ethnicity, marital and parental status, height, and weight and only then, by gender. The third suggestion was to forbid verbal comparison by gender in the first month of the course by teachers, students, and commanders. In short, I suggested creating a community without gender as the main organizing principle.

Constant comparisons of women and men are insidious because they assume essential male and female natures. They do not recognize the extent to which masculine and feminine characteristics are situational, interactive, or simply stereotypical. They also fail to see that gender is part of the intersectionality of multiple and simultaneous sources of privilege and disadvantage.[9]

USING GENDER: A CONTINUUM

Degendering fits into a continuum of the ways feminists have used gender to frame research questions and political actions.

Gender visibility attends to the extent to which societies, cultures, groups, and individuals are gendered and how this process comes about and is maintained through the policies and practices of governments, work organizations, educational systems, the media, religions, and other major social sectors. Gender visibility is a corrective to gender neutrality, which is a perspective that ignores gender biases and allows the dominant group to prevail. A major success of feminism in the last thirty-five years has been to make gender visible as a social phenomenon.

Gender balance attempts to redress the small numbers of women in various arenas, particularly in politics and positions of power. It is also used to encourage men to enter formerly all-women professions, such as nursing. Gender balance takes gender visibility to its extreme in that the categories "women" and "men" become the focus of balancing strategies. For example, affirmative action in workplaces and universities and mandated quotas to increase the number of women in government are common gender-balancing policies.[10]

Gender balance presumes that women and men have different views and attitudes and both should be represented. However, the appointment or election of women and men from the same political party shows that they are rarely far apart in their views. A second false assumption is that women and men can be treated as homogeneous categories for purposes of achieving equal numbers. For example, a *New York Times* article talked about how women's colleges that have gone coed have tried to attract men students by upgrading their economics and mathematics courses and building new gyms.[11] My son chose Sarah Lawrence, formerly an all-women's college, because it offered excellent writing courses. He started a thriving alternative newspaper with like-minded men and women friends and never, as far as I know, set foot into the gym. Similarly, classes divided by gender to provide learning atmospheres congenial to boys' and girls' temperaments—supposedly, boisterous versus thoughtful—neglect the thoughtful boys and the boisterous girls.[12]

Gender diversity recognizes that women, men, boys, and girls are not homogeneous groups but intersected by cultures, religions, ethnicities, social class, sexualities, bodies, and other major characteristics. Gender diversity frequently becomes a problem in strategies for achieving gender balance as it becomes evident that balance on gender alone ignores within-gender dominance issues. And because gender, racial ethnic groupings, and social class intersect, there are many people with conflicting statuses—high on some, low on others. Madeleine Albright, for example, was secretary of state but also a woman. When her Jewish heritage was revealed, her high-status identity became even more compromised. People with complex sets of statuses often become "outsiders within" who critique and break up established hierarchies. Thus, African American women debated the feminist goal of simple gender balance, pointing out that the balance had to include racial identity as well; otherwise they would be visible as women but invisible as *Black* women.[13]

Gender freedom has as its goal living outside the binary sex/gender system. Some examples include bisexual men and women who have same-sex and opposite-sex relationships, "pre-op transsexuals" who take hormones to alter some body characteristics but have no intention of undergoing surgical alteration of genitalia, female-to-male (FTM) homosexuals, and male-to-female (MTF) lesbians. Gender rebels attempt to live their lives free of or against the grain of gender norms and expectations, but without concerted political action they cannot change bureaucratic gender rules. Legal gender statuses are particularly restricting to intersexuals (people born with ambiguous genitalia) and transitioning transsexuals who need medical and social services or are incarcerated. Ki Namaste argues that the playful gender rebellions celebrated by queer theory have little relevance for a battered transgendered individual who needs emergency medical care and a shelter and is bounced between being treated as a man and as a woman.[14] Poor trans people and those who are members of disadvantaged racial ethnic groups are the least likely to experience gender freedom. Despite their bravado, gender outlaws and transgender warriors know they are vulnerable to violence and ostracism.[15] Their lives are often focused on survival, not on a gender revolution.

Degendering calls on the so-called gender normals—biological, sexual, and gender "straights"—to make the revolution by becoming gender deviants. It is up to those who practice gender within the basic institutions of a society to start the process of degendering by challenging the binary gender system in work organizations, families, schools, religions, cultural institutions, and politics. Effective degendering would remove only one of the barriers to full equality, but it is one with tentacles in every sphere of social life.

WHY IS IT SO IMPORTANT TO DISMANTLE THE SOCIAL INSTITUTION OF GENDER?

Gender is so deeply embedded in our lives because it is a *social institution*. It creates structure and stability, seeps into the practices of many social roles, has a long history, and is virtually unquestioned.[16] In addition to gender, the basic social institutions are family and kinship, technology and the economy, language and culture, values and religion, power and politics. Modern societies also have systems of law, education, medicine, the military, and mass media. Gender is an intrinsic part of all of these other institutions and systems.

Institutions are ways of doing things that are so longstanding that they are rarely questioned. These entrenched ways may not be the best practices; very often they produce inequalities, conflicts of interest, and severe power differences. But they are so pervasive in a society and learned so early by its members that they seem impervious to change. Nonetheless, institutions change as societies change. A society that transitions from an agrarian economy to an industrial economy goes through a revolution. The institutions that change are technology and the economy, but other institutions, such as the family and the political structure, change as well.

Institutions can also be changed by political movements— one of the most important ideas of modern society. The change from government by royal succession to government by elected officials came about not through evolution but through rebellion and armed conflict. Politics and power underwent major transformations, which were consolidated and reinstitutionalized in carefully constructed constitutions. Slavery was a major European and American economic institution until its abolition in the nineteenth century—another deliberate change that happened only through organized resistance and violent battles. One hundred years later, slavery's heritage in the United States, racial segregation, had to be similarly dismantled.

The institution of gender has certainly evolved in Western

societies; women and men now have *formal* equality in all the major social spheres.[17] No laws prevent women from achieving what they can, and many laws help them do it by preventing discrimination and sexual harassment. More and more countries are ratifying laws to protect women's procreative and sexual rights and to designate rape, battering, and genital mutilation as human rights crimes. Despite formal and legal equality, however, informal discriminatory treatment of women still occurs regularly in Western criminal justice systems, education, the economy, and especially politics. Where gender equality has not significantly penetrated the family, conflicts over who takes care of the children spill over and are exacerbated by gender inequities in the paid job market. Women have not gained the power or economic resources in most Western societies to ensure the structural bases of gender equality, and so their successes can always be undermined by the vicissitudes of the economy, a war, or the resurgence of religious fundamentalism.

Social construction gender theory argues that as a social institution, gender produces two complementary but unequal sets of people—"women" and "men." This binary division bureaucratically overrides individual differences and intertwines with other major social statuses—racial categorization, ethnic grouping, economic class, age, religion, and sexual orientation—to create a complex hierarchical system of dominance and subordination. Gender's thrust is structural in that it orders the processes and practices of a society's major sectors—work, family, politics, law, education, medicine, the military, religion, and culture. Gender also permeates social relationships in families, kinships, friendships, and other informal networks. A gender schema is built into our perceptions of ourselves and the world around us. Gender is a system of power in that it privileges some groups of people and disadvantages others in conjunction with other systems of power (racial categories, ethnicity, social class, and sexual orientation). Gendered thinking and symbolic representations form much of language, art, and other cultural productions. Gender is so intertwined with language that even in English, where only the pronouns are gendered, it is hard to speak of a nongendered God. In some languages, nouns and verbs are gendered, and there are no neutrals.

Gender is constructed and maintained by both the dominants and the oppressed because both ascribe to its values in personality and identity formation and in appropriate masculine and feminine behavior. Gender is hegemonic in that many of its foundational assumptions and ubiquitous processes are deliberately kept invisible, unquestioned, and unexamined. But it starts with the division of people into two—and only two—legal, bureaucratic statuses, and that division is where the gender revolution should start.

DOING GENDER AND CREATING STRUCTURE

The social construction perspective on gender recognizes the equal importance of agency (what people do) and structure (what results from what they do).[18] Gender simultaneously gives individuals status and identities and shapes their everyday behavior and is a significant factor in face-to-face relationships and organizational practices. Each level supports and maintains the others, but—and this is the crucial aspect of gender—the effects of gender work from the top down. As a building block of social orders, gender gets built into organizational structures, floods interactions and relationships, and is a major social status for individuals. Gendered norms and expectations pattern the practices of people in workplaces, in families, groups, and intimate relationships, and in creating individual identities and self-assessments. People's gender conformity supports gendered practices and gender as a social institution; people's gender diversity and deviance challenge it.

The gendered social order, however, is highly resistant to individual challenge. Its power is such that people act in gendered ways based on their position within the gender structure without reflection or question. We "do gender" and participate in its construction once we have learned to take our place as members of a gendered social order. Our gendered practices construct and maintain the gendered social order. Our practices also change it. As the social order changes and as we participate in different social institutions and organizations throughout our lives, our gendered behavior changes.[19]

I am arguing here that we have to go beyond changing gendered practices and modifying the content of the gendered social order to achieve gender equality. To have a gender revolution, we have to challenge the whole institution and its binary divisions.

The binary divisions of gender are deeply rooted in every aspect of social life and social organization in most societies.[20] They remain even as the content changes. The gendered division of work has shifted with changing means of producing food and other goods, which in turn modify patterns of child care and family structures. Gendered power imbalances, which are usually based on the ability to amass and distribute material resources, change with rules about property ownership and inheritance. Men's domination of women has not been the same throughout history and across societies but varies with political, economic, and family structures. In medieval Europe, politically astute aristocratic women, such as Eleanor of Aquitaine, amassed lands, raised armies, and made marriages that gave them considerable power within a patriarchal feudal society.[21] From the fifteenth to eighteenth centuries, women like Elizabeth I of England, Catherine the Great of Russia, and Maria Theresa of Austria inherited thrones in the absence of male heirs in reigning dynasties.[22] In the sense of an underlying principle of how people are categorized and valued, gender is differently constructed throughout the world and throughout history.[23] But the basic principle—a social order built on two sets of different types of people—remains.

At the present time in the Western postindustrial world, the gendered social order persists without much rationale. Women and men have legal equality, supported by a public rhetoric of equal rights and equal responsibilities for family support, household maintenance, and child care, as well as for individual economic independence. The "Mars and Venus" debates over tastes and emotions have morphed into degendered gadgets and metrosexual men with androgynous grooming styles.[24] There are still occasional claims for men's "natural" domination over women and women's "natural" subordination, ostensibly backed by research on brain organization, hormonal input, or personality structure, but these claims are increasingly delegitimized by the presence of women prime ministers, governors, and university presidents.

Unfortunately, the rhetoric and legality of gender equality

mask the underlying structure of gender inequality. Modern machinery and computers even out the discrepancy in physical capabilities between men and women, but jobs are assigned as if upper body strength mattered. Women are often better educated than men, but the postindustrial gendered social order still reproduces gender inequality in the job market and in wage scales.[25] Men can run vacuum cleaners and change diapers, but women are still the main household workers and managers and the primary parents. Heterosexual men still think they have a right to women's bodies and exploit them sexually. Laws made by governments dominated by men restrict women's procreative choices.

Women's presence in the political arena varies widely. In 2003, Finland had a woman premier and a woman president, and 37.5 percent of the members of its one-house parliament were women. Sweden was even better, at 45 percent. In Rwanda, a new democracy, 48.8 percent of the lower house and 30 percent of the upper house were women. In contrast, in the United States, 14.5 percent of the House of Representatives and 14 percent of the Senate were women.[26] In the Scandinavian countries, women's points of view are valued in the political process, and so they are encouraged to run for high office. Many new democracies have structured their constitutions and election systems for gender equality and equal representation, just as they protect the political rights of all disadvantaged religious and ethnic groups. In the United States, gender parity in governing bodies is not a priority, and the political process at the national level is heavily weighted in favor of people with money and still tainted by the idea that women can't lead the country.

The continued gendered division of labor in the job market and in the home creates the conditions for gender inequality. As workers, women are lower paid, but hardworking and responsible even when they are also maintaining a family.[27] They are an advantage to postindustrial economies because they, and not the employer, pay the economic cost of their other contribution to postindustrial society—motherhood.[28] Mothering work is used to legitimate women's lower pay and slower advancement up career ladders. Because of her truncated financial resources and job prospects, it is difficult for a mother to argue with a better-paid father for equality in child care, in turn making it difficult for her to claim higher wages and promotions on the job. Her double workload becomes a major barrier to her achieving a position of authority or pursuing a political career. Thus, you have a self-reinforcing structure of gender inequality based on the gendered division of workers who do paid and unpaid work. At the very least, the gendered division of family work and the gendered practices of work organizations and their interconnections need to be degendered if we are to create true and permanent gender equality.

Dismantling the Gender Structure

As pervasive as gender is, because it is constructed and maintained through daily interaction, it can be resisted and reshaped. The social construction perspective argues that people create their social realities and identities, including their gender, through their actions with others—their families, friends, and colleagues. Gender is a constant performance, but its enactment is hemmed in by the general rules of social life, cultural expectations, workplace norms, and laws. These social restraints are also amenable to change, but not easily because the social order is structured for stability. Many aspects of gender have been changed through individual agency, group pressure, and social movements.[29] But the underlying structure has not changed.

We need gender troublemakers to challenge the way gender is still built into the Western world's overall social system, penetrating the organization of the production of goods and services, kinship and family, sexuality, emotional relationships, and the minutiae of daily life. Gendered practices have been questioned, but the overall legitimacy of the gendered social order is deeply ingrained and currently bolstered by scientific studies on supposed inborn differences between females and males. The ultimate touchstone is pregnancy and childbirth. Yet procreative and other biological differences are part of the gendered social order, which is so pervasive that the behavior and attitudes it produces are perceived as natural, including women's greater predisposition to nurturance and bonding. This belief in natural—and thus necessary—differences legitimates many gender inequalities and exploitations of women.

Feminist movements have focused on the inequalities and exploitations, especially in the gendered work world and the domestic division of labor, but have found that as one set of gendered practices is eliminated, others rise to take their place. To keep women down, socially constructed differences from men must be maintained and used as a rationale for women's inferior status.[30] Feminists have either minimized gender differences, to little effect, or maximized and valorized them, also to little effect. The problem is that the focus has been on differences between women and men as individuals or as social actors. These differences are a means to an end—legitimation and justification of gendered social orders. It is the foundation of gendered social orders—gender itself, gender as a social institution—that must be delegitimized.

But aren't biological sex differences the ultimate barrier to degendering? And what about sexuality? Won't degendering founder on sexual desire for a member of the opposite or the same gender? My argument is twofold: biological sex and sexuality in themselves are not clear binary opposites, and both are deeply intertwined with the social aspects of gender.[31] The complexities of the gender system—it is a hierarchy of race and ethnicity and social class as well—complicate the categories of biological sex, sexual identities, and sexual desire. None of those categories are binary, and none produce gender.

Sex Differences

Female and male physiology are produced and maintained by both testosterone and estrogen, so sex is more of a continuum than a sharp dichotomy.[32] The changing physiological characteristics of children and adults at different stages of the life cycle and according to physical abilities multiply the two sexes. Women's biological states change, depending on whether they are pregnant or nonpregnant, between periods or menstruating, pre- or postmenopausal. Men's biological states change with fluctuations in testosterone levels and other hormonal cycles. If we are going to use bodies to set up social categories, we should have many more than two.[33]

Despite these multiplicities, we tend to think of bodies as consistently male or female because they are socially constructed in deeply gendered societies. Even bodies that are ini-

tially biologically ambiguous are quickly gendered, because a
gender-neutral or androgynous or "unisex" body is anathema in
a world where people must know quickly and precisely where
to place others they encounter for the first time or in short face-
to-face interactions. Thus, children born with ambiguous-
looking genitalia (intersexed children) are often surgically
reconstructed to look "normally" female or male even though
there is ample evidence that clitorises, vaginas, penises, and
testicles vary considerably in size and shape.[34] Of course, in
most interactions, gender is displayed through appearance and
presentation of self; the congruity of the body beneath the
clothes is taken for granted.[35]

As viewed from a social construction perspective, gender
is not an overlay on biology; rather, biology itself is socially
constructed *as* gendered. Sex differences do matter, but the
way they matter is a social phenomenon.[36] Menstruation,
menopause, pregnancy, and childbirth are biological phenomena that are mediated and experienced socially. Female and
male bodies are gendered for femininity and masculinity
through sports, exercise, and physical labor. Gendered eating
patterns have physiological consequences. Men's rates of coronary heart disease rose precipitously after World War II in
Western industrialized countries because they had the privilege
of eating more scarce red meat.[37] In many postindustrial countries, there are major physiological differences between women
and men in their sixties and older, but their sense of self becomes more androgynous, less gendered.[38]

In sum, genes, hormones, physiology, and bodies (what are
summarized as "sex differences") are socially constructed as
gendered in Western society; they are not the source of gender

as a social status. The conceptualization of male and female bodies as intrinsically and consistently different and as the main marker of social status is not universal. In fact, the enormous male-female body divide we see as so unbridgeable is a relatively recent Western concept.[39] In the past in Western society, hierarchies of birth (aristocrat versus peasant, freeborn versus slave) were more important status markers and just as embodied as gender is considered to be today.

A society does not have to be organized around gender. Oyèrónké Oyěwùmí points out that the feminist assumption that gender's salience is universal replicates biological reasoning.[40] Citing Yorùbá's nongendered language, she argues that precolonial Yorùbá society was ordered not by gender but by relative age, which determined relationships and hierarchies. She says:

> Unlike European languages, Yorùbá does not 'do gender'; it 'does seniority' instead. Thus social categories—familial and nonfamilial—do not call attention to the body as English personal names, first-person pronouns, and kinship terms do (the English terms being both gender-specific-body-specific). Seniority is highly relational and situational in that no one is permanently in a senior or junior position; it all depends on who is present in any given situation. Seniority, unlike gender, is only comprehensible as part of relationships. Thus, it is neither rigidly fixated on the body nor dichotomized.[41]

Oyěwùmí's account of precolonial Yorùbá's genderlessness bolsters the social construction contention that gender is not based in biology and that gender divisions in Western society can be minimized, if not entirely erased.

Sexualities

Like bodies, sexuality is socially gendered but has multiple manifestations that create more than one "opposite sex." Studies of sexual orientation have shown that neither heterosexuality nor homosexuality is always fixed for life and that bisexuality, in feelings and in sexual relationships, is widespread.[42] Sexuality is "scripted" differently at different times and places and intertwined with gender, racial, and class statuses.

These multiplicities of sexual behavior and identities take place within a gendered social order, taking us back to the binaries. Lesbians, gay men, and bisexuals identify as men or women, and their sexuality is influenced by their gender and by the gender of their intimate partners. Women and men bisexuals prefer women partners for emotional intimacy and men partners for physical assertiveness.[43] Gendered norms influence ideals of feminine and masculine sexual attractiveness and the kinds of sexual behavior acceptable for women and men of different social classes, racial ethnic groups, religions, and ages. These norms are most starkly seen in aging women and men and those with visible disabilities. Many economically secure and powerful men retain their sexuality; few women of the same status do.[44] In most societies, permitted and tabooed sexual behavior is embedded in gendered hierarchies of power, prestige, and economic differences.[45]

In short, sexuality follows gender scripts; it does not create them. If sexual behavior were the source of gender categories, there would be many more categories than straight man, straight woman, gay man, lesbian woman.

TRANSGENDERING: DOING OR UNDOING GENDER?

Radical gender benders, who sometimes call themselves queers, do not claim identity with men or women, heterosexuals or homosexuals. Queers openly subvert binary gender and sexual categories through their deliberate mix of clothing, makeup, jewelry, hairstyles, behavior, names, and use of language. By not constructing gender and sexuality in expected ways, they make visible, in Judith Butler's term, the *performativity* on which the whole gender order depends.[46] They parody and play with gender but don't kill it. In fact, queer performances, like drag, need visible contrasts of masculine and feminine dress and behavior to parody and play with.[47]

The phenomenon of transgendering (transvestism, living in a gender that is different from that assigned at birth, and transsexuality, surgical transformation of the body to change gender) is an arena that amply illustrates multiplicities of bodies, sexualities, and genders but, like drag and queering, paradoxically reflects the gender binaries. Transgendering is meaningless without established gender categories. If gender statuses were not so pervasive and determinative of so many other aspects of our everyday lives, there would be no need to pass as a member of a different gender in order to live and work in a way that is compatible with personal desires. The goal of many transgendered people is to "pass" as a "normal" gendered person, a goal that is necessary for solving problems of daily life but not one that disrupts the gendered social order.[48]

Those who successfully construct their gender as different from their birth assignment, whether through cross-dressing or surgical alteration of genitalia, in order to live as a member of their chosen gender, reaffirm the conventional categories of man and woman even as their behavior subtly sabotages the solidity of the categories.[49] When a transgendered teacher, scientist, economist, travel writer, police officer, novelist, or physician and tennis player, openly declares that she was wrongfully a man but now is rightfully a woman, is she saying that she is the same person professionally, with the same knowledge and expertise?[50] She has changed her body, name, legal status, relationships, clothing, hair, cosmetics, voice, speaking style, and personality but not her education, occupation, racial ethnic status, or social class. She declares that she is now the person she always felt she was, a "woman." What does that mean?

Deirdre McCloskey, an economist, claims that women make better economists than men, who dominate the field, because they take social factors into consideration, especially family relationships.[51] McCloskey thought economics was more rhetoric than abstract mathematics when she was man. Was that because she was, deep down inside, a woman? Or can men as well as women think "like a woman"?

What is the core of gender? Transgender transformations indicate that it is legal status, body, and gender display. If the legal status of gender were removed, would trans people need to change their bodies and gender display? In *The Transsexual Empire*, Janice Raymond insists that male-to-female transsexuals are still men because they were socialized as men and absorbed all the privileges of patriarchy. In "The Empire Strikes Back," Sandy Stone, a transsexual, admits complicity with the conventionalizing gender order and its medical control agents. She felt it was necessary to pass as "normal" to mitigate the dangers of visibility as a "posttransexual." But, she says, *not* passing as "normal" would be transformative:

> This is a treacherous area, and were the silenced groups to achieve voice we might find, as feminist theorists have claimed, that the identities of individual, embodied subjects were far less implicated in physical norms, and far more diversely spread across a rich and complex structuration of identity and desire, than is now possible to express.[52]

Transgenders who do want to live *as transgenders* end up degendering. A recent newspaper report described "a new kind of campus activism: transgender students and their allies who are convincing colleges to meet needs that include private bathrooms and showers, specialized housing and sports teams on which students who don't identify themselves as either male or female can play."[53]

A similar phenomenon occurs in intersexuality. In order to fit into the gender binaries, intersexed bodies are surgically and hormonally reshaped.[54] Parents and doctors make significant decisions on behalf of intersexed babies and children long before the intersexed children can do so for themselves. Doctors urge parents to let them create "normal-looking" genitalia as quickly as possible even though "normal" genitalia vary widely in size and shape. Parents are not put in touch with parents of other intersexed children or representatives of the Intersex Society of North America.[55]

In contrast, the current political goal of adult intersexuals is to live *as intersexuals,* that is, without "clarifying" genital surgery that transforms ambiguous genitalia into "normal," gender-identifiable clitorises, vaginas, penises, and scrotums.[56]

Unaltered intersexuality would not only undercut gender categories but would also undermine Western societies' putative foundational source of gender—naturally sexed bodies. To have a structural effect, this revolutionary behavior needs to be acknowledged in the basic bureaucratic categories of Western societies. What could become a landmark case of degendering has already taken place. In January 2003, Australia issued a passport to an X, an intersexual named Alex MacFarlane. Alex is a 47XXY, a form of androgyny shared by about one in every fifteen hundred to two thousand babies. Now forty-eight years old, Alex has been fighting bureaucratic misrepresentation since reaching adulthood. Alex says, "Intersex individuals should not have to break the law, by pretending to be male or female, in order to vote, marry, hold a license, or own property."[57]

Open intersexuality, transgender queering, and sexual fluidity, deliberately ambiguous, nongendered presentations of self, *and* refusal to accept the ubiquitous bureaucratic gendered classification that begins and maintains gendering might undo gendering at the personal level. But as long as the gender categories order our lives, parents and grandparents who don't immediately offer the expected information about the "flavor" of the newborn will be asked the question within five minutes. Indeed, in these days of prenatal imaging, the gendering begins with the sexing. "I don't know" is a bureaucratic limbo. "I can't decide" is an interactive quagmire. "Other/neither/both" is, to psychiatrists, a disease called gender identity disorder.[58] These phenomena attest to the intransigence of the binary structure of Western postindustrial gendered social systems and its implicit two-sex biological basis.

Doing Multidimensional Research

If gender were no longer a bureaucratic category, how would we do research or shape policy on gender inequality? Social science research that recognizes the multiplicity of genders, sexes, and sexualities has the problem of needing categories to order data while critically deconstructing them. We know that the content and dividing lines for genders, sexes, and sexualities are fluid, intertwined, and intersected by other major social statuses. How, then, do we do research without reifying the conventional categories?[59]

We can adapt categories to particular research questions, intersecting sex, sexuality, and gender with each other and with other relevant social statuses. That method releases research designs from traditional "opposites," but it does not go beyond the conventional categories. To do that, we have to first determine what we want to know. Then we can decide on the categories for comparison. What we consider inevitable opposing categories are actually variable cultural and temporal constructions of "opposites." Michael Kimmel told the following anecdote, which illustrates the problem of "opposites" very well:

Occasionally, Zachary (my three-year-old) and I play a game called "opposites" in which I tell him a word and he tells me its opposite. These are incredibly simple, and he loves it. One evening, my mother was visiting, and she played with us. Scratchy/smooth, tall/short, high/low, ugly/beautiful, fast/slow—well, you get the idea. Then my mother asked, "Zachary, what's the opposite of boy?" I clenched. Every fiber of my gender-theorizing body tensed up. Uh oh, I thought, here it comes, gender binarism, heterosexual dimorphic reasoning, gender schematized ideation. I braced myself. Zachary took a few seconds. "Man," he said.[60]

In addition to carefully choosing comparison categories, social scientists can do multidimensional research by examining the behavioral patterns that emerge from processes and social location without the overlay of status categories, examining what people do to and with whom and how these processes construct, maintain, or subvert statuses, identities, and institutional rules and social structures. Organizing data without reliance on the conventional dichotomous categories does not confine researchers to single-case analysis or a limited number of in-depth interviews; quantitative methods will still be applicable.

Social scientists have developed methodologies that do not rely on polarized categories. Among them are analysis of positions in a social network, letting patterns emerge from the data, as recommended by grounded theory, and the critical deconstruction of social texts.[61] The familiar categories can be used in the next level of analysis to see whether the emergent network positions, typical behavior, and subtexts are characteristic of those of different genders, racial ethnic groups, and social classes, and they can be taken to a third level, describing how they relate to power and resource control. Or they can be dropped entirely in favor of category names more descriptive of empirical content. Using grounded theory to analyze the varieties of behavior of male cross-dressers, Richard Ekins distinguished patterns related to sex ("body femaling"), sexuality ("erotic femaling"), and role behavior ("gender femaling").[62]

Letting patterns emerge from the data, the methodology long recommended by ethnomethodologists and other qualitative researchers, permits the analysis of processes within structures. These patterns can be used for quantitative comparisons, as in Mary Clare Lennon and Sarah Rosenfeld's statistical analysis built on Arlie Hochschild's data in *The Second Shift,* on the extent of housework done by husbands and wives where the woman was the greater earner.[63]

The common practice of comparing females and males, women and men, or homosexuals and heterosexuals frequently produces data that are so mixed that it takes another level of analysis to sort out meaningful categories for comparison. Such comparisons have to include bisexuals, people who are transitioning and may not go all the way to the other gender, trans people who are successfully living as members of the chosen gender, intersexuals who identify themselves as intersexuals, and queers who refuse categorizing. In order to do this second level of analysis, the sample groups have to be heterogenous on the conventional categories in the first place—and they have to include racial ethnic, social-class, religious, and other statuses.

Thus, the familiar categories do not have to be dispensed with entirely, but their use in analysis can be bracketed until other differentiating variables have been revealed. These differentiating variables are likely to break up and recombine the familiar categories in new ways that go beyond the conventional dichotomies but do not remove the category from our lexicon. We can continue to compare women and men, but we need to be careful to specify which women and which men, by social class, racial ethnic group, age level, sexual orientation, and other variables of interest. Gender may turn out to be a less significant variable than other statuses.[64] A more radical methodology, however, would throw out the conventional categories entirely and do ethnographic research to discover who people think they are and why and then use community-based categories to develop statistical data.[65]

It is worth applying to gender research Donna Haraway's warning that "there is no category independent of narrative, trope, and technique. . . . To pretend otherwise is symptomatic of an advanced case of hardening of the categories."[66]

PRACTICING DEGENDERING

Degendering as a viable form of resistance has to be deliberate, structural, and independent of sexed bodies if existing gendered social orders are to be transformed. Degendering needs to be focused on how people are sorted and allocated tasks in work organizations, schools, small groups, families, and other familiar social groupings. Degendering means not assigning tasks in the home and workplace by gender. Degendering means not grouping children by gender in schools. Degendering means confronting gender expectations in face-to-face interaction and underplaying gender categories in language (saying not "ladies and gentlemen" but "colleagues and friends"). Many people already use the degendered and legally neutral terms "partner," "constant companion," "significant other," or "beloved" for the other person in their long-term emotional relationship. Degendered kinship designations, such as "child," "parent," and "sibling," could liberate us further from stereotypical gendered expectations. Especially important is to stop comparing children by gender and not ever saying "boys will be boys" or "just like a girl."[67]

Where language itself is built on gender categories, developing gender-neutral ways of addressing and referring to people will be a major and revolutionary enterprise, but its accomplishment would go a long way toward structural degendering.[68] Similarly, in theocracies where the dominant state religion separates women and men and treats them markedly unequally through religious law, degendering cannot take place unless personal status laws are secularized and made gender-neutral. Nonstate religions should be free to continue to separate women and men, but their rules should not influence secular society.

Even with degendering, people who wished to could continue to identify themselves as men, women, girls, and boys and to display femininity or masculinity, as they defined it, in names, clothing, and behavior. Displays of dominance or aggression, however, would not be a prerogative of men, nor would displays of subordination or submission be confined to women; with degendering, such currently gendered behavior could be expected of anyone. People could be uniform in their gender presentation and display in all phases of their lives or uniform in some situations, mixed in others. The focus of self-presentation, identity, group membership, and politics might be a gender, or it might be a racial or ethnic category, an occupation, an age group, a religion, a sexual orientation, a country, or one or more of these. What is most important about degendering is that formal bureaucratic categories and the formal structures of organizations should not be built on gender divisions, nor should workplaces, households, and child care.

As degendering agents in our everyday lives, we can confront the ubiquitous bureaucratic and public gender binaries just as trans people do—by thinking about whether we want to conform or challenge. We could stop ticking off the M/F boxes at the top of every form we fill out or ask about the need for them. Shannon Faulkner, a girl, got into the Citadel, an all-boys military school, because the admission form did not have an M/F check-off box; it was assumed that only boys would apply. All her credentials and biographical information qualified her for admission, but when the Citadel administration found out she was a girl, she was immediately disqualified. The person didn't change; her qualifications remained the same. The *legal status*—and all of the stereotypical baggage about capabilities that comes with it—changed. It was on that basis that she successfully claimed gender discrimination and challenged the all-male status of the Citadel.[69] That is precisely what degendering would do.

Another potent way to degender is to "liberate" public bathrooms. Many single-use bathrooms have already been made unisex; any designation of M/F on such bathrooms should simply be ignored. But multiple-use bathrooms could also be unisex, even those with urinals, if we didn't stay locked in conventional thinking. If all bathrooms were unisex, people who did not want to see others urinating or be seen urinating could use the stalls-only bathrooms.

Degendering boxes and bathrooms is not a trivial goal nor a problem only for trans people. Both are intrinsic parts of the bureaucratic structure and the process of control of public space.[70] Gender-divided bathrooms replicate the supposed biological base of the gendered social order and the symbolic separation of men's and women's social worlds. They are also constant evidence of gender inequity, since there are never enough ladies' rooms in public spaces.[71] However, other body characteristics besides sex may be salient in determining the need for public facilities. The long lines in front of men's rooms that I've seen recently at cultural events is an indication of an aging population; older men frequently have prostate problems. We know that we need a lot of bathrooms where children congregate; the same is true for older people. Dividing such bathrooms by sex hardly seems necessary.

Degendering does *not* mean ignoring bodies or the effects of biological sex, particularly in procreation and illness. However, sex is not always the critical factor. A high rate of maternal mortality decimates child-bearing *women*, but availability of prenatal care and emergency childbirth services depends on the resources of the whole health-care system. Women gestate and give birth, but men often have the social power over abortions, sex selection, and timing and number of children. An enormous amount of feminist criticism and analysis has shown how pregnancy, childbirth, and motherhood have been used to delimit women's opportunities in the public sphere and increase their dependence on an individual man or on the chancy welfare benefits of patriarchal governments. Feminist critiques of the Western health-care system have shown how women's physiology has been either ignored or stereotyped in male-centered health-care curricula. Gendered analyses here are necessary to tease out the social construction of bodies, men's as well as women's, and to document the loop-back effects of biology, environment, and social patterns.[72]

In societies where all women are disadvantaged, degendering may not be the best strategy to achieve women's rights. Gender sensitivity may be necessary to bring attention to how seemingly neutral policies are insidious for women. It may also be necessary to compare women and men in the economic sphere, but here the effects of education, income, and social-class standing often mean that women and men cannot be treated as homogeneous global categories. The paths of transmission and the procreative implications of AIDS are highly gendered, but invidious social policies and lack of treatment have had equally detrimental effects on the lives of poor, rural women and men in many countries.[73]

If we are going to conduct a campaign of degendering, it must be everywhere and ongoing, because gender so imbues our lives. If this sounds like the "good old days" of pervasive personal politics, it is—but rather than just fighting sexism or the oppression of women by institutions dominated by men, it includes men and attends as well to other subordinating social statuses. Most of all, degendering directly targets the processes and practices of gendering and their outcome—gendered people, practices, and power. Deliberate degendering is not ignoring gender, which allows gendered processes and practices to proceed unhindered. To deliberately degender, you have to attend to those processes and practices in order not to do them. You have to use gender to degender. In *Gender Trouble*, Judith Butler dared us to go beyond the obviously possible:

> The task here is . . . to redescribe those possibilities that *already* exist, but which exist within cultural domains designated as culturally unintelligible and impossible. . . . Cultural configurations of sex and gender might then proliferate, or, rather, their present proliferation might then become articulable within the discourses that establish intelligible cultural life,

confounding the binarism of sex, and exposing its fundamental unnaturalness.[74]

These are the goals of degendering:

- eliminating gender divisions in the family and the workplace
- looking for multiplicity in depictions of gender
- doing multidimensional politics in coalitions of diverse women and men
- imagining a social order without gender divisions

The rest of this book will take up each goal in turn.

Chapter Two
NO MORE MOTHERS AND FATHERS: DEGENDERING PARENTING

> *Fathers are*
> *more fathering*
> *these days they have*
> *accomplished this by*
> *being more mothering.*
> —Grace Paley[1]

EVERY YEAR ON MOTHER'S DAY, the U.S. media carry feature articles on overfamiliar themes—mothers' enchantment/disenchantment with newborns, mothers' conflicts over working outside the home, stepmothering, the costs of motherhood, the costs of nonmotherhood, and so on. And every year on Father's Day, the U.S. media carry feature articles on equally overfamiliar themes: the joys/woes of single fatherhood, taking/not taking paternal leave, searching for/bonding with father. The articles are all on the individual parent-child bond divorced from the bonds between and among the child's caretakers. Stories on shared parenting are rare; stories on nannies and day care are "horror" tales. The relationship between parents and how parents relate jointly to the child seem to get discussed mostly in pieces on gay and lesbian parents.

The current ideology in the Western world assumes that for heterosexual parents, the division of labor in the home will be gendered—the mother will be the primary parent, the father the primary breadwinner. The unexamined subtext is that the mother will have a greater investment in and attachment to the child than the father; thus, the story for her is how to have "a life" while prioritizing motherhood; for him, it is how to be a father without seriously interfering with his ongoing life outside the home. Shared parenting between women and men partners is acknowledged as a good idea, and evidence that men are capable of intimate fathering is often presented as support of that utopian goal. But there is a contradictory conviction that given the demands of quality parenting and "greedy" careers, the two are incompatible.[2] Workplace pressures are thought to be unchangeable, so the burden of innovation falls on the family. It is newsworthy if the parent who is better at child care is the man or if the parent who earns a higher income is the woman. When heterosexual couples reverse parental roles, however, stay-at-home fathers suffer from ostracism and isolation because the domestic world is so gendered.[3]

To get beyond these gendered assumptions of modern parenting in Westernized nuclear families, we need a different language frame. Commenting on a study of working parents, James A. Levine, director of the Fatherhood Project at the Families and Work Institute, said that as long as "working parent" means only the mother, there will not be a significant shift toward shared parenting. He recounts a conversation with a woman executive who complained that she was always the one to stay home if her two-year-old child was sick. He asked why her husband couldn't take a turn. She said, "His company wouldn't allow it." Levine said, "Has he ever asked?" The woman didn't think he ever had. Levine then asked her if she had ever asked him to ask. She said no, it had never occurred to her. To break these symbolic boundaries—what Levine calls collusion—would take "challenging the implicit assumptions that drive current business practice. That challenge is the responsibility of men and women, and employers and employees."[4]

New ways of talking about parenting would dramatize new values that recognize the importance of infant care by fathers and their capacity for nurturant behavior and would help counter the underlying assumption that the mother should be the primary child carer. Also necessary are workplace policies that support fathers and mothers who care for children while earning a living. But what is crucial to relieving mothers' burdens is more equally shared parenting, where both the father and the mother "mother." What I mean by this was expressed by Thomas Laqueur, a professor of history. Commenting on himself as a father, he said:

> I am far guiltier of the stereotypical vices of motherhood—the neurotic worry about [my daughter's] physical and mental well being, unfounded premonitions of danger, excessive emotional demands, and general nudginess—than is [my wife]. In short, my experiences . . . make me suspect the naturalness of "mother" or "father" in any culturally meaningful sense.[5]

WHY PARENTING HAS TO BE DEGENDERED TO ACHIEVE GENDER EQUALITY

The two main social institutions in Western societies that are built on and maintain gender inequality are the family and its division of labor and the workplace and its allocation of jobs, career advancement, and financial rewards. Work and family form a gendered loop that disadvantages women who are mothers. They pay a price in lowered wages, reduced lifetime earnings, and minimal pensions because of part-time and interrupted work. When they want to return to full-time work or get off the "mommy track," they are discriminated against in hiring and promotions. Although everyone in a society benefits from good parenting, when it is mostly done by women, these lost work opportunities amount to what Ann Crittenden calls a "mommy tax." This tax is about 7 percent of women's earnings for each child. The unfair distribution of the costs of parenting are evident if children are looked on not as the property of the parents but as the future citizens of the whole society. Michelle Budig and Paula England, who documented the wage penalty for motherhood, say:

> Good parenting . . . increases the likelihood that a child will grow up to be a caring, well-behaved, and productive adult. This lowers crime rates, increases the level of care for the next generation, and contributes to economic productivity. Most of those who benefit—the future employers, neighbors, spouses, friends, and children of the person who has been well reared— pay nothing to the parent. Thus, mothers pay a price in lowered wages for doing child rearing, while most of the rest of us are "free riders" on their labor.[6]

Many Western industrial countries absorb some of the costs of child rearing with child allowances, subsidized day care, free health insurance, and paid parental leave.[7] But even if the workplace is family friendly and governments or employers provide financial benefits for raising children, mothers with jobs often carry the full load of paid work and responsibility for running their households. If the load is too burdensome, they drop out or cut back on their paid work, constricting their family's standard of living. Wives of high-earning husbands may experience fewer financial constraints, but motherhood often jeopardizes their place on professional or managerial career ladders. Men who are primary parents also experience these penalties, but since fewer men than women are in that position, it is mothers who pay most of the price of parenting. They get to be there at the first smiles and first steps, and that may be reward enough. But mothers who want to do other work may feel they have given up half their life, just as fathers working long hours may feel that they, too, are losing a great part of their lives by missing those first smiles and first steps.

To most people, it is perfectly natural that men do paid work and women do housework and child care. So are the assumed reasons—women bear children and are biologically programmed to take care of them. Men, because they don't bear children, are responsible for providing the food or the financial support for their wife and children. In postindustrial societies, this complementarity assumes a heterosexual, nuclear family household and a "family wage"—high enough wages or profits on the part of the man who is the head of household to support the whole family. Heterosexual families where the woman is the main earner and families headed by a woman are dependent on the woman's earning capacity. The assumption that all women are secondary providers disadvantages these women in the job market.[8]

According to marxist feminist theorists, the loop-back effects of the gendered family structure on the status of women and men are at the heart of capitalist patriarchy:

Low wages keep women dependent on men because they encourage women to marry. Married women must perform domestic chores for their husbands. Men benefit, then, from both
higher wages and the domestic division of labor. This domestic
division of labor, in turn, acts to weaken women's position in
the labor market. Thus, the hierarchical domestic division of
labor is perpetuated by the labor market, and vice versa. This
process is the present outcome of two interlocking systems,
capitalism and patriarchy. . . . The resulting mutual accommo-
dation between patriarchy and capitalism has created a vicious
circle for women.[9]

Other feminists have pointed out that in socialist economies
and welfare states, where the government provides income and
services for single mothers and low-income families, women
may be just as dependent on a paternalistic state as they are on
paternalistic husbands in capitalist economies.[10]

In practice, there are many breaches in the work-family
gender divide throughout most of the postindustrialized world.
African American middle-class women have long contributed
substantially to the family income in order to buy the con-
sumer goods the modern household relies on, while at the same
time managing the household and child care. For many poor
families, sharing parenting and economic resources among
the members of a social-support network is essential to their
survival. The mothers rely on other women for child care
while they earn a living—"allomothers," "othermothers," "co-
madres." They rely as well on "otherfathers," men relatives and
lovers who are not the biological fathers, to share parental care.

Many young heterosexual couples choose part-time work or staggered shifts so they can share child care and financial support. Gay and lesbian parents have a variety of shared responsibilities for earning money and taking care of the children.11

Yet in the Western world, social policies are based on the belief that mothers and mothers alone are naturally the best parents for their biological and adopted children. Workplace and government policies may permit women to combine parenting with a job, and husbands may help with the child care, but the expectation is that the mother will be the primary parent. Salary scales, promotions, and political involvement for women are geared to this expectation, which rubs off on women who are not mothers or the primary parent. Mothers who create, do research, go off to war or into space, and head governments are admired, but they are considered a deviation from the "normal."

Supporting this underlying view of the gendered division of labor at home and in the workplace is the conviction that it is a natural outcome of women's and men's biology and personality structures. The extent to which the social environment structures, shapes, and induces this gendered division of labor is ignored.

Biological Hurdles to Degendered Parenting

In 1964, Alice Rossi, a prominent feminist sociologist, saw women and men as interchangeable in parenting potential. In 1977, she shifted to a biosocial perspective and linked the hormonal input during pregnancy and lactation to the development of mother-child bonding and women's superior child-care skills. In 1984, she placed more emphasis on male and female styles of parenting, which she claimed are "rooted in basic sexual dimorphism" that gives women greater sensitivity and consequent fine-tuned acuity to infants' cues for attention. Thus, they would make better parents for adopted children as well as biological children.[12]

The biosocial argument Rossi used to explain gendered responses to children is twofold: nurturing capabilities are prenatally "hardwired" into female brains, and aggressiveness is similarly incorporated into male brains, through a combination of genetic input and hormonal flooding of the fetus during pregnancy. In adolescence and adulthood, these same sex hormones reinforce the previously laid down predispositions for masculine and feminine behavior. Organizational/activational theory became popular with psychologists and neuroendocrinologists in the 1960s, but the linear connective pathways on which the theory relies have never been directly shown in any brain-organization research.[13] More interactive models use a loop-back interchange of body, behavioral, environmental, and social factors. For example, in a natural experiment, a troop of usually aggressive and belligerent baboons was transformed into a peaceable group when the alpha males died after accidentally eating diseased meat that only they had access to. The resulting predominantly female troop developed a more affectionate and mutual grooming mode of social interaction that has lasted through several generations, supposedly through the socialization of new male members by the resident females. Physiological tests on the current adults in the troop indicated much lower levels of stress than those documented when the troop was first studied twenty years ago.[14]

Recent research has shown that a biological mechanism for male and female parental behavior could be related to different responses to stress. A study on stress that was the first to focus on adult women found that they don't have a "fight-or-flight" response but rather have a "tend-and-befriend" reaction. In situations provoking fear or anxiety, men tend to stand and defend themselves physically or run away to protect themselves. Women often seek out support from other people, or they protectively look after their children. The biological complement of stress responses in men is testosterone; in women, it is oxytocin, the same hormone that induces labor in childbirth and milk letdown in breast-feeding. The high oxytocin levels may be an effect of learned maternal protectiveness rather than a cause of it—or, more plausibly, there may be a loop-back effect. Similarly, in men, socially approved acts of aggression raise testosterone levels, and these raised levels in turn produce more aggressiveness.[15]

Evolutionary theorists argue that a natural gendered division of parenting comes from our primate ancestry and evolutionary history. The feminist evolutionary argument is that men's parental behavior evolved from the woman's choice of sexual partners who would be likely to protect and feed her and her children. The evidence from primate behavior is that the successful mother is independent, ambitious for high tribal status on her own, and a competitor for material and social resources; these traits give her children and grandchildren survival advantages. Part of her survival strategy is her choice of mates who will invest in her children; she frequently chooses more than one sexual partner to ensure that there will be responsible male parents for all her children, although men in turn devise strategies to claim only some of their mate's children.[16]

The hormonal and evolutionary views together would argue that the "tend-and-befriend" propensity in women encourages sharing between women and men. In prehistoric human foraging societies, according to current anthropological research, men and women gathered, hunted, and scavenged foods and shared them among all the tribe's adults and their children, not just between a heterogendered pair; child care was also a group activity.[17] Extended families sharing economic resources and domestic labor have been the norm throughout human history and are the preferred family structure in most kin-based societies today. Even in societies where the nuclear family of mother, father, and children is the ideal, shared financial support and child rearing among adults who are not necessarily biological kin are widespread.[18]

Breast-Feeding and Shared Parenting

Another stumbling block often placed in the way of sharing parenting is breast-feeding. Yet breast-feeding has little relationship to labor-force participation of women and involvement of fathers in child care. When bottle-feeding became popular in the United States in the 1930s and breast-feeding declined precipitously, the innovation did not induce middle-class mothers with working husbands to go out to paid work in greater numbers, and middle-class fathers did not start sharing child care. The resurgence of breast-feeding in the United States in the last generation has coincided with more and more mothers of young children entering the paid work-force.[19]

Breast-feeding can be combined with work outside the home in different ways: shared breast-feeding, paid wet nurses, on-site nursing facilities, and expressing or pumping breast milk for bottle-feeding. Several women nursing several babies is a longtime human-survival tactic but uncommon in post-industrial societies. Crèches were situated at U.S. work sites during World War II but abandoned when the women workers returned home.[20] As part of a concerted campaign to get all mothers to breast-feed, working mothers in Norway are given two hours off a day to breast-feed at home or at work, even at their desks. Norway recently reported that 99 percent of new mothers breast-feed their infants at birth, and 80 percent continue for at least six months after, the highest rate among ten industrial nations.[21]

Unlike women of past centuries, today's employed women do not use wet nurses to breast-feed their infants when they are not able (or willing) to breast-feed them. Instead, they use pumps to supply breast milk that can be fed to babies in bottles, and they store the milk in refrigerators, freezers, and picnic bags. It may be onerous, but it's doable.[22] The bottles of breast milk can then be fed to babies by fathers or other caretakers.

But breast-feeding is not only a way to provide nourishing and safe milk, as it is in developed countries and was in developing countries before the AIDS epidemic. It also affords infants skin-to-skin tactility and gives them comfort. Are men precluded from offering babies if not the breast, then a comforting chest and shoulder during and after a bottle-feeding? In arguing for separating nurturance—"the mother acts"—from gender, Barbara Katz Rothman described her own experience sharing with her husband the parenting of two birth children and an adopted child. She says:

> I offered the comfort and security of the breast. And Hesch offered the comfort and security of his shoulder—holding the child's head on his shoulder as month by month, year by year, the legs came to dangle down longer and longer. I've seen my very young children, both the boy and the girls, offer a doll the breast, and I've seen both of them hold a doll on their shoulder, walking back and forth in sharp imitation of Hesch.[23]

Jules Law, talking about the politics of breast-feeding, points out that infant feeding "is a social activity in which the bodies, prerogatives, obligations, and interests of multiple citizens converge."[24] It will certainly be done by more than one child carer and can certainly include fathers, older brothers, and other men kin.

As adoptive parents know, competence, nurturance, and love come from hands-on care, not from hormones, birthing, or suckling. If the intensities of parenting are more common in women than men, it is because women are usually the primary child carers and nurturers in a family. They may be so because it is in their genes, evolutionary history, hormones, or unconscious, but the biological substrata neither make them parent no matter what their other circumstances may be (many women are voluntarily childless), nor do they prevent men from parenting intensively when they choose or are forced by circumstances to do so.

PSYCHOLOGICAL HINDRANCES TO DEGENDERED PARENTING

Taking a different approach to gendered parenting, psychoanalytic theorists claim that gendered personality structures are laid down in childhood in response to relationships with emotionally close mothers and emotionally distant fathers and that women and men reproduce those relationships in their own parental behavior as adults.[25]

Psychoanalytic theory links the division of parenting in the heterogendered Western nuclear family to the gendering of women's and men's personalities—objectification and emotional repression in men's psyches and emotional openness and nurturance in women's psyches. Both emerge from the primacy of women in parenting. Boys' separation from their mothers and identification with their fathers lead to their entrance into the world of men's dominance, but those processes also necessitate continuous repression of their emotional longings and fear of castration. Girls' continued identification with their mothers makes them available for intimacy; their heterosexual coupling with emotionally distant men produces their desire to become mothers and reproduces the gendered family structure from which gendered psyches emerge.[26]

In psychoanalytic theory, gendered parenting reproduces not only the structural division of child care in heterosexual nuclear families but also the power structure of the larger society. Boys' identification with their fathers is identification with their father's social dominance in a world that values objectivity, distance, control, coolness, aggressiveness, and competitiveness over intimacy, warmth, caring, and sharing—the characteristics that women develop in their hands-on parenting. It also reproduces a defensiveness in men against women's incursions into their spheres of domination. Degendered parenting would presumably undercut the development of gendered personality structures that are the outcome of the mother's primary parenting, but only if fathers "mother."

It is questionable, however, whether degendered parenting and degendered personality structures would alter men's domination of most positions of power. Empathy and emotional displays in men leaders have been accepted in recent years without undercutting their authority; women leaders, in contrast, have had to display coolness under fire. The gendered allocation of power is more firmly embedded in men's control of wealth and networking resources than in their personality structures or emotions.[27]

MEN'S TURN TO PARENT

Describing revolutionary parenting, bell hooks said:

> Structured in the definitions and the very usage of the terms father and mother is the sense that these two words refer to two distinctly different experiences. Women and men must define the work of fathering and mothering in the same way if males and females are to accept equal responsibility in parenting.[28]

Pregnancy, birth, and breast-feeding are often invoked as insurmountable barriers to men's parenting, seeming to give women bonding advantages that deepen their psychological leanings toward intensive mothering. Yet many men accompany the mother of their child to obstetric checkups, listen to the baby's heartbeat and look at the sonograms along with the mother, take prenatal classes, coach the mother through the birth, hold the baby immediately after, and even, without paid parental leave, take a week or two off from work after the birth. Many reports of shared parenting describe fathers waking up with the mother during night feedings and diapering and burping the baby, thus sharing the breast-feeding work and the bonding.

These forms of bonding are modern versions of *couvade,* where the father imitates the mother's procreative behavior and socially claims the child. In conflicts over custody, a father's involvement in child care bolsters paternal claims against the presumption that the mother is the primary parent.[29]

In most Western countries, fathers at least "give a hand," by changing diapers, putting children to bed, and comforting crying babies. Michael Lamb, in assessing the amount of child care performed by fathers throughout the world, described three levels of involvement with children: *child minding*—being on call near the child but not directly engaged in care; *one-on-one care*—holding, feeding, bathing, dressing, playing with, helping with homework, reading to the child, and so on; and *responsibility*—thinking about the child's emotional, social, and physical development and welfare and making arrangements for nonparental care, sick care, doctor visits, school visits, and playtime.[30] What brings men to sharing one-on-one care and responsibility for their children with their women partners?

Many of the men who share parenting start early, sharing the decision to have children and getting involved in fertility issues, prenatal checkups, preparation for birth, birthing, and infant care. Continued involvement is then not a major issue, especially for those couples where both parents are child centered and believe that mothers should not have to do it all. But co-parenting men also want to be intimate fathers to their children for their own sake. Scott Coltrane was surprised by how many of the co-parenting fathers he interviewed said it was

> a rare opportunity to develop the sensitive, vulnerable, and caring parts of themselves. Many talked about discovering a new form of love and experiencing the world in different ways since they became fathers. Some also talked about how being a parent was helping them to work through unresolved emotional issues with their own fathers.[31]

Diane Ehrensaft claimed that the middle-class urban and academic heterosexual couples whom she studied shared parenting chores fairly equitably, but the mothers tended to take on more of the psychological and emotional management—to worry more. They felt they were on call for their children all the time while the fathers could let them cry. The mothers felt they had to struggle for separation, the fathers for closeness. Women, she said, *are* mothers; men *do* fathering. Yet in the course of fathering, the men had fallen in love with their children and wanted to be with them because they were so fascinating and lovable. The intensity of the men's feelings for their children reversed the conventional parental triangle; instead of the fathers' being jealous of the time the mothers spent with the children, mothers felt left out of the father-child "couple."[32]

For women and men, the skills of parenting are learned, usually "on the job." Expertise is the *result,* not the cause, of gendered parenting. If women are better than men at parenting, it's because they do it more. Men who are single fathers or who do a significant amount of child care become good at it, too. Coltrane's study of twenty dual-earner heterosexual couples who shared the care of older children found that the men felt they were learning to "construct and sustain images of themselves as competent fathers." They had started out with the expectation that they could be nurturant, and "the successful practice of sharing child care facilitated the development of beliefs that men could nurture like women." Barbara Risman interviewed men who became single parents out of necessity, because their wives had died or left them with the children. These single fathers did not have previous beliefs about their capacity for intimate parenting, but they developed fully nurturing relationships with their children.[33]

The psychoanalytic perspective on parenting focuses on the emotional intimacy of mother-daughter bonds and on the repressive effects of emotionally distant fathers on sons. If little girls learn to mother intensively through emulation of their mothers, from whom do boys learn to be emotionally present fathers? Leonard Pitts, Jr., a *Miami Herald* journalist who interviewed African American men about their troubled relationships with their fathers, says that for him and others, there are always role models: "fathers, black men, *family* men who came up on hard streets, sired by disappointing dads, yet get up every morning and do the hard work of raising and supporting their children." If men's child-care clumsiness is genetic, evolutionary, hormonal, or psychological, it is not that hard to modify in adult life by learning through doing. As Pitts says, "The point isn't that it's easy, getting around the debts of a bad upbringing, but that it's *possible*."[34]

Parenting by men goes from being possible to being probable through practiced family routines. It becomes standard through cultural expectations and governmental policies—the social politics of fatherhood. As Barbara Hobson and David Morgan point out in their introduction to a six-nation critical study, fatherhood in Western postindustrial society is in a state of flux and competing interests: between fathers and mothers, biological and social fathers, individuals and governments. These interests split over the dimensions of fatherhood and its evolution from "cash" to "care." "Cash" is the obligation of fathers to give their children economic support; "care" is the obligation of fathers to be with their children and to give them emotional support. Fulfillment of either obligation gives fathers rights to authority over their children or participation in decisions, visitation, or custody.[35]

State policies influence the cash-versus-care dimensions of fatherhood, either directly or through support or nonsupport of mothers and children. The U.S. government, for example, limits state-provided financial support of single mothers with small children to five years and enforces fathers' financial support of biological children through legal establishment of paternity and garnishment of the wages of divorced and never-married fathers. Sweden, in contrast, moved from a similar cash policy to encouragement of care by biological fathers through direct state allowances for children, paid parental leave with a "daddy month" that fathers must take or forfeit, ensured visitation rights, and compulsory joint custody. These policies of paternal-care responsibilities and rights apply to married, non-married, cohabiting, nonresidential, and divorced fathers. Legal acknowledgment of biological paternity is usually voluntary but can be forced through DNA testing.[36]

Sweden's fatherhood policies have been actively promoted

by men's and women's feminist groups as part of an ideological commitment to gender equality and have been strengthened by government commissions and media campaigns. But they have run up against a gendered labor market and wage scales and the persistence of the cultural assumption that men will be the primary breadwinners. Men in Sweden frequently convert their "daddy month" into long weekends or extended vacations instead of using it to bond intensively with, and be responsible for the care of, their newborns.[37] Women are expected to take their guaranteed leave and are looked on as bad mothers if they do not. When Swedish mothers return to work, they do a double shift of work at home, with fathers' help. Swedish men's parenting is participatory but not equally shared.

Sharing Parenting

Fathers' involvement in caring for children is becoming a familiar phenomenon. Men with babies or small children in tow, nongendered family rooms in public places, and workplace parental-leave policies have become fairly routine in postindustrial Western societies. Equally shared parenting, however, is still novel. When a couple truly shares parenting, the children have two primary caretakers. Although some parents share child care because each holds a full-time job, other parents share by choice, because both want intense involvement with their children. Each doesn't do the same thing, but they divide chores and the time spent with the children equitably and share decisions about their upbringing.[38]

For couples whose goal is an egalitarian family, achieving a scrupulously even or equitably fair division of household work, paid work outside the home, and child care takes conscious negotiation and arranging. The pull of biological motherhood needs to be balanced by the involvement of the father in child rearing in such a way that the father is in many ways the social equivalent of the "other" mother in lesbian couples and the "other" father in gay couples. This restructuring of the family constellation in the form of genuine co-parenting is evident in studies of heterosexual and lesbian and gay parents. It not only takes organizing the household for equality but also involves creating new parenting roles and identities in opposition to the conventions of gendered mothers and fathers for heterosexuals and in the absence of legal and blood kin ties for gays and lesbians.[39]

Equalizing heterosexual parenting entails downplaying conventional gender expectations. Egalitarian fathers devote extensive physical and mental energy to their children while also earning a living, and egalitarian mothers contribute substantial economic support to the family while also caring for and giving emotional support to the children. Same-gender parents presumably don't have to go against the grain to the same extent, since they have already challenged the gendered family structure, but gender norms about manhood and womanhood emerge even in same-gender households.[40]

One study of twenty-six lesbian and twenty-six gay couples found that, just like many heterosexual couples, lesbian and gay couples tend to exaggerate the extent to which they share domestic work equally. Separate in-depth interviews with both partners about the details of their domestic work, combined with observations of several hours within the household, revealed that the more affluent partner tended to do less of the work that maintains family life, and the partner in a lower-paid, lower-prestige occupation tended to do more. The gay men doing more domestic work and the lesbians doing less were more likely to claim the division of labor as equal, since each was violating a gendered norm as well as the image of the egalitarian same-gender household.[41] However, when it comes to staying home full-time to be the primary child carer, homosexual men are more likely to do so than lesbian women, even at the cost of giving up economic independence.[42]

Francine Deutsch's *Halving It All* (a superb title, for which Deutsch credits her husband) is a primer for equal parenting (its subtitle is *How Equally Shared Parenting Works*). It is based on lengthy interviews of eighty-eight heterosexual couples divided by how much actual child care they did. Couples were designated "equal sharers" if the father did at least 45 percent of the work on twenty-four of thirty-two specific parenting tasks. Some couples alternated the same tasks and some divided the tasks according to convenience or likes and dislikes. In working-class families, each parent tended to do all the care at alternate times ("mother and Mr. Mom"). Some shared equally from the birth of their first child; others, when the mother went back to work, sometimes after several years of being the prime parent. Some used child-care facilities outside the home; others did not.

In Deutsch's study, the correlation of income with extent of sharing child care was telling. Among the couples where the mother did more child care, the husband earned an average of about nineteen thousand dollars a year more than the wife. Among the equal sharers, the discrepancy was only six thousand dollars, and 30 percent of the wives earned more than their husbands. Among those who alternated shifts, the difference was eleven thousand dollars. These discrepancies, Deutsch claims, were as much the result as the cause of how much child care was shared. Decisions about what jobs husbands as well as wives took, how much time they spent working, and their interpretations of the demands of those jobs were part of the negotiations on child care. Most of the wives could earn what their husbands earned; it was commitment to equal sharing of child care versus gender-based norms that influenced time spent in paid work and in domestic work. Among working-class alternating-shift couples, even when the wife was the better earner, the husband worked more hours and the wife did more child care; thus they maintained the gender-appropriate roles of primary breadwinner and primary parent.[43]

Barbara Risman's study of shared parenting focused on deliberately "gender-fair" heterosexual families. An extensive search process turned up only fifteen families that met the equality criteria: a forty-sixty or better split on sharing household labor, equal responsibility for breadwinning and child rearing, and a self-assessment that their relationship was fair. (Their gender fairness was reflected in their family surnames.) They tended to divide housework by preference and competence without much discussion or argument (and with supplemental paid cleaning help). The majority of the couples had dual careers—both were career oriented, and each felt that the other's career was as important as his or her own. Two of the couples were what Risman called dual nurturers, less career oriented than focused on home and family. Another family, with older children, was deliberately structured for sharing domestic tasks equally among all five members of the household.[44]

In Anna Dienhart's study of eighteen couples with young

children and a commitment to sharing, all were dual nurturers devoted to the basic goal that each parent be intimately involved in the physical and emotional work of child rearing. Within this commitment, Dienhart's couples had a variety of work-family divisions: dual incomes, job sharing, mother or father doing part-time work, and mother or father as stay-at-home parent with a home-based business. For some couples, the parenting work was fully interchangeable; for others, it was partly specialized. For some, negotiations on who does what were flexible; for others, it was based on equity accounting. Dienhart calls their structure tag-team parenting. All the couples were strong, well-matched teams with confidence in each other's child-rearing skills. They could, therefore, equally share and trade off the work and responsibility of parenting.[45]

Adults' relationships are often strengthened by their shared involvement with their children. They spend a lot of time talking about raising the children, comparing and improving each other's skills. The downside is that neither partner gets to have a conventional "male career" because neither has a "wife" to do the work at home. Both are workers in both spheres; both get the rewards of their work and of hands-on parenting. Both also get the fatigue, the boredom of performing household chores, the time crunch, the guilt that they are spending either too much or too little time with their children or on their work.[46]

How widespread is equal parenting likely to be among heterosexual couples in the United States? African American fathers are more likely to share parenting than White fathers, because of the need for two incomes. Circumstances certainly dictate how the family can be structured, but a study based on two waves of the National Survey of Families and Households

(1987–88 and 1992–94) found that "the modal division of labor in contemporary marriage is more gender-traditional than egalitarian, especially after the initiation of parenthood."[47] For more couples to share parenting equally, women have to give up being the chief child-care expert, and men have to learn how to be one. Also necessary are gender-equal pay scales, "family-friendly policies" in workplaces *and* encouragement of their use, and access to an affordable system of supplemental high-quality child care outside the home.

DOES DEGENDERED PARENTING BEGET DEGENDERED CHILDREN?

Susan Moller Okin argues that a genderless family would encourage children's sense of justice. She says that "the example of co-equal parents with shared roles, combining love with justice, would provide a far better example of human relations for children than the domination and dependence that often occur in traditional marriage." Francine Deutsch says that the advantages of equal parenting for children are higher self-esteem and two knowledgeable, responsible adults who can substitute and fill in for each other.[48]

Barbara Risman assessed the children in her gender-egalitarian families as "growing up to be happy, healthy, and well adjusted" but not especially gender-free. In interviews and observation of twenty-one children ranging in age from four to fifteen, Risman found a complex combination of gender-egalitarian values and gendered identities. The children, like their parents, believed that women and men were equal in capabilities and should be equal socially, but from their experiences at school and with their peers, they got the message that boys and girls were totally different. She says, "It almost seems as if these children believe that boys and girls are opposites but that men and women are magically transformed into equal and comparable people." In their own interests and activities, six of the children were more stereotypically gendered while fifteen crossed gender lines. The girls tended to recognize when and how their behavior was nongendered; the boys tended to ignore their nontraditionality. Risman predicts that for all the children, the parents' egalitarian, nongendered values relating to adult responsibilities in the home will be models for their own adult behavior.[49]

What of nonheterosexual parenting's effects? In a careful review of studies that claimed few or no differences between children raised by heterosexual and "lesbigay" parents, Judith Stacey and Timothy Biblarz found that "children with two same-gender parents, and particularly with co-mother parents, . . . develop in less gender-stereotypical ways than . . . children with two heterosexual parents." They are also more open to homoerotic relationships, and the girls are more sexually experimental. They are, however, no more likely to become gay or lesbian as adults than children raised by heterosexual parents.[50]

It may not take strictly egalitarian households to encourage children to plan on degendered family roles. Kathleen Gerson argues that today's young adults are already children of a gender revolution that has changed attitudes and behavior. Her life-history interviews with 120 women and men of diverse racial ethnic and social-class groups, aged eighteen to thirty-two, found that as a result of divorce and remarriage, most had lived in nontraditional households before they were eighteen years old. For themselves, they wanted autonomy and commitment, love and work, and egalitarian relationships. However, the men she interviewed would settle for "modified traditionalism," where they were the primary breadwinner and had a partner to do most of the domestic work while also contributing financially. The women, in contrast, would forgo marriage (but not children) rather than be economically dependent.[51]

Deutsch claims that equal sharing does not take special people; rather, "it is a by-product of the negotiations over all the details of everyday life in a family." In light of Gerson's findings that men are more inclined to the conventional family division of labor, these negotiations may take strong women. Deutsch found that in unequal households, wives live by myths that mask their own ambitiousness and their husband's power to resist their pleas for help; on the surface, at least, they claim their family pattern is their own choice. They are "ambivalent about what they are entitled to at home, ask for less, and ask less directly." Conversely, "equally sharing women feel entitled to equality," and they negotiate their family patterns openly and directly. They are "also not afraid to use power, and the language of power." Some had insisted that they wouldn't get married, stay married, or have children if their husbands wouldn't take on half the child-care load; others refused to cook or clean until the husband pitched in. Older children are certainly aware of family myths and family negotiations, which serve as negative and positive models.[52]

STRUCTURING DEGENDERED HOUSEHOLDS FOR EQUALITY

Discussing what she calls the postmodern family, Judith Stacey says that "the complex patterns of divorce, remarriage, and stepkinship" create a "New Age extended family" that links a household of adults and children with kin outside the household who have varied economic responsibilities and caring duties for those in the household. These households, whether headed by heterosexual women or lesbians, tend to be woman-centered, but they could be degendered. Any grouping of adults could share both the income from paid work and their domestic labor and thus provide economic support and nurturing care for the children, elderly, and sick in a household. As Stacey says:

> In theory, the postmodern family condition of pluralism and flexibility should represent a democratic opportunity in which individuals' shared capacities, desires, and convictions could govern the character of their gender, sexual, and family relationships.[53]

The fluid households of divorced parents, poor and working-class single mothers, African American families, immigrant families, stepfamilies, and gay and lesbian co-parents are today considered deviant family forms in Western postindustrial societies. Although some governments have extended the legal benefits of marriage to cohabiting heterosexual and nonheterosexual couples in domestic partnerships, the complexities of second-parent adoption and other ways of ensuring that adults who are not related by blood can have legal permanent relationships with children are only beginning to be explored. A group of adults and children living together could legitimately be a family if there were a way of sharing legal responsibility for each other in a nongendered civil union.[54]

Alternatively, Martha Albertson Fineman proposes that the basic legal family unit be a "mother" (caretaker) and "child" (dependent). It would be the only unit given legal protection and the benefits of the welfare state. The parents and siblings of the mother could be discretionary members of her household, but the core unit would be the mother-child dyad. Sexual affiliations would be private concerns. Men are not excluded:

> Men can and should be Mothers. In fact, if men are interested in acquiring legal rights and access to children (or other dependents), . . . they *must* be Mothers in the stereotypical nurturing sense of that term—that is, engaged in caretaking. Second, the Child . . . stands for all forms of inevitable dependency—the dependency of the ill, the elderly, the disabled, as well as actual children.[55]

My preference would be a legal civil union or domestic partnership among adults with specified responsibilities for each other and the children with whom they claim bonds. The adults and their children would be state-designated kin for citizenship, taxes, health care, and welfare benefits. They could share a family name as well as keep their own surname. What they called each other in kinship terms would be a private matter or evolve gradually in linguistic public discourse. Simple solutions would be to use first names at home and "life partner" and "co-parent" with others. Sexual relationships among adults would be private, although state regulations would forbid sexual abuse of children. The state would not issue marriage licenses but would ratify contracts for civil unions. The breakup of a civil union, or one partner leaving a multiple-partner union that remained in effect, would be equivalent to a legal divorce, with specified continuance of financial support and visitation rights. Weddings would be social or religious ceremonies that were neither sanctioned nor forbidden by the state.[56]

No matter what the core legal unit, if you have a household of adults who share income generation and care work but who have different duties and responsibilities, you need a way of ensuring that no one is economically dependent and no one is overworked.[57] All household income could be pooled and allocated first to the necessary household expenses, such as food, clothing, shelter, transportation, medical care, school fees, and so on. After that, income could be allocated to household discretionary expenses, such as charitable donations, gifts, entertainment, vacations, and savings for large purchases and emergencies. To assure equal personal resources, the remainder could be split evenly among the adult members of the household for their individual use. Each adult in a household should be able to claim the same amount of discretionary income, regardless of earnings, since that surplus buys the freedom as an individual to donate, give gifts, entertain, travel, work on private projects, save, and so on. Any earnings from the discretionary income should belong to the investor who is risking her or his own individual portion of the household money. Individuals should also be able to give what they have accumulated to whomever they want.

Any household work not done through paid services, as well as responsibility for paid services—hiring, overseeing, and providing transportation—would have to be evenly split or allocated by desirability, competence, convenience, and time. If all adults shared responsibility for domestic work, each ought to be able to have equivalent time for educational and occupational advancement and political work.

If the economic system and the political system were also structured for equality (by equitable income distribution and rotated positions of authority), the egalitarian structure of domestic life would support and be supported by the egalitarian structure of work and government. Such a utopia is remote, but workplaces could be restructured in degendered ways that would eliminate work-family conflicts.

Equal sharers of parenting may be more pragmatic than ideological; personal equality rather than gender equality may be their goal. But whether or not gender rebellion is intended, the accomplishment of equally shared parenting has important implications for the gendered structures of our social worlds.[58] By suggesting the interchangeability of women and men and of biological and nonbiological parents in a domain as central to people's lives as caring for infants and raising children, shared parenting challenges one of the major gender divisions on which so much of modern society is still based. The legal recognition of extended nongendered and restructured family unions would solidify this revolution.

Chapter Three
WORKERS HAVE FAMILIES:
DEGENDERING THE WORKPLACE

*Radical reforms, perhaps even demolition and starting again from
scratch, will be necessary to remove gender from the allegedly rational-
legal-technical gender-free workplace.*

—Patricia Yancey Martin[1]

THERE IS A SCIENCE FICTION STORY by Stanislaw Lem about a
planet of Phools, where new machines are built that can produce goods endlessly, without any human intervention. The
machines replace the Drudgelings, who starve because the
owners of the machines, the Eminents, refuse to give away
the mounds of food, appliances, and other goods necessary to
sustain daily life. In the face of the inevitable rioting by the
displaced Drudgelings, the Eminents declare themselves too
emotional to keep order and commission a "purely rational,
strictly logical, and completely objective Governing Machine
that does not know the hesitation, emotion, and fear that be-
fuddle living minds." The machine produces myriads of small
black robots, which buy the surplus goods and empty the ware-
houses. Then they build a beautiful building and invite the
Drudgelings in for food and drink. The Drudgelings never
come out. The robots turn them into disks that they arrange in
orderly patterns all over the planet. The Eminents end up with
the same fate, but as the "Voluntary Universalizer of Absolute

Order" points out, it was all rational, logical, and efficient, and besides, everyone had a choice.[2]

I start with this story because we live with the fictions that workers are quasi robots without families, that organizations are run by principles of rational choice, and that emotions and empathy have to be banished from the workplace. The reality is closer to the meshed commitments of work and family described by Lisa Belkin one Mother's Day in her *New York Times* "Life's Work" column. She talked about the way her mother, a professor, was caring for her seriously ill husband and attending to her teaching duties while her daughters—Belkin and her sisters—took time off from their jobs to fill in for their mother by taking their father to doctors, leaving their husbands to care for the children when they came home from work.[3]

The fiction that workers (and employers) are "rational men" who make decisions based only on cost-benefit calculations has been critiqued by feminists and some economists. They argue that decisions as to who does what in the workplace and in the home are not made "rationally" in response to available jobs and salary scales but are heavily influenced by familial and community pressures and are often the "least worst alternative."[4] A woman making a much higher salary than her husband may cut back on her work to take care of small children because of moral pressures on her as a woman while he will feel he needs to be the breadwinner because he is a man. A study of 144 married physicians who reduced the hours they worked to attend to family demands found that most were women, even when their husbands' job prospects were unstable and they made half what their wives made. The decision to cut back was not the wives' preference but a response to "social acceptability."[5]

In postindustrial societies, men and women workers are not that different; both act and choose as workers emotionally as well as rationally, but they are treated differently, most especially as family members. The heart of the difference is the assumption that women workers have families and men workers have wives. In this assumption, all workers have families, but only women should be encumbered by them. Child care and household management are their responsibility, so the work-family conflict is their problem. In contrast, as workers, men are enhanced by their families. Their responsibility for economic support goads them to work hard, make more money, and get promotions. When the production-reproduction unit is the individual nuclear family and there is no extended family or government system that can bear some of the burdens, the gendered system of organizing family responsibilities and paid work is guaranteed to create time pressures and unpalatable decisions by women and men who want to both work and spend time with their families.[6]

In the last chapter, I explored the possibilities of degendered parenting. In this chapter, I will explore the possibilities of degendering the workplace to make degendered parenting (and other domestic responsibilities) more possible. How we think and talk about work and workers—the discourse that reflects gendered assumptions and values—needs to change. Work practices need to recognize that all workers have second shifts—their work as family maintainers, caretakers of children and other kin, community and political volunteers. Professionals and managers have a third shift—as collaborative colleagues, supportive mentors, and competitive self-promoters. To treat workers as humans, not robots, work organizations need to structure into their schedules twenty-first-century ways of using place and time more flexibly.

WORK, FAMILY, AND CITIZENSHIP

The production of goods and services for pay or sale, feeding and maintaining adult workers, and care of children, the sick, and the elderly are the everyday occupations of most of us. It is all *work*. In nonindustrial parts of the world, the different kinds of work occur at the same time and place—on farms and in small residential businesses. Workers have also lived and worked in large communal units, such as Israeli kibbutzes, with shared child care, food preparation, and laundries. In much of the postindustrial world, paid workplaces and family residences are separate, and the logistics of travel between them, time schedules, maintaining the household, preparing meals, and taking care of children, the sick, and the elderly are personalized.

Some governments have institutionalized policies that recognize family caretaking as work that takes time, energy, thought, and skill and incurs costs and benefits to unpaid care-takers, paid workers, family members, and the whole social order. All adult men and women are considered "caring citizens"; women, however, may do most of the hands-on family work. To translate caring citizenship into both work and family practices, they have to be structured interactively. Work hours have to allow for family time, and family duties have to be shared or outsourced to day-care centers, paid help, and domestic services.[7] To degender caring citizenship, the adults in a house-

WORKERS HAVE FAMILIES   73

hold, men as well as women, have to share family work and be able to balance it with their paid work time.

In opposition to the reciprocal interaction between work and family that constitutes caring citizenship is commitment to an enterprise—a high-level organizational position, a professional or creative career, politics, activism, international work—that takes people away from their families. As Mary Blair-Loy describes devotion to work, these commitments take allegiance, intensity, and single-mindedness. The rewards are challenges and excitement, status, and "the euphoria of successfully working with like-minded devotees toward a common goal."[8] This kind of involvement makes the participant an "organizational citizen."

Organizational citizenship demands time, energy, and involvement in the informal collegial networks where ideas are generated, people are evaluated, and careers are advanced. For those trying to maintain a balance between work and family, it is, as Arlie Hochschild terms it, the third shift. Cutting back on work commitments usually means cutting out that third shift and may mean downgrading a career to a job.[9]

What also throws work and family out of balance is an equally intense commitment to child rearing. Trying to maintain the intensity of commitment to both work and care of a family often causes burnout. Trying to work intensively and be an intensive parent is probably impossible. The gendered choices have been for mothers to parent intensively and fathers to work intensively, giving men the advantages of status, power, and financial independence. An ideal degendered solution would be for work-intensives to live with family-intensives, without regard to gender. A more likely degendered solution is for sharing parents to devote time and energy to work and to children, providing intensive parenting through their teamwork and perhaps alternating time devoted to intensive work. Children differ on the extent to which they need intensive care, and their needs change as they grow. Careers, too, have downtimes and uptimes. Indeed, their whole shape has changed. Close studies of career paths find that they are no longer linear, individualized, employer-responsive, and separate from family and community, but for both women and men careers are "multiplex." They are relational, driven by employee needs, and intertwined with family and community.[10]

Attitudes toward women's roles have changed. Married mothers with good educations now have social approval for the lifelong, full-time pursuit of prestigious careers as well as the freedom to quit "for the sake of their family." Women's seeming always to "come home" is the outcome of a gendered division of labor that consistently discourages and does not reward their total immersion in public life.[11] For most women in postindustrial societies whose households are not totally economically dependent on them, the work-family combination remains what it has been since the Industrial Revolution took the production of goods and services out of the home and placed them in factories and offices—their paid work is fitted around the care of children and the maintenance of households. More and more, even for women with small children, that paid work is a full-time job.

What seems like personal choice is heavily influenced by government policies. Many European countries and Israel have policies of maternal leave and subsidized child care that encourage women with small children to stay in the paid workforce, but because they have the organizational and emotional responsibility for their families, women are discouraged from competing with men for high-level, better-paid, full-time positions. Should they do it anyway, they incur informal undercutting by men who feel they have enough competition from other men. Countries that subsidize mothers and children but do not provide child care encourage women to stay out of the paid workforce. Countries that subsidize neither mothers nor child care—as is the case in the United States—make the "juggling act" a responsibility of individual families.[12]

A society's attitudes toward the importance of having children greatly influences attitudes toward organizing work time around family responsibilities. In the United States, men and women working in jobs where men are the predominant workers are the most likely to sacrifice family duties and the least likely to forgo a promotion or working extra hours for the sake of their family.[13] In Israel, where having children is a mandate for men as well as women, divorced men in high-tech industries who plead that they need flextime to be able to see their children are usually granted it. Women executives in those industries also have gained enough clout to organize their work schedules around their children.[14]

The ideal worker, from the point of view of the boss, is one who needs the job for survival or to support a family but whose family does not interfere with the job. That ideal ignores the extent to which workers juggle work and family responsibilities. A study of American workers showed that women and men, young and old, all cut back on their work when they had to care for family members. Among 870 workers aged twenty-five to sixty-four who were interviewed every day for a week,

30 percent cut back on at least one day, and 5 percent needed to cut back on three or more days.[15]

Without unions that can bargain collectively for higher pay, better working conditions, sick pay, and vacations, workers are exploitable. But unions in the United States have rarely bargained for maternity leave, so pregnancy and childbirth have to be categorized as illness or disability to qualify for paid leave.[16] Caretaking time is neither, and paid leave time for it is rarely on the bargaining table. In the United States, the Family and Medical Leave Act, passed in 1993, protects men's and women's jobs for a maximum of twelve weeks without pay. Much more generous time off with pay to care for children, an ill spouse, or an elderly parent has been mandated by governments in many other Western industrial societies, but the concept of the unencumbered ideal wage worker still persists in the structure of work organizations. Workers may be treated as if they had no family life, but single, childless people are not so valued by employers, since they are thought to be too footloose and independent.

The conventional solution to having a full-time job and a family has been for one partner to work outside the home and the other to be the "wife," a stay-at-home parent who cares for the children, runs the household, keeps in touch with kin, organizes a social life, and attends to the working partner's emotional and sexual needs. This arrangement often means that the partner in the labor force has to work longer hours to support the whole family, and the stay-at-home partner is economically dependent. Dual-career families need a homemaker if both careers are to proceed equally, or one partner may opt for a less pressured full-time position, one that does not demand long hours, traveling, or intense commitment. The parents in two-job families with small children often work alternating shifts, so one parent is always available at home. Another common arrangement is for one parent to work part-time and manage the household while the other works full-time and for the couple to supplement parental care with schools, day-care centers, kin, or paid domestic child carers. These arrangements also occur where couples are divorced or have stopped living together but continue to have caretaking and financial responsibility for their children.

None of these solutions for managing home and long work hours are ideal, but they would not culminate in gender inequality if as many fathers as mothers were the partner who opted for part-time work or a less pressured job or became the stay-at-home partner. Unfortunately, the discourse, practices, and structuring of work organizations and families assume that for men the prime family responsibility is to provide economic support and for women it is to take care of home and children. The reasoning starts with the unexamined belief that mothers are better at parenting than fathers and that mothers suffer more from separation from the children they have "fallen in love with." Given a real choice, more men might show their superior parenting skills and refuse to be limited fathers. More families might divide child care and economic support equitably, so that each partner benefits from intimate parenting *and* the rewards of paid work.

Without such degendering of family and work commitments, mothers make less money, are more likely to be fired, achieve fewer positions of authority and prestige, and have much less chance to wield social power. Those who cut back or leave the workplace are socially downgraded and lose marital bargaining power. Working-class single mothers may end up on welfare. At the upper end of the occupational scale, women lawyers who leave large firms that feed into the government, judgeships, and politics to teach, work in advocacy, or start alternative small law firms make significant social contributions, but they won't be seen in the current corridors of power. Women managers and executives also fall out of the prestigious career pipeline:

> A selection process that winnows women out of this stream has the effect of keeping a disproportionate number of qualified women out of top government jobs, off the bench, and out of the loop for corporate directorships and other leadership positions.[17]

GENDERED WORKPLACES

Our assumptions that women and men workers are significantly different underlie the gendering of the organization of work. Workplaces are more or less gendered on several levels. One is the extent of gender segregation and stratification, which can be assessed by the demographics and hierarchies of a workplace. In many organizations, women and men do not work together in the same physical space. They don't do the same jobs, or they do the same jobs with different names and salaries. Men usually boss women and men, but women usually supervise only women.

Other aspects of gendering are cultural and evaluative. When workers are recruited, gendered characteristics influence the search process for candidates who have "masculine," "feminine," or "neutral" traits. In Westernized cultures, "masculine" would be physical strength, rationality, objectivity, aggressiveness; "feminine" would be dexterity, emotional sensitivity, psychological perceptivity, ability to mediate and compromise. "Neutral" would be intelligence, honesty, experience, mental agility. The gender designation of the attributes is culturally contingent, and the skills needed for a job are frequently regendered as the gender composition of the workforce changes. Thus, when most bankers were men, it was argued that only men knew how to handle large sums of money. Now, bank tellers, branch managers, and financial-services providers are routinely women because it is believed that they are good with customers and clients, but global financiers are almost all men. The same jobs can be stereotyped as masculine "dangerous work" in one country and feminine work needing "nimble fingers" in another. The corollary of the attribution of desired characteristics is the valuation of men workers over women workers, men's jobs over women's typical jobs, and "masculine" over "feminine" work capabilities.[18]

Workplaces are gendered, jobs within workplaces are gendered, recruitment is for women or men, and desired attributes are "masculine" or "feminine." Whatever way you consider gender, the economic outcome seems to be stubbornly uniform in advantaging men. Salaries are highest in jobs where men are the predominant workers, whether the worker is a woman or a man, and lowest in jobs where women are the predominant workers, again whether the worker is a man or a woman. Looked at from the perspective of the worker, men have the advantage no matter what the gender composition of the job or workplace. Men earn more than women in jobs where men are the majority, in jobs where women are the majority, and in gender-neutral jobs. In 2002 among full-time, year-round workers in the United States, women earned 74.3 percent of men's wages. Full-time, year-round workers who are fathers earn more than childless men; mothers earn less than women without children.[19]

The extent of gendering depends on the decisions, policies, and history of the particular workplace. These factors produce a structure: allocation of jobs, salary scales, advancement criteria, evaluation of workers, leave and return policies, type of control (rule based, top down, collegial). This structure is maintained through the interactions of the workers as colleagues and as bosses and underlings and through their decisions and choices as they evaluate and work within the organizational system. The structure is legitimated by rationales for the selection and placement of new workers and the advancement of some and not others.[20]

Tacitly or openly, the underlying assumptions of family responsibilities influence the recruitment, retention, and advancement policies of workplace managers:

> For men, real, imagined or potential domestic responsibilities were usually evaluated as a positive indication of stability, flexibility, compatibility and motivation, while for women, they were often viewed negatively as confirmation of unreliability and a short-term investment in work. However, these selector assumptions could be reversed, where the jobs on offer were low paying, low status, and mundane with little career potential. For such jobs, it was often decided, on the basis of the stereotype of the dependent female homemaker, that women would be more stable, flexible and able to "fit in."[21]

Such stereotyping disadvantages men and women in couples who share parenting and breadwinning, whether they are heterosexual or homosexual, and leaves single parents, women or men, virtually out of the loop.

These discriminatory practices persist even with equal opportunity guidelines because so much of recruitment and evaluation is interactive, and interaction between women and men is steeped in gendered beliefs and ideologies. Gender is a "superschema," an "invisible hand," a set of cultural rules that pattern face-to-face encounters.[22] This taken-for-granted frame works as long as the participants look and behave appropriately, that is, by gendered rules. Resistance, rebellion, and transgression may be tolerated by people who know one another well and in public celebrations of difference (such as gay pride parades), but the workplace is the least acceptable place for a man to be noncompetitive or a woman to be an assertive "bully broad."[23] I would argue that for a man to be a father first and a worker second or a woman to be a worker first and a mother second is a major workplace transgression. Even a presentation of oneself as someone with equal commitment to work and to family goes against the gender grain.

The pervasive cultural beliefs about women and men workers that perpetuate gender inequality support the devaluation of women's competence by men. Women themselves help to sustain the devaluation because they frequently compare themselves with other women, not men, at the same level. The unequal salary scales and opportunities for career advancement thus seem fair because there are no challenges to the beliefs that sustain them. The process producing gender inequality in the workplace is interactive and structural. As Cecilia Ridgeway says:

The result is a system of interdependent effects that are everywhere and nowhere because they develop through multiple
workplace interactions, often in taken-for-granted ways. Their
aggregate result is structural: the preservation of wage inequality and the sex segregation of jobs.[24]

Gendered Workers

One of the classic feminist dilemmas has been how to degender
the workplace without turning women into men. Feminists
want men to parent the way women are supposed to—with
thought and emotional attention to children's needs—but
don't want women to work the way men allegedly do—single-
mindedly, competitively, without regard for feelings, objec-
tively, purely rationally. The truth is that men don't work that
way. Women and men workers act pretty much the same. They
form inner circles, look out for their friends and undercut their
enemies, cover for each other, use work time for showing off
their accomplishments and gossiping about colleagues and
bosses, recommend and hire their friends and compatriots.

This informal organization of work circles encourages gatekeeping that excludes workers of different racial ethnic and religious groups. It certainly perpetuates separating women from
men in persistent and almost irradicable gender segregation of
jobs and work sites. When women and men do work together,
men often act as if the women were invisible, secretaries, or sex
objects, unless the women act the way men are supposed to—
stay late, go out for drinks after work, talk sports. Women who
go home to their children and talk about their children at work
are "different." So are men, but they are far less likely to
do so.[25]

To counter the discriminatory outcomes of the informal organization of work, feminists have pushed for affirmative action policies that counteract clone hiring. Sexual harassment guidelines and policies have been formulated to protect workers from unwanted sexual approaches, sexual attacks, threats of retaliation for refusing sex, and inappropriate sexualization of the workplace environment. Young women workers have been taught how to play the networking and mentoring game, and older women have been urged to sponsor younger women protégées. Women who work mostly with other women, as nurses do, seem to know these career-enhancing practices without special lessons. They have no trouble attaining positions of leadership and authority; ironically, they don't hold men back either.[26]

Thus, it is not substantial differences in the work practices of women and men that sustain the gendered workplace; rather, it is that these practices produce inclusion and exclusion. Those whose social characteristics are the same as most of the other workers are believed to be more trustworthy. They can be counted on to abide by the informal norms of the workplace—pace of work, what should not be made public, what the higher-ups don't need to know, and so on. As Everett Hughes said thirty years ago about trust and loyalty in work organizations: "These factors conspire to make colleagues, with a large body of unspoken understandings, uncomfortable in the presence of what they consider odd kinds of fellows."[27] The Western world does not wall off women from men or cover them with veils, but it creates separation and invisibility through practices and language that designate men as "normal" workers and women as the "oddballs."

It is no accident that many corporate whistle-blowers are women. Many women who work in organizations dominated by men are "outsiders within." The concept conveys being inside but not one of the insiders and so feeling alienated and isolated. But there are some advantages to being an outsider within—you can see things the insiders take for granted, such as not-quite-legal compromises, shortcomings, and wrongdoings. The three women whistle-blowers who were chosen as *Time*'s 2002 Persons of the Year were just such corporate outsiders within.

Coleen Rowley was the critic of the FBI's practices that led to its neglect of suspicious flight-school students in the summer of 2001. Cynthia Cooper uncovered the falsified financial records at WorldCom. Sherron Watkins went public with Enron's accounting fakery. After their whistle-blowing hit the headlines, Rowley said that none of her e-mails to FBI headquarters suggesting new investigative and legal strategies received a substantive response. Cooper was kept at a distance by the senior executives at World-Com. Watkins is making a living with lectures and book and movie deals. Commenting on its choice of these courageous women, who took a lot of flak for their open criticisms of the FBI, WorldCom, and Enron, *Time* said:

> Their lives may not have been at stake, but Watkins, Rowley and Cooper put pretty much everything else on the line. Their jobs, their health, their privacy, their sanity—they risked all of them to bring us badly needed word of trouble inside crucial institutions.

Lest you think they had high-earning husbands to fall back on, their outsider position was true of their personal lives, too.

All three were married with children and the breadwinners in their families at the time they risked their careers. What's more, Cooper's and Rowley's husbands were full-time stay-at-home dads. To quote *Time* again: "For every one of them, the decision to confront the higher-ups meant jeopardizing a paycheck their families truly depended on." They weren't so different from most of the men in their organizations who were invested in their careers and supporting families. Yet their gender was crucial—not because women are more honest or less committed to their careers or need their paychecks less than men do. Their gender was crucial because they were oddball sisters in the organizational brotherhood—as women with families and, even more oddball, with homemaking husbands.[28]

Exclusionary gender tactics may sound outmoded for the twenty-first century, when men have encountered women co-workers and leaders in many situations. Few men these days would put down women's capabilities. They don't have different interests—women can easily talk sports and sex; men can easily talk babies and schools. Many single women and men are equally free of family responsibilities. The big difference is between mothers and fathers. The working mother is suspected of divided attention and insufficient career commitment even though research shows that women who work full-time and take care of families are more productive than men who do only one of those jobs.[29] If a working mother asks for a temporary flexible or part-time work schedule, she jeopardizes her chances for advancement on resuming full-time work. Men who might want to take parental leave or cut back on their work to spend more time with their children are discouraged even more by the "parent track" stigma and by negative responses from colleagues, relatives, and friends.

THE HEAD-ON CLASH: CHANGED FAMILIES AND UNCHANGED WORKPLACES

Against these gendered assumptions about men and women workers with children is the postindustrial phenomenon of married mothers who have small children and husbands in the workforce and are working full-time because the family needs the income and because they are committed to careers.[30] Despite the cultural lag in public opinion and unchanged workplaces, most of these women don't opt out. They organize their work and family life to be able to do both.

An article on professional development in the *Journal of the American Medical Women's Association,* aptly titled "In Search of Balance: Medicine, Motherhood, and Madness," gave explicit advice for constructing a "strategic life plan." The advice included the evaluation of positions not only on their work demands but also on location (near home is best) and on the family friendliness of future colleagues. Other advice was to pick a partner who would be flexible and responsive to family demands and who would share child-care and household duties, as well as finding, keeping, and monitoring "excellent, reliable, and stable child care." But most of the advice was for the woman herself: time management, organization, delegation, reasonable goals, and planning everything—pregnancy, breastfeeding, time with children, and meals—and then learning how to bend with the inevitable emergencies.[31]

These complex time demands are experienced by women of all occupational levels, not just doctors who expect to work eighty-hour weeks. As Jerry Jacobs and Kathleen Gerson point out in their analysis of household "time binds," in the majority of married couples today, both adults work full-time. Their analysis of the work hours of 24,125 couples in the United States in 2000 found that 59.6 percent were dual earner, with husbands working about forty-five hours per week and wives about thirty-seven hours per week. This allocation to paid work held for wives of all educational levels and for those with one to three children under the age of eighteen.[32] Cross-national comparisons of postindustrial countries using a different data set showed that the highest percentage of dual-earner couples was in Sweden, with 85.1 percent, followed by Finland, with 80.6 percent. In this data set, the United States came next, with 72.3 percent. The percentage of dual-earner couples in Canada and France was over 60 percent; in Belgium, Germany, and the United Kingdom, it was over 50 percent. The lowest was Italy, with about 45 percent.[33]

The division of work time between men and women in dual-earner couples is not enormous, and the work-family time crunch is experienced by men as well as women, even men with stay-at-home wives. In fact, men whose wives are not employed would prefer to work *less* than those whose wives have outside jobs. Reports from U.S. workplace surveys found that women with full-time jobs work only about 6 hours less than men with full-time jobs and that both would prefer to work about 10 hours less a week. Married men with employed spouses and married men with unemployed spouses work about 48 hours per week; the former's ideal would be 9.9 hours less; the latter, 11 hours less. Married women with employed spouses worked about 41 hours per week; their ideal was 11 hours less; married women with unemployed spouses worked 38.5 hours and could afford to wish for only 5.7 hours less. Children under six added an hour to men's preferred reduction in work time but did not change women's. These averages blur educational and occupational differences: the trend is that managers and professionals want to work less; those at the bottom of the socioeconomic scale would like to work more.[34]

The time crunch is experienced similarly by men and women in the United States. The U.S. National Study of the Changing Workforce found that 59.8 percent of the men and 55.5 percent of the women surveyed attested to conflict in balancing work, personal life, and family life. The differences were not by gender but by parenthood. Among women, 65 percent with children under eighteen felt the conflict, compared with 45 percent of those without children that age. Among men, 75 percent with children under eighteen were pulled in too many directions, compared with 50 percent of men without young or teenage children. Work flexibility, autonomy, and supportive supervisor and workplace culture eased the burdens on parents with economic and domestic responsibilities.[35]

Cross-national comparisons show that economic factors, state-provided benefits, and family structure (single, married, with or without children) all influence workers' desires for more or fewer hours of work. Men and women in the United States put financial need before family in their desired work hours. In Sweden, where family benefits are generous, part-time work is attractive for women with family responsibilities; Swedish men would also like to work fewer hours, but not because of family obligations. Germany encourages women to stay home when they have children; only childless men with a partner who works want fewer hours. Japan has the fewest mis-matches between desired and actual work hours: most women do not work full-time, and most men work long hours.[36]

The dramatic change in women's labor-force participation in postindustrial countries in the last thirty-five years, espe-cially among the more highly educated, who tend to be career-oriented professionals and managers, is only one part of the work-family balance problem. The other parts are the rigid workplace, men's varying degree of participation in household labor, and nonexistent social services or maternal-support poli-cies that encourage gender inequities. The burden of balance is on the individual woman rather than on the couple, the work-place, the community, or the government. Families have been transformed by the permanent full-time labor-force participa-tion of married women with small children, but even when fa-thers want to be equal participants in family life, there is little encouragement. As Jacobs and Gerson conclude:

> In short, whether they are mothers or fathers, parents who as-pire to balance and share the important work of earning a liv-ing and caring for a new generation face clashing, potentially irreconcilable expectations and demands. . . . We need a work-place transformation commensurate with the family transfor-mation that has already taken place.[37]

FROM "WOMEN'S TIME" TO GLOBAL TIME

In the challenge of restructuring work to match twenty-first-century postindustrial family structures, time is the battle-ground and the prize. Time is a delimited and valued resource whose uses are socially constructed, often around gender.[38]

Women's procreative work—bearing and caring for children—
takes priority when many have to be born for a few to survive.
But mothers have to feed their children, so they may have to
give first priority to production work. In agricultural societies,
procreative work and food and goods production for the family
and for the market all go on at the same time.[39] The work itself
may be gendered, but time use is governed by the sun and the
seasons, not gendered norms.

In the Western world, production work moved out of
the household and into factories and offices in the nineteenth
century and, with artificial light, spilled into night work.
Nineteenth-century protectionist laws in the United States for-
bade employers to assign women factory workers to night
work. The issue of women working at night ostensibly centers
on their physical protection, but it also protects men's monop-
oly of better-paid overtime.[40] Whole families worked long
hours at home in "cottage industries" that were unregulated
until twentieth-century child-labor laws mandated school at-
tendance.

With global time and twenty-first-century portable technology, work once again seems to be taking place at all hours
and is back in the home.[41] The self-employed have home offices, but many professionals and managers also take work
home. Academics in particular are prone to the long hours of
"cottage industries": household partners edit each other's work,
university e-mail addresses do double duty, and disks, data, and
hard copies of students', colleagues', and personal work are in
constant transit between a professor's home and college offices.
As a result, eighty-hour weeks are the norm for getting tenure
and promotion.[42]

On the domestic side, the growing numbers of married women working full-time have had an impact on the gendered allocation of time spent on household work in postindustrial European and North American countries, as have changing attitudes and media representations. From 1960 to 1997, women spent almost an hour less on cooking and cleaning; men spent about twenty minutes more.[43] Women still spend more time on housework than men, but it is not the feminist battleground it was in the 1970s. The postindustrial conflicts over time use are more over what counts as "work hours"—physical presence in a designated place, time in front of a computer screen, overtime, output, billing—and who gets the credit for them.

Time use is increasingly round-the-clock as round-the-world economic exchanges become routine. Workplace interactions that take place around the globe—by phone, e-mail, instant messaging, and data transport—are transforming face-to-face interactions from local to global "conversations" and from colleague communities of "embodied presences" to "response presences." As defined by Karin Knorr Cetina and Urs Bruegger, "response presence corresponds to situations in which participants are capable of responding to one another and common objects in real time without being physically present in the same place." In their ethnographic description of virtual financial trading markets, they argue that the same microstructural rules that govern face-to-face interactions pattern "face-to-screen" interactions—evolving intersubjectivity, reciprocal exchanges, and interpersonal evaluations. Engagement evokes emotions, and language is earthy, sexual, and aggressive, transposing male physicality into metaphor—the classics,

"don't fuck with me" and "I got shafted." Instead of disembod-
iment leading to degendering, sex, sexuality, and gender have
become the lingua franca of computerized workplaces, easily
re-creating the gender inclusion and exclusion of embodied
colleague communities and the stratification of work and
workers.[44]

The permeation of gender in virtual interactions extends to
time use. With global markets, trading can take place around
the clock, generating long hours for dedicated workers. Work
done at home can be meshed with family time, or it can dis-
place it. Alternatives are easy to organize, especially since data
are instantly transportable. Teams can work fixed hours in
shifts, making it possible for more married women with children to participate.[45] Other simple solutions to allow for more
flexible time use are stores that are open at night and on weekends, school holidays that coincide with work holidays, workplace cafeterias that provide full meals throughout the day and
evening, on-site child care and routine medical services, and
better transportation between residential areas and work centers. The more workers there are on the job around the clock
and all week, the more services there will be for them, creating
more 24/7 jobs. The number of hours and days are a given;
what humans do with them is not.

STRATEGIES FOR RESTRUCTURING WORK

Integrated work and family lives are not individual accomplishments but depend on formal company policies and informal norms for workplace presence and absence. As Jerry Jacobs
and Kathleen Gerson point out, the situation for many workers

who need to mesh family time with work time is equivalent to nineteenth-century workers who got sick or wanted to observe a religious holiday—bargaining was between the boss and the worker, and the worker was often penalized. In postindustrial countries, workers are so used to contracts for a certain number of work hours and paid sick days, vacation days, personal days and a certain amount of disability and unemployment insurance and, in most European countries, health insurance as well that they consider anything less sweatshop conditions. They are, of course, the privileged workers of the world, but they are also the standard-bearers for workers in developing countries. What we need now, Jacobs and Gerson say, is similar collective, legal guarantees of the rights of parents to workplaces structured for integrating family life and work life.[46]

Employers throughout the world have already instituted strategies for restructuring the workplace to be family friendly without penalizing the individual worker. A study tour of Japan, Australia, Sweden, Germany, the Netherlands, and Italy during 2000, sponsored by the Economic Policy Institute, based in Washington, D.C., obtained information on these policies from government officials, academics, union representatives, and employers' associations.[47]

These employers routinely make innovative use of flexible work time for all workers, not just parents. One strategy is to allow employees to work at home one day a week or to leave early and finish their work later on in the evening. International firms working on varied time schedules probably already expect their employees to follow clients around the clock. One law firm in Sydney outfitted home offices with laptop computers, fax machines, extra telephone lines, and cell phones. Employees may still be working long hours, but the autonomy and flexibility reduce the time-crunch burden.

Autonomy and flexibility can also be achieved by giving workers a choice of shift lengths within a fixed number of weekly hours or a choice of eight-hour days spread over a thirty-two- to thirty-six-hour workweek. Swedish law gives workers the option of a six-hour day until their children are eight years old or in the first grade. Pay is prorated, but the government covers the balance to ensure that workers are making a full-time salary. Other strategies also get away from the nine-to-five Monday-to-Friday mind-set, such as averaging weekly hours over several weeks or a month and letting employees work longer and shorter weeks.

Such strategies are transformative if they restructure time schedules for all workers, not just those with family needs. If jobs are structured on the assumption that a worker should be full-time and on site at the same time as all other workers, part-time work, off-site work, and flextime are all deviant. Workers who do not adhere to "conventional" hours (which may include overtime, travel, and weekend work) are stigmatized for not being fully committed to their jobs. Taking time away from the job to care for children or family members, whether sporadically or by establishing a new schedule, is seen as a special favor, a career-breaking choice, or a prerogative only of well-paid, highly placed personnel.[48] Joan Williams, a feminist lawyer, argues that "jobs designed around an ideal-worker schedule discriminate against women on the basis of their inability to command the flow of family work that supports most male ideal workers."[49] They also discriminate against men who want to share family work.

An obvious alternative is normalizing flextime—a solution to the double burden of work and family that is at least a generation old. Flextime offers employees a choice from a cafeteria of schedules and production goals with commensurate salary scales and with a guarantee of equal benefits, such as health insurance (if provided by the employer), advancement possibilities, and seniority tracks. Such choices would allow all workers to mesh their paid work with family responsibilities, family budgets, and personal interests, such as getting further training or education, buying time out to pursue a creative project, engage in politics, or do community work. Evaluation of workers would depend on their meeting their chosen work goals, which might include a certain amount of face time with clients and colleagues. Some workers, even those on a career track, might put face time with their children first, letting advancement slide for a while.

Given the round-the-clock hours of so many types of work, flexible schedules may be the actual norm, even though we still think in terms of a nine-to-five-day, five-day-a-week job as "full-time." Williams documents the ways that large and small firms employing manufacturing and service workers have benefited from flexible work schedules and staggered staffing in increased productivity and worker retention. Vacations, sick leave, and emergency absences from work can be covered without hiring temporary workers; there are fewer gaps in production and customer service and greater coverage during busy times. She argues that accepting flexible schedules as the norm, rather than dividing workers into "full-time" and "part-time," might also stop dividing them into "mothers and others."[50]

Degendering Discourse about Workers

The solutions to gendered time use seem so obvious and easy to organize. What, then, are the barriers? Cynthia Fuchs Epstein points to the constraints of gendered time norms and the power of time ideologies to evoke sanctions and guilt when they are transgressed, even if they are contradictory.[51] Norms of intensive mothering preclude multitasking, an about-face from the common practice of cooking, cleaning, and telephoning while children play. Carrying responsibility for multiple roles is today thought to lead to stress, burnout, and not doing any of them well even though most people easily move from task to task and think about one while doing another, both in the workplace and at home. Sometimes the spillover effects are positive, sometimes negative, but they do not necessarily create feelings of failure.

The Cornell Couples and Careers Study of 979 dual-earner, middle-class couples found that most felt "reasonably successful" in work and family life. Both men and women reported higher levels of family success (84.5 percent) than work success (79.3 percent). The women in the study were more likely than the men to feel they had successfully balanced work and family life, but both reported reciprocally positive interactions between these major parts of their lives. The authors sum up: "Thus, contrary to popular conceptions, we see positive spillover in various aspects of successful living."[52]

How can we change the prevailing discourse about mothers and fathers and paid work so that it reflects twenty-first-century reality? One way is to change the way work and workers are framed. Frames are assumptions that funnel discussions about the feasibility and evaluation of practices. They construct a reality that seems "natural" but is changeable. As Erving Goffman says in *Frame Analysis,* "Social frameworks . . . provide background understandings for events that incorporate the will, aim, and controlling effort of an intelligence, a live agency, the chief one being the human being."[53] Social frameworks legitimize or demonize transformations, and this evaluation in turn encourages or discourages new policies and structural changes. The responses of Sweden and the United States to mothers' mass entry into the labor market demonstrate the power of frameworks.[54]

In Sweden, women's labor-force participation through the life cycle is seen as a social contribution in light of a small population and diminishing birth rate. The country therefore supports women as workers by providing services and benefits to them as mothers. Mothers are encouraged by a generous but term-limited paid maternity leave to go back to work after having a child. Fathers are encouraged by paid paternal-leave allocations to share child care. In addition, all workers are entitled to paid sick leave and paid leave to attend to sick children and shorter working hours when children are young. A byproduct of expanded social services is the proliferation of employment opportunities in the public sector, jobs held mostly by women. This symbiotic relationship between the state's support of women as mothers and its need for them as workers has somewhat undercut gender equality—men hold the higher-level public-sector jobs and dominate manufacturing, professional, and managerial positions in the private sector. In short, the new frame continues the gendering of workers and just reconstructs women as mother-workers. Men are formally reconstructed as father-workers, but informal norms still expect their full-time commitment to work.

In the United States, the employment of married women is seen as an individual choice for personal satisfaction or to supplement household income at a time of men's diminishing job opportunities. Children are not valued as future citizens, so child care by the mother or a paid worker is devalued.[55] There is no policy for any of the social supports families in most postindustrial countries take for granted, such as subsidized parental leave, child care, or health insurance. The husband is still considered the main wage earner even though the majority of households have two or more adult earners. Paid and unpaid work are privatized and priced at market value. Long hours of paid work pay off; care of children and the elderly goes cheap. Gender equality—on the job and in the home—depends on the ambition, motivation, and negotiating skills of the individuals involved.

The model of paid work and family work on which policies are framed has to move beyond the concept of separate or overlapping spheres. The prevalence of dual-career and two-job families and single parents who juggle work and child care needs more integrative models that include paid or unpaid helpers. These models assume the embeddedness of the individual worker in a family and a community. What happens in each partner's workplace and the family demands of paid child carers and other domestic supports all have an impact on one another. Increased demands in one workplace upset the balance, as can the loss of one adult's job. The effects can be mutually supportive and energy enhancing, or the whole system can fall apart in a domino effect if one adult gets the flu or a child gets chicken pox.

Enlightened corporations and governments have for a long time provided flextime, parental leave, on-site child care, and referral services for care of children and the elderly. But they have not offered them without penalties in advancement or the stigmatization of "mommy tracks." Nor have bosses considered the impact of their seemingly trivial decisions on their employees' family life. An emergency early-morning meeting, last-minute travel, mandatory weekend or holiday work, and relocation take an enormous toll on carefully organized work-family systems. Formal policies and informal practices need to reflect awareness of the whole life of every worker if the transformation in families is to be met with transformation in the workplace.[56]

ROUTINIZATION OF THE RADICAL

As long as work-family balance is the burden of mothers, there will be little radical change. The costs of family friendliness on the job will come out of the wages and careers of parents, meaning mothers because few men will feel they can afford, economically and psychologically, to jeopardize their ability to support their family financially. Similarly, few mothers will feel they can live with the burden of guilt for neglecting their children in light of the continuing moral imperative to be a good (that is, intensive) mother.

Radical change paradoxically comes with routinization. As a young Israeli professional said to me, "When the government provides child care and everyone uses it, not just poor mothers, then there's no question about leaving your young children so you can go to work."[57] When state-subsidized early-childhood care is high quality, everyone uses it, and there are few critics. When the boss becomes a father and stops calling dinner meetings, going home while the children are still awake becomes routine. When employers offer flexible work schedules to everyone on the first day, not as a reward for "good behavior" or as a special, temporary favor to a new mother, the nine-to-five mind-set disappears. When two or more people are routinely assigned to a function or task, they are able to cover for each other, just as the adults in a household do when they share domestic work and child care.

The solution to the work-family conflict lies in a frame that assumes that all workers have dual life responsibilities and commitments and that those responsibilities have to be shared within families, communities, and nations. Sharing involves money, in the form of taxation and paying for subsidized child care and elder care, schools, health care, income support, and paid parental leave. Sharing involves time, and it is important that no one bear all the burden of care of a child or an elderly parent alone. Work-family balance is probably impossible; neither family demands nor work demands stay fixed. Children have different time needs as they grow up; grandparents age and need more attention; careers blossom and wane; jobs become available and vanish.

The better word is *interweaving*.[58] The family-work weave has to be degendered and has to include government services as well as a restructured workplace and a household where domestic work, child care, and economic support are shared among the adults. Degendered households are extremely difficult to sustain in a conventionally gendered work world. In turn, degendered workplaces and government-supported parental leave, child care, health care, and other supports for families encourage degendered and egalitarian households. They are all pieces of the elusive goal—gender equality.

Chapter Four
HEROES, WARRIORS, AND BURQAS: GENDER AFTER SEPTEMBER 11

In a time of fear, the only battle that matters is the broad-stroked cultural mano a mano over who's most macho.

—Frank Rich[1]

WE LIVE OUR WORK AND FAMILY LIVES in a cultural climate, or *zeitgeit,* a spirit of the times, sometimes stormy, sometimes becalmed. September 11 and its aftermath have been a storm of violence.

Feminists have long argued that the physical, political, and economic oppression of women reflects a society's inherent violence. The destruction of the World Trade Center and part of the Pentagon by suicidal plane hijackers on September 11, 2001, and the killing of thousands of people were, to many feminists, prime examples of masculine violence. In their eyes, the hijackers were not only fundamentalist Muslim men who used violence as a weapon against Americans, but they were also fundamentalist believers in *shari'ah,* religious laws that violently oppress women. But to many feminists, American men were no better. They had perpetuated a masculine global politics of imperialism, oil, and war. Post–September 11, feminists deplored the American paternalistic rhetoric of masculine protection that justified the bombing of Afghanistan, the invasion of Iraq, and the violation of American civil liberties.[2]

In the U.S. media, the post–September 11 picture was a conventionalizing idealization of American women and men, a propagandistic demonization of Muslim men, and a sentimentilization of Muslim women. The gender rhetoric heard over and over in the media portrayed American men as heroes and Islamic men as terrorists, American women as sad widows and Islamic women as equally sad oppressed wives. There were few attempts by journalists or feminists to build a composite picture that included both within-gender and between-gender similarities and differences, even though American and Middle Eastern women and men behaved in ways that were unconventionally as well as conventionally gendered.

Instability and powerlessness in a nation or group seem to encourage a cultural reversion to traditional gender norms—in the West, women's nurturance and men's combativeness; in Islamic countries, veiling and segregation for women, fundamentalism and martyrdom for men. These were the gender characteristics that framed the post–September 11 discourse in the U.S. media. There were stories and responses that countered the ongoing gender stereotyping, but they did not make much of a dent in the main Western media narrative of working-class heroes, grieving widows, fanatic Muslim men, and veiled Muslim women. Tolerance of gender diversity and exploration of change are more likely to flourish in either a time of calm and peace or a time of power and arrogance. The shifts in depictions of women and men in the U.S. media reflected changes in the national mood: they were conventionalized during times of vulnerability, degendered during times of powerfulness.[3]

HEROES

In the United States, the media heroes of September 11 were the firefighters and the cops, and they all seemed to be men. The heroism of the men in uniform who died at the World Trade Center spread over the cleanup crews that practically lived at ground zero for nine months. They, too, seemed to be mostly working-class men. As described by William Langewiesche in *American Ground: Unbuilding the World Trade Center,* the recovery site was "an outer-borough New York blue-collar scene—overwhelmingly Irish, Italian, and male."[4] Just as there were women rescuers on September 11, there were many women at ground zero in the months after—police, doctors, nurses, emergency medical technicians, counselors, and clergy —but it was the men who found bodies and body parts who were featured in news stories. Although the firemen at the "pile" were far outnumbered by the construction crews, they were especially valorized by "the powerful new iconography that was associated with the disaster—these New York firemen as tragic heroes, these skeletal walls, these smoking ruins as America's hallowed ground."[5]

In the months after September 11, working-class manliness was back in style. According to Maureen Dowd, in her November 28, 2001, *New York Times* column, entitled "Hunks and Brutes":

> Feminism has done a back flip. Once men in uniform were the oppressors. Now they're trophy mates. Once cops were pigs. Now they're foxes. Once firemen were the guys you brought home if you couldn't snag a doctor. Now they're the most sizzling accessory.[6]

Leslie J. Calman, an executive vice president of the National Organization for Women, countered Dowd's version of the macho hero in a letter to the editor:

> How many of us are aware of Terri Tobin, the Police Department veteran who had concrete lodged in her skull, a shard of glass in her back and a fractured ankle? Yet she pulled three people out of the rubble, helped evacuate an apartment building and gave up a spot on an ambulance so that a photographer with multiple fractures could get to a hospital.[7]

Other letters criticizing Dowd for her praise of machismo noted the heroism and deaths of women police and Port Authority officers.

On December 5, a few days after Dowd's column appeared, a front-page *New York Times* story on the police officers who died in 2001 began with an account of the police department's Medal of Honor being awarded to the husband and daughter of Moira Ann Smith, who was killed in the collapse of the World Trade Center. A picture of the father and daughter was prominent on the front page.[8] Writing about Smith and other women heroes of September 11, Peggy Drexler said:

> They offer a generation of boys and girls a new definition of heroism—a definition that doesn't transcend one gender or another but offers both genders the qualities conventionally associated with each: the nurture and fellowship of women, the command and courage of men.[9]

A book published on the first anniversary of September 11, *Women at Ground Zero: Stories of Courage and Compassion,* told the stories of thirty women survivors and three women who died in the line of duty. Its intent was to make sure that "current and future generations of children [would not] grow up believing that only men are strong, brave, and heroic."[10] But recognition of the women heroes of September 11 and afterward by feminists did little to shake the pervasive macho imagery of muscular men in uniform storming up the stairs of the World Trade Center and burly men in hard hats digging through the night into the smoking rubble.

WIDOWS

There was parallel imagery of sorrowing widows. It was a false image of helplessness, since some of the women formed an aggressive activist group that became known as the Widows of September 11. The *New York Times* described "the widows" on November 25:

> A new political group has emerged from the cinders and ash of the World Trade Center disaster site. It is a group that no city official wants to offend, one whose broad powers are only beginning to be realized by its members. In the verbal shorthand of these troubled days, it is known simply as "the widows."[11]

In the months after the collapse of the Twin Towers, "the widows" fought successfully against a cutback in the number of firefighters at ground zero and pushed for the search for bodies and body parts to continue around the clock and on holidays. Their long-term goal was to have a say in what kind of memorial the site will have and what kind of rebuilding it will undergo, but by the end of 2002 the influence of the victims' families over the plans had waned. A small group of widows of financiers who had worked for Cantor Fitzgerald were the goad behind the creation in 2002, and the public hearings in 2004, of the 9/11 Commission of inquiry into the events surrounding the attack.[12]

The partners of lesbian and gay men who died in the Pentagon bombing on September 11 became another activist group. While their stories were reported, gay and lesbian victims did not have a visible place in the collective mourning or memory. They did sue successfully to be recognized as family members by the federal September 11th Victim Compensation Fund of 2001, but they were a sidebar to the main story of conventionally gendered men heroes and the widows of heterosexual men.[13]

Women are heroes in disasters in many ways that don't get into the newspapers, as Elaine Enarson and Betty Hearn Morrow point out in the introduction to their book, *The Gendered Terrain of Disaster:*

> Typecast as helpless victims protected and rescued by vigilant men, women are in fact also present in every disaster response as mitigators, preparers, rescuers, caregivers, sustainers, and rebuilders. Focusing on women's status as dependents in the relief process and excluding them from community recovery . . . is myopic and misguided.[14]

But it is women's emotional nurturance and caregiving in disaster work that usually are the focus of media attention.[15]

For the United States after September 11, the widows were a double-sided gendered image of womanly strength in adversity and feminine vulnerability. The widows provided a way to restore blue-collar masculinity. The firemen who survived could take a manly comfort in their maternality, and they could also be protective. When the wars in Afghanistan and Iraq provided the imagery of men's heroism, the widows faded from the front pages. Then, when conditions in Iraq were in a meltdown in May 2004, the widows were featured in the media once again, in quite a new light. They were dethroned as brave and assertive heroines and depicted as financially greedy adulterers. The accounts of several affairs between firemen's widows and married firemen who had survived September 11 took on the tone of national betrayal that was permeating the news. One account said:

> Later, Charlene's widow friends would be thought of as the unappeasable widows, the wealthy widows, the lustful widows. But at the start, when they were assuming their new roles, the widows were the perfect virgins of grief, which was how they were supposed to stay.[16]

WOMEN WARRIORS

When the United States went to war in Afghanistan, the macho imagery of the firemen and police shifted to the military. Once again, the heroism of men was emphasized, and the presence of women was not remarked on. Yet a woman marine, Sgt. Jeanette L. Winters, was one of seven marines who died in the crash of a military tanker plane in Pakistan on January 9, 2002. The presence of women in the U.S. military campaign in Afghanistan may have been downplayed because the American public felt too vulnerable to think about women fighting their battles.

When the media focus on terrorism shifted to Israel, the news of the first woman Palestinian suicide bomber, twenty-seven-year-old college-educated Wafa Idris, made global head-lines in January 2001 as a startling challenge to Muslim women's traditional roles. The second woman suicide bomber blew herself up at a checkpoint just a month later. She was a twenty-two-year-old college student, Darin Abu Eisheh, who said in her farewell videotape that she believed women should take their place beside their men in fighting the Israelis. She described herself as following in the footsteps of Wafa Idris, who had been praised in some of the Arab-language media as an Islamic Joan of Arc.[17]

The Palestinian women suicide bombers were an odd turn of events given the instability in the Middle East, but I would argue that they reflect the sense of power of Arab terrorists after September 11. Participating vicariously in the severe wounding of the United States (consider the destruction of two 110-story buildings as a kind of castration), Palestinian Arabs could encourage unconventional behavior in their women.[18]

In contrast to the lack of attention to women in the military in Afghanistan in the spring of 2002, in the war in Iraq in 2003 women soldiers, pilots, marines, and prisoners of war were very much in the news. There was an extraordinary set of twelve photographs in the *New York Times* on the day the war started. Entitled "Facing Combat," the caption was "These are some of the men and women of the First Marine Division head-quarters company photographed hours before they went into Iraq." The photographs showed twelve young people in full battle gear, complete with rifles. What was extraordinary was that seven of the twelve were women and half were people of color. What was *not* extraordinary was that the two top officers—first sergeant and captain—were White men and the only ones with Anglo-Saxon names. The other names were Italian, Indian, Black American, Hispanic, Polish. The photographer was Ozier Muhammad.[19]

During the first months of the war, when America seemed to be in full control, the stories about U.S. military women's visible presence in Iraq treated them as frontline soldiers; in the later period, when troops, the UN, and European agencies were attacked and bombed, the stories became increasingly gendered. At first, women soldiers became the representatives of America's good side. In a column entitled "A Woman's Place," Nicholas Kristof began and ended this way:

> The only time I saw Iraqi men entirely intimidated by the American-British forces was in Basra, when a cluster of men gaped, awestruck, around an example of the most astoundingly modern weapon in the Western arsenal. Her name was Claire, and she had a machine gun in her arms and a flower in her helmet. . . .
>
> One of the reasons we go to war is to uphold values—like equality for all. We transmit that message every time our troops encounter foreigners, particularly when our soldiers have flowers in their helmets and names like Claire.[20]

The quintessential heroic woman soldier was twenty-year-old blond, beautiful, wounded Pfc. Jessica Lynch, rescued from an Iraqi hospital in a commando raid on April 1, 2003. Her story was supposed to exemplify the bravery of both women and men soldiers in Iraq, but the glory and heroism of Private Lynch and her men rescuers were diminished considerably as the story unfolded. She had not been in battle but had been a supply clerk, and she had not shot her gun when she and her group were ambushed. She wasn't being held prisoner, raped, or beaten; she was protected by Iraqi doctors who were going to take her to a military hospital as soon as she was stabilized. Their protectiveness and the men commandos' rescue feminized her. So rather than the "Rambo" representation of American heroism, Lynch became a "maiden in distress" threatened by "savages." This story mirrored the plight of embattled American soldiers stuck in Iraq, picked off by incessant guerilla attacks, which was certainly not the intention of the original "saving Private Lynch" scenario.[21] It was, however, closer to the conventional gendering brought on by a resurgence of American vulnerability.

Women warriors can be brave and nurturing—God's handmaidens. But events in Iraq showed they can be the devil's handmaidens, too. U.S. women soldiers were deeply implicated in the torture and abuse of Iraqi prisoners at Abu Ghraib: Brig. Gen. Janis Karpinski was in charge of the military police that ran the military prisons, and Pfc. Lynndie R. England appeared in a number of the photographs, engaged in sexual and physical humiliation of naked men prisoners. Commenting on the use of sexual humiliation by women soldiers as part of the torture of Abu Ghraib prisoners, a columnist said, "One could not have designed a more symbolic representation of the Islamist warning about where Western freedom ultimately leads than yesterday's *Washington Post* photo of a uniformed American woman holding a naked Arab man on a leash."[22] Karpinski's ability to command was called into question and she was dismissed; England was sent home, pregnant and in disgrace, portrayed as the ugly opposite of Jessica Lynch.

According to Frank Rich, who writes on the media for the

New York Times, the symbolic juxtaposition of Private Lynch as "the heroic poster child for Operation Iraqi Freedom" and Private England as "the hideous, leering face of American wartime criminality" used both women for their gender and sexuality. Lynch's "profile in courage" was deliberately constructed by the United States to counter the degenerating military situation in Iraq. Private England's "profile in sadism" became, to critics of the war, the way Iraq corrupts young people; to supporters, one of the "bad apples" playing at pornography; and to the Arab press, a perfect example of the horror of Western women.[23]

The gendering of women warriors thus seems to fluctuate with social stability. They may be unmarked as different from men in stable times, but in times of unrest they are stereotyped as soldiers with charm, damsels in distress, incompetent leaders, cruel Jezebels. Given America's social instability as conditions in Iraq deteriorated, there was little chance for either "the widows" or women in the military to upset the conventional Western gender order.

The Uses of Masculinity

In the conventional gender order, *masculinity* means strength and solidarity, no matter how it is manifest. Times of upheaval and uncertainty seem to lead to a resurgence of nostalgia for gender certainties. Among men deposed by new political and economic orders, Michael Kimmel notes, the response may be violent rage, fanatic fundamentalism, and the mobilization of masculinity in reactionary movements: "Efforts to reclaim economic autonomy, to reassert political control and revive traditional domestic dominance thus take on the veneer of restoring manhood."[24] Both of these uses of masculinity—bonding and vengeance—occurred in the events of September 11.

In "Declarations of War," Kimmel reflected on the meaning of masculinity after September 11. Remembering the firefighters' rescue efforts, the men who stayed with disabled friends, and the way so many men called their wives, lovers, and mothers and fathers before they died, he said:

> Traditional definitions of masculinity certainly have their imperious sides, brimming with homophobia and sexism. But they also contain the capacity for quiet heroism, selfless sacrifice, steadfast resolve, deep wells of compassion and caring, and, yes, a love that made these men magnificent.[25]

In a eulogy for a colleague who was killed on September 11, Capt. James Gormley defined *comrade*. He said:

> It's harder to be a comrade than a friend. It's different than being a brother. Friends and brothers forgive your mistakes. They are happy to be with you. You can relax and joke with them. You can take your ease with them—tell them tall tales. Comrades are different. Comrades forgive nothing. They can't. They need you to be better. They keep you sharp. They take your words literally. . . . Some people equate camaraderie with being jovial. It is anything but. Camaraderie is sharing hardship.[26]

These are moving words, but they apply as well to the comradeship of terrorists whose religious zeal and political commitment were fostered in Al Qaeda training camps.[27] Then the dark side of camaraderie sends a chill into Western hearts. Solidarity and willingness to sacrifice oneself for a larger cause characterized the firefighters and the heroes who forced the hijackers of the flight bound for the White House to crash into a field in Pennsylvania—*and* the hijackers who flew that plane and who rammed other planes into the Twin Towers and the Pentagon.

The description of the enemy as self-sacrificing comrades threw into sharp relief the self-sacrificing comradeship of the firefighters and other American heroes. They could not be cut from the same masculine cloth. In the months that followed September 11, the coalescing of emotions around American heroes and Middle Eastern terrorists suppressed the similarities and exacerbated the differences in ways that Niza Yanay says are characteristic of collective love and collective hatred.[28]

In the biographies in the U.S. media, American heroes had work families and home families and were devoted to both; the Middle Eastern plane hijackers ignored their kin and created families as false fronts. Comrades on the American side were mostly White men—but we were assured they were tolerant; Middle Eastern comrades, we were told, could not tolerate the openness of Western civilization. American religious ceremonies were glorified as creating a Durkheimian national community rallying for a "just war"; Middle Eastern religious ceremonies, equally a means of creating community, were vilified as an incitement to holy war. And so, as in most wars, Americans were presented with a careful construction of two very different types of masculinity—the *good doers* and the *evildoers*.

Even homosexuality was put to differential use. The American gay hero Mark Bingham, one of the main resisters on the flight that was crashed in Pennsylvania, was "a popular, brawny, 6-foot-5 rugby player who could have played any sport, just as he could have talked his way into any room," according to a story in the *New York Times*.[29] In other words, a manly man, gay or not. The masculinity of the hijackers was demeaned by hints of homosexuality, but the Taliban, who punished homosexuals with death by crushing, seemed the essence of machismo, with their beards, guns, and misogyny. So what are we to make of this description of Pashtun men in an article about Afghanistan by Jon Lee Anderson in the *New Yorker*, a liberal magazine?

> Pashtun men, Kandaharis in particular, are very conscious of their personal appearance. Many of them line their eyes with black kohl and color their toenails, and sometimes their fingernails, with henna. Some also dye their hair. It is quite common to see otherwise sober-seeming older men with long beards that are a flaming, almost punk-like orange color. Burly, bearded men who carry weapons also wear *chaplis,* colorful high-heeled sandals. I noticed that to be really chic in Kandahar you wear your *chaplis* a size or so too small, which means that you mince and wobble as you walk.[30]

Anderson went on to describe the photo portraits left by Taliban fighters, some holding hands with friends, most with eyes heavily lined with kohl. In his feminization of the Taliban, he ignored the fact that in Afghanistan and other Middle Eastern societies, hand-holding, kissing, and displays of affection between men are not homosexual behavior and that beauty in men is not incompatible with virility. Kohl and henna are worn by everyone for their medicinal properties, and small, ill-fitting shoes are what's available.[31] There is a tradition of transgenerational homosexuality in parts of the Middle East, between older and younger men or boys, but it does not preclude marriage or incur a stigma.[32]

What was going on was the feminization of the enemy, devaluing its masculine characteristics and, in the process, emphasizing the true masculinity of American men.[33] That emphasis is one reason why macho blue-collar workers were valorized after September 11.

AMERICAN MEN'S STATUSES

In looking at masculinities, R. W. Connell has contrasted hegemonic, or dominant, men and subordinated men. Hegemonic men have economic and educational advantages and institutionalized patriarchal privileges, and their characteristics are the most valued attributes of masculinity. Subordinated men, such as blue-collar workers, are not necessarily devalued, but they have fewer opportunities for advancement and little of the power, prestige, and wealth of hegemonic men. As Connell says:

> To recognize diversity in masculinity is not enough. We must also recognize the *relations* between the different kinds of masculinity: relations of alliance, dominance and subordination. These relationships are constructed through practices that exclude and include, that intimidate and exploit, and so on. There is a gender politics within masculinity.[34]

Using this analysis of within-gender hierarchies, we can see that the firefighters' camaraderie is the bonding of subordinated men—White, working-class men with strong Irish and Italian identities. Many brothers, uncles, fathers, and sons worked and died together. The distinction Captain Gormley made between blood kin and comrades is a lived experience—how to love and trust those who are not brothers but might as well be, since the racial ethnic homogeneity of the New York Fire Department has not been dented very much by affirmative action. This "tribalism" was evident during the search for bodies and body parts at ground zero. Langewiesche notes that the firefighters "treated their own dead with a reverence not accorded others."[35] The way firefighters close ranks against outsiders and look to each other rather than the outside society for their trusted and loyal allies suggests their subordinate status in the gender hierarchy of men.

Ironically, the men the firefighters were likely to have trusted the least were those they lost their lives trying to rescue—the hegemonic men in the upper-floor World Trade Center offices of the upper echelons of finance and investment. Symbolically, they met on the stairs of the World Trade Center buildings—the financiers going down, the firemen going up. The firefighters' lack of reverence for civilian bodies and body parts in the months of recovery may very well have reflected their anger with this class cleavage.[36]

The mostly White financiers who were so many of those killed when the Twin Towers fell were part of the dominant class in the United States. They were not for the most part born to their dominant status; indeed, many lived in the same parts of New York and New Jersey as the police and firefighters. But they had the advantages of college educations and entry into upwardly mobile career positions. Langewiesche was struck by the upscale cars left in the World Trade Center underground garages: "A disproportionate number of the cars were BMWs,

Jaguars, Lexuses, and the like—indicating, if nothing else, the preponderance of a certain culture that had thrived there."[37]

In *Masculinities*, Connell describes how hegemonic masculinity is produced through college education, where young men are trained to be rational and technically expert, and reproduced in professional and managerial careers in hierarchically organized workplaces, where hegemonic men expect eventually to have positions of authority over other men. Modern society continues to produce this hallmark elite group. Even though the seeds of change are in the values of reason and technology, which form the basis of credentials available to all who can get a good education, social networks and cultural capital give certain groups of men privileges denied to those less well connected.

This hierarchy was overturned at ground zero in the nine months of demolition following September 11, when firemen and cops on overtime, hands-on engineers, and three thousand well-paid, unionized construction workers ran the operation. The who-you-know modes of recruitment, informal leadership, and innovative and risky practices all came out of blue-collar culture. There was a dark side of guns, fist fighting, and looting as well. But for the most part, it was an astounding opportunity for working-class men to experience the exhilaration of battle, to test themselves in new leadership roles, and to make a lot of money besides. As Langewiesche sums it up, the macho atmosphere at ground zero felt to many like "going to the moon," with everyday routines and responsibilities and traditional lines of command left far behind.[38]

In sum, American society provided secure niches for friendship and family and a stable income to blue-collar men. However, their version of masculinity was not as highly valued as that of upwardly mobile college-educated men. What September 11 did was to valorize the masculinity of the socially subordinated men—especially the firefighters—by raising them culturally to the same dominant, hegemonic status as the financiers. They became the symbol of American strength in the face of adversity. The valorization of the firefighters as heroic icons has become international, but their economic and political status in New York City is what it always has been—blue-collar, unionized workers fighting for jobs and salary raises in a time of restricted city finances.[39] Forgotten in this picture of heroes and victims were the poorer, non-White, working-class men—the cooks, dishwashers, and busboys of the World Trade Center restaurant, the mail handlers and maintenance personnel of the buildings—the strata in the least desirable jobs, many of whom were immigrants. Their masculinity was not valued enough to be called heroic—or American.

MIDDLE EASTERN MEN'S STATUSES

Successful religious revolutions in Islamic countries have established new pecking orders for men, but the Middle Eastern theocracies have not privileged working-class or college-educated men. In Iran after the overthrow of the shah, as Shahin Gerami notes, new masculine prototypes were in favor —mullahs as the leaders of revolution, martyrs as its soul, and working-class men as its beneficiaries. With the region's high birth rate and low levels of economic development, college-educated men found that urban jobs were hard to come by or paid little. An alternative route to a proud masculine status was to become a heroic soldier and martyr, protector of women and their country's honor. If martyrs died heroically, their families were elevated in status and prosperity.[40]

The terrorists of September 11 were middle-class, college-educated children of prosperous families who were willing and able to send them to Europe and America to study or work. What radicalized them? Thomas Friedman described a typical biography of the key September 11 plane hijackers and other Al Qaeda agents:

> He grew up in a middle-class family in the Arab world, was educated, went to Europe for more studies, lived on the fringes of a European society . . . , gravitated to a local prayer group or mosque, became radicalized there by Islamist elements, went off for training in Afghanistan and presto—a terrorist was born. The personal encounter between these young men and Europe is the key to this story.[41]

Friedman and others contend that émigrés coming from religious, patriarchal societies find it hard to adapt to Europe's more open social rules and retreat to the familiarity of the mosque. The same pattern is claimed for alienated Muslim men in the United States. In a letter to the *New York Times* commenting on Friedman's column, Lakshmi Bandlamudi, a professor of psychology, described the émigré students in her classes at LaGuardia Community College:

> When their core beliefs are challenged, men respond in a variety of ways. Some genuinely struggle and strike a healthy balance, some live with a split identity, some shed their ethnic identity and some freeze their sense of religion and ethnicity and desperately and even forcibly affirm their identity.

> The anger brewing within them is so potent that there is an
> adamant refusal to acknowledge a pluralistic society, and only
> the money and freedom are desirable and the rest must be dis-
> carded. This kind of identity politics is most dangerous for
> their personal well-being and for the society at large.[42]

Of course, their anger and alienation are just as much rational
responses to the discrimination and lack of opportunity they
face in Western societies, which are in reality far less than open.

The biographies of many of the September 11 suicide pilots
show that they were downwardly mobile, unable to get jobs
commensurate with their education and class backgrounds.
Like the American White supremacists that spawned Timothy
McVeigh, Kimmel points out, they had every reason to be re-
sentful of their loss of middle-class male privilege. And to an
alienated young man like Mohammed Atta, as to McVeigh,
terrorism could be a route back to masculine pride: "Someone
else—some 'other'—had to be held responsible for the terrorists' downward mobility and failures, and the failures of their
fathers to deliver their promised inheritance. The terrorists
didn't just get mad. They got even."[43] In the eyes of anti-
Western Middle Easterners, they also raised the status of Arab
men.

ISLAMIC WOMEN'S STATUSES

The political shifts that reversed Islamic men's gender hierarchies, bringing dominant status to formerly subordinated men,
made college-educated and professional women, who were dominant over some men, subordinate to all men. Formerly subordinated poor, religious women could attain positions of dominance

over other women as enforcers of purity codes of dress and behavior, but the prevailing pattern was subordinate gender statuses for women.[44]

In the last century, the struggle over women's status and rights in Muslim countries has been intertwined with nationalistic and revolutionary movements that have produced pendulum swings of Westernized, secular regimes and the counterestablishment of tradition-based theocracies. In general, women have had a more equal status with men under secular regimes and have lost many rights with theocratic revolutions. Whether the emerging state is secular or religiously conservative depends in part on the strength of kin-based tribal factions, as Mounira Maya Charrad found for postcolonial Tunisia, Morocco, and Algeria.[45]

The political changes in Iran and Afghanistan in the past twenty years offer a counterpoint of shifts in women's status.[46] In Afghanistan in the 1980s, a secular government imposed by the Soviet Union on a tribal society attempted to abolish patriarchal inheritance and marriage practices, make education compulsory for girls as well as boys, and give women rights to divorce and custody of their children. Women were active in the government, the professions, and various unions and other NGOs.

In Iran at that time, the overthrow of the shah in 1979 brought to power a theocratic revolutionary government whose goal was eradication of Western decadence. The ayatollahs imposed compulsory veiling of women; public gender segregation; polygamy, divorce, and child custody as prerogatives of husbands only; early marriage for girls; restrictions on women's employment and travel; illegalization of abortion; the diminishment of inheritance for women to half that for men; and the death penalty for adultery and homosexuality. Yet women continued to vote and hold government office, be educated, and work outside the home, and they were the providers of women's health care.

When the religious rulers took over in Afghanistan at the beginning of the 1990s, they imposed a set of Islamic rules more restrictive than Iran's. These were tightened and brutally enforced in the theocratic dictatorship of the Taliban that began in 1996. The result was the total expulsion of women from the public sphere, and many women and men fled the country. By that time, Iran had loosened its restrictions on women, and women were increasingly visible in Iran's public life.

The life of the 2003 Nobel Peace Prize winner, Shirin Ebadi, an Iranian Islamic fighter for human rights, especially for women and children, sums up these political contradictions. A judge under the shah, she was deposed by the postrevolutionary Iranian theocratic decree that women couldn't be judges. She stayed in Iran to work as a lawyer, writer, and university lecturer. She has been criticized by conservative Islamic women in Iran for her liberal views and by Iranian émigré feminist activists for her compromises with Iran's ruling clerics, but in her Nobel Prize acceptance speech she was critical of the human rights violations of both Islamic theocrats and Western governments.[47]

Throughout these shifts, women's private and public resistance to Islamic restrictions had more scope in urbanized Iran than in tribalized Afghanistan. In Iran, a mothers' movement and journals with a large readership among educated women mounted public debates on women's issues. In Afghanistan, the Revolutionary Association of the Women of Afghanistan (RAWA) and other women's organizations had to work clandestinely to provide desperately needed services, like minimal education for girls and some health care, as well as to publicize women's plight under the Taliban. Even though the legal restrictions on their political activity have been lifted, Afghan women are still struggling for adequate representation in the national government and for a loosening of traditional tribal practices. In Iraq, many urban, educated women were professionals, but it remains to be seen whether women will gain or lose in the post-Saddam social order.[48]

I would expect that the status of women in Afghanistan, Iraq, and Iran will depend on the stability of those countries' governments—the more stability, the more likely it is that women will gain in status.

ISLAMIC FEMINISM

Islamic feminists have had to develop theories and political practices that deal with complex issues of individual rights and kinship obligations, modernization and religious traditions. Three trends in Islamic feminism reflect the political debates among scholars and activists over the status of women in Islam.[49]

One trend is Islamist, part of the political movement that valorizes Islamic history, culture, and beliefs as a counter to Westernization. A search for Islamic rootedness and legitimation has led Islamist feminists to interpret the Qur'an from a woman's perspective. Using these readings, they argue that Islam is inherently gender-equal, so a theocratic state need not subordinate women. Islamist feminists do not want gender equity (separate but equal spheres). For a model of a gender-equal Islam, they go back to a prestate Islam, in which women, notably Muhammad's wives, were influential in shaping the religion and its rules. For these feminists, Islam and gender equality are fully compatible.

The second trend in Islamic feminism is secular, part of the movement for modernization and democratization. Secular feminists argue that the goal should be a separation of civil laws from religious rules, a clear split between clerical authority and the state. Laws governing personal status (such as marriage, divorce, child custody, and inheritance) should be gender-equal. The public sphere (education, law, politics) should be open equally to women and men. Islam as a religion should be respected, but it should not be the basis of state laws and policies, which should be democratically derived.

The third feminist trend is to seek a middle way that would be Islamist but would also offer gender equality in public and in the family. Transcending East and West, these feminists advocate changing personal status codes to give women equal rights, as do secular Muslim feminist movements. The more specifically Islamist focus is to create a discourse based on the inherent gender equality in Islam. Its goal is to give Muslim women an Islamic way of achieving gender equality. As recently defined by Margot Badran, "Islamic feminism is a feminist discourse expressly articulated within an Islamic paradigm, and behaviors and activisms inspired by it are enacted in Islam's name." But it has "also articulated itself within nationalist, humanitarian/human rights, and democratic discourses." In this view, says Badran, "Islamic feminism argues that women may be heads of state, leaders of congregational prayer, judges, and muftis." As evidence that the middle way is possible, she points out that "in some Muslim majority countries, Muslim women function as judges, some as prime ministers, and one is a head of state."[50]

The stubborn question is the viability of a third way that incorporates individual rights with political, economic, and gender equality and is also respectful of indigenous cultures and multiple religious traditions. As Farida Shaheed points out in her discussion of the international network Women Living under Muslim Laws (WLUML), the social codes and norms of local communities can be more powerful than civil laws. When they are in conflict, local rules often prevail. A secular, formal, legal system that runs counter to religious cultural practices and is enforced will be seen as oppressive and destructive by traditionalists. Women and girls have often been caught between these two systems and have made international appeals for support in resisting ritual genital cutting, executions by stoning for adultery, paternal child custody, and polygyny.[51] When secular national governments are not strong or stable enough to sustain gender equality in the face of tribal resistance, women lose ground.

The opposite situation confronts Islamic women who want to wear the veil, and who are living in countries that maintain the separation of state and religion. They confront laws forbidding teachers, students, and parliamentarians to wear a religious symbol in a public institution. Some have invoked the Western ideology of individual and religious freedom and cultural diversity to support their right to veil; others have opted for integration into secular society. Religious Islamic men in diaspora communities are apt to use Western rhetoric to support their desire to have their wives and daughters wear head scarves and modest Islamic dress, a way of establishing their authority in states where they have no establishment power.[52]

In sum, the fluctuations in Islamic women's status reflect the conflicts between religious and secular movements, tribal and urban local practices, and nationalism and assimilation in diasporas. Islamic feminists struggle to reconcile these conflicts theoretically; politically, they run up against gender practices and policies that emphasize gender divisions and "women's place" in turbulent times and places.

WHAT IS THE NEW NORMAL?

Times of upheaval, when feminists hope that changes will erase some of the bases of gender inequality, may instead reawaken old gender stereotypes in attempts to restore social order. Depictions of American women and men in the mass media after September 11, a time of great vulnerability, were quite gender-divided. Greater gender heterogeneity during the 2003 Iraq War, which was declared by President George W. Bush as visible evidence of American power, reverted to gender stereotypes in the embattled guerrilla-war period.

Yet there was an undertone of change in these depictions. In the post–September 11 period, men were macho firefighters who cried, and women were grieving widows who fought aggressively for their causes. In the months of official war, U.S. women joined men soldiers as heroes; in the months of guerrilla attacks, they became representatives of democracy but also maidens in distress. Bush himself became a symbol of these gender shifts. In May 2003, when he declared America's mission accomplished, he swaggered on the deck of a battleship in a flight suit. In November 2003, when American troops were hunkered down against bombings and ambushes, he appeared in a mess hall with tears in his eyes, bearing a big platter of Thanksgiving food.[53]

Post–September 11, gender in the Middle East has undertones of change as well. Women struggle for political representation in Afghanistan and Iraq, and they have gained seats on the transitional councils. Shirin Ibadi predicts that the conferring of the Nobel Peace Prize on an Iranian woman "will be an inspiration to the masses of women who are striving to realize their rights, not only in Iran but throughout the region—rights taken away from them through the passage of history."[54] The political debates over women's positions in Islamic societies are imbricated in the controversy over the benefits and costs of secular modernization versus religious nationalism and in the larger debates over Western cultural imperialism and economic hegemony—the political ground zero of September 11.

As much as we may have mixed feelings about women in the military and deplore women suicide bombers, they remind us that men are not always the aggressors. Men's tears for their lost companions and sons and fathers and brothers at ground zero remind us of their emotional vulnerability. Middle Eastern women's political battles remind us that women are entitled to seats in governments—with or without their heads covered.

The "new normal" doesn't take us back to the first millennium or, indeed, to the second. But if it is to take us on the way to a better third millennium, one that allows some progress in gender relations, then we had best heed Shirin Ebadi, who said:

If the twenty-first century wishes to free itself from the cycle of violence, acts of terror and war, and avoid repetition of the experience of the twentieth century—that most disaster-ridden century of humankind—there is no other way except by understanding and putting into practice every human right for all mankind, irrespective of race, gender, faith, nationality or social status.[55]

Chapter Five
PARADOXES OF GENDER IDENTITY: STRATEGIES OF FEMINIST POLITICS

Feminism without borders . . . acknowledges the fault lines, conflicts, differences, fears, and containment that borders represent. It acknowledges that there is no one sense of a border, that the lines between and through nations, races, classes, sexualities, religions, and disabilities are real—and that a feminism without borders must envision change and social justice work across these lines of demarcation and division.

—Chandra Talpade Mohanty[1]

THE GOAL OF FEMINISM has been to turn the possibility of gender equality into a probability. The simple version of this goal is to make women equal to men. But men are not all equal, and women don't want just to emulate men. More important, "men" and "women" are not uniform, global categories. The unity of these identities—*woman, man*—has been challenged by recent feminist theory, research, and politics. Multicultural, socialist, and postcolonial feminists have shown how women and men are divided by national allegiances and social-class differences. The social construction perspective in the social sciences sees multiple forms of femininity and masculinity produced in everyday interaction and through organizational practices. Poststructural critiques have destabilized the concepts of permanent identity and sense of collectivity.

Theories aside, the lived reality of people's experiences is that they belong to many different groups and have multiple identities. We are, in Nira Yuval-Davis's words, "multi-layered citizens."[2] In modern societies, gender, race, ethnicity, social class, degrees of able-bodiedness, nationality, religion, and the varieties of sexuality intersect each other, and each of these can produce a sense of identity in an individual. As Barbara Katz Rothman says, "I have a thousand identities. They're like hooks that stick out all over me, catching strangers and finding connections."[3] Where the group is disadvantaged or stigmatized, these identities can become the core of collective politics; conversely, involvement in a social movement can evoke or intensify an individual's identity with a group.[4] However, the new boundaries may create conflicting loyalties and intragroup tensions, as happens with women of different ethnic, racial, and religious groups. In such situations, women who at one time worked together for peace, like Israeli and Palestinian feminists, have become enemies.[5]

Being a woman may be a major social identity, but it may not be a rallying point of political activity for everyone. Iris Marion Young argues that gender, racial category, and class are *series*—comparatively passive collectives grouped by their similar social conditioning.[6] These locations in social structures may or may not become significant sources of self-identification or political action. Barbara Smith describes her multiple political identities:

> Objectively I'm African American. I'm female. I'm a lesbian. I come from a working class family, but I am highly educated. And I'm a radical. I'm a socialist and a Black feminist. By

Black feminist, I don't mean a feminist who is Black. I mean the politics of Black feminism.[7]

The shift in focus from women and men in the unitary sense creates a tension between *gender visibility* and *gender diversity*. At the beginning of the second wave of feminism, thirty-five years ago, the ubiquity and power of gender were made visible through attention to the ways in which societies, cultures, groups, and individuals are gendered and how this process comes about and is maintained through the practices of institutions, cultures, groups, and individuals. More recently, the feminist focus has been on diversity—the ways in which women and men, boys and girls, are not homogeneous groups but are intersected by other major social statuses, most prominently, nationality, social class, and racial ethnic and religious identity. The effect of focusing on gender visibility is to foreground women's experiences, as standpoint feminism urges. The effect of focusing on gender diversity is to incorporate diverse women's experiences, as multicultural feminism urges.

There may be a common core to women's experiences, but feminist politics cannot ignore the input from social statuses that may be as important as gender. Global feminist politics today is often strategically degendered—it includes disadvantaged men and uses the experiences of women of different social classes, educational levels, racial ethnic and religious groups, marital and parental statuses, sexual orientations, ages, and degrees of able-bodiedness. This strategy does not fragment standpoints into individual perspectives. The experiences of multiple domination, of status conflicts, of shifting degrees of power and powerlessness, are shared by others; thus they are vital sources of varied worldviews and political agendas. Diverse and intersecting perspectives become both a source of knowledge and a source of political activism.[8]

Intersecting group memberships and multiple identities are not a weakness in the feminist movement, but a strength. When they become a basis for national and international coalitions, intersecting group memberships and multiple statuses are powerful feminist weapons.

MULTIPLE SYSTEMS OF DOMINATION

Throughout the twentieth century, social critics have argued about which aspect of inequality is the most damaging. Leila Rupp and Verta Taylor argue that twentieth-century feminism was always potentially fragmented by national and class differences, but there was a social-movement community and a collective identity for those who had a consciousness of gender and the goal of women's equality.[9] But while feminists focused on women's oppression, civil rights activists reacted to the plight of men and women in disadvantaged racial ethnic groups. Marxist and socialist men and women have been in the forefront of working-class political struggles. Multicultural feminism argues that all of these aspects of subordination have to be fought at the same time.

The important point made by multicultural feminism is that a member of a subordinate group is not disadvantaged just by gender or racial category or ethnicity or social class but by a multiple system of domination—the intersectionality of subordinate statuses. Multicultural feminism is therefore critical of feminist theories that contrast two global groups—women and men—because in multidimensional societies, no one is just a woman or just a man. The combination of social statuses makes for a particular group standpoint and a particular culture, a set of values, sense of appropriate behavior, and outlook on life (which may be completely distinctive or may overlap that of other groups). Since the dominant group's standpoint is the one that prevails in the definition of social problems, in the attribution of their causes, in allocation of resources to conduct research, and in the power to create political solutions, members of disadvantaged groups, including women, have to fight to have their points of view heard. In the political arena, however, diverse women sometimes band together, but women sometimes ally with men of their own social group. The politics of identity is a complex of shifting sides.[10]

WHO BELONGS WITH WHOM?

Standpoint theory in feminism argues that women's viewpoints must be privileged in order to counteract the domination of men's perspectives. Whoever sets the agendas for scientific research, shapes the content of higher education, chooses the symbols that permeate cultural productions, and decides political priorities has hegemonic power. Standpoint feminism therefore insists that women's perspectives, women's ways of seeing the world, be privileged in the production of knowledge and culture and in setting political agendas.[11]

But are all women's experiences the same? Donna Haraway claims that all knowledge is partial, dependent on social location. Sandra Harding, who did the groundbreaking work on bringing women's standpoint into science, raised the question of fractured standpoints in 1986 and now argues for the multicultural aspects of science. Feminists in developing countries critique the negative effects of first-world science on the local sciences of African, Chicana, Asian, Indian, Native American, Indigenous Australian, Maori and women. Their technologies of food production and their manufacture of objects of daily living that fit their environment are ruined by imported technologies that ignore local needs and local conditions.[12]

Another problematic issue for feminist politics is that sometimes the discrimination disadvantaged women experience is specific to them as women, and at other times they share class and racial and gender ethnic oppression with the men of their group. In the United States, African American women, Latinas, and Asian American women all encounter racial and gender prejudice in social encounters, but they have markedly different experiences in schools and in the job market, and so their strategies for action have to be different.[13] Since class, racial ethnic, and gender identity are intertwined, political unity with the men of the same group can severely undermine a consciousness of gender oppression. As Dafna Izraeli wrote about the suppression of a separate women's movement among some Zionists in prestate Israel in the early 1900s, "The network of social ties that linked the feminists of the second wave with the male leadership of the labor movement discouraged the development of a 'we-they' dichotomy."[14]

In other situations, women's loyalty, identification, and politics may not be joined with those of the men of their own racial ethnic group if the men are oppressive because of a traditional patriarchal culture or because they themselves are oppressed by men at the top of the pyramid. Men's and women's standpoints within the same group may differ considerably even though they may share a sense of injustice on account of their mutual racial ethnic status. In the U.S. civil rights movement, women, White and Black, had very different experiences from those of White and Black men.[15]

Politically, however, oppressed women of oppressed groups may feel they have to stand by their men. Lynn Chancer tells the story of the Portuguese working-class community in which a Portuguese woman was gang-raped on a pool table in a bar while other men watched. All the men were Portuguese. The women of the town first rallied around the woman who had been raped. But when the national media came in and began to vilify the men racially, the women turned on the rape victim, accusing her of sexual looseness and child neglect, and they supported the men at the trial. After their conviction, the woman who was raped was so ostracized that she left the town to live a thousand miles away.[16]

Drucilla Cornell says that in the quest for equality, the question of who is compared with whom is crucial. If disadvantaged women achieve equality with the disadvantaged men of their group, they have not achieved very much. If they outperform them, as has happened with African American and Hispanic American women college and professional-school graduates in the United States, then the men in the same groups are seen as endangered.[17] Women may feel they are in a double bind and can't win if they raise themselves as women, leaving their men behind, but they don't want to subordinate themselves to their men, either.

Feminist Identity Politics

Feminists throughout the world are confronted by many cleavages that have created conflicts over coalitions and political strategies. Some of these divisions have been among those of different racial ethnic categories and religions, with further divisions within religions and between those who are religious and those who are militantly secular. Socioeconomic statuses—women on welfare, professionals, working class, middle class, traditional elites—create different political interests. Other divisions are among feminists of different sexual orientations and among those who are single, married, divorced, in heterosexual or same-gendered couple relationships. Those with children of different ages and those without children, by choice or not by choice, have different perspectives on family life. Those who need environmental and personal assistance to live normal lives have different political agendas from the able-bodied. Even "fat" is a feminist issue that distances those who are thin and athletic from those who are not.

The boundaries of who belongs with whom shift depending on what identity you are talking about and what the political issue is. And since many of these identities emerge from life experiences, the identities themselves shift over time. The politics of identity sometimes exacerbates and sometimes patches over internal differences. As Sylvia Walby says:

> The politics of difference, or of location, assumes that it is possible to separately identify holistic communities each with their own distinctive values, but this is a dubious proposition. . . . Given the engagement of most people in multiple group social practices with which they have varying degrees of involvement at different times, the identification of clear communities is highly problematic.[18]

Can feminists recognize gender diversity and continue to rally around the flag of womanhood? Judith Butler says,

"Surely, it must be possible both to use the term, to use it tactically . . . and also to subject the term to a critique which interrogates the exclusionary operations and differential power-relations that construct and delimit feminist invocations of 'women.' "[19] I do not think it is possible to conceptualize "Woman" as a stable category and to use the experiences of women with varying other important identities at the same time. The multiplicity of identities forces us to go way beyond the gender binaries in our theories, research, and politics—and that means confronting the question of whom you choose to stand up with.

Rather than identity politics, where membership in a particular social category is required for activism, Susan Hekman argues for a "politics of identification." She advocates identification with political causes and activism for political goals without regard to personal status.[20] This kind of inclusion requires not only that "outsiders" see others' causes as important to fight for but also that the "insiders" accept the "outsiders" as legitimate political actors. Working together against the differences takes more than recognition; it takes transformation. As Dale Bauer and Priscilla Wald said:

> Coalition politics does not offer a united front of feminism. . . . The differences are always in view and always potentially disruptive. . . . So when we coalesce—come together—we have to give up any secure sense of self. We merge, and we change. And we cannot count on a supportive environment. A coalition comes together to get some work done, not to nurture.[21]

PARADOXES OF GENDER IDENTITY

The politics of identity demand that you know who is "us" and who is "them." As William Connelly says in *Identity/Difference,* "Identity requires difference in order to be, and it conveys difference into otherness in order to secure its own self-certainty."[22] In gender politics, that hardens the boundaries between women and men; in sexual politics, it hardens the boundaries between lesbians and gays and heterosexual women and men; and in multicultural politics, it hardens the boundaries between the dominants and all the disadvantaged and each disadvantaged group against the others. If we want to erase boundary lines, the politics of identity presents several paradoxes.

- *The first paradox is that to erase boundaries, one must first recognize them, thus confirming them.*

Joan Wallach Scott calls it an inevitable feminist paradox that to fight to erase the effects of sex differences, you have to invoke them:

> To the extent that it acted for "women," feminism produced the "sexual difference" it sought to eliminate. This paradox— the need both to accept *and* to refuse "sexual difference"— was the constitutive condition of feminism as a political movement throughout its history.[23]

To create a politics around a unifying concept of "Woman," feminism often ignores important other statuses, in particular, racial ethnic, religious, social class, and sexual. The assumption that all women suffer the same oppressions and want the same forms of liberation has resulted in an ethnocentric politics. An obvious example is the liberal feminist critique of marriage, economic support by a man, and full-time domesticity. As African American and Latina feminists pointed out, these forms of "oppression" look like liberation to poor, single mothers cleaning other women's houses and taking care of other women's children in order to feed their own children.[24]

- *The second paradox is that without clear categories, not only can't you have a politics of identity, but you also can't have a politics of resistance or rebellion.*

If boundaries are erased, distinctiveness may also be obliterated. Jan Wickman found that there were two factions in the transgender community he studied in Finland: adapters and rebels. Adapters wanted to fit into the heterosexual community and sought medical and surgical solutions to resolve their cross-gender identity. Their goal was a body and appearance that could pass for "normal." They wanted to obliterate the boundary lines between themselves and heterosexuals, and so they separated themselves from the gay community. The gender rebels, in contrast, saw themselves as one of many types of gendered sexuality. They allied with the gay movement to gain acceptance for being different and for support of alternative lifestyles.[25]

- *The third paradox is that identity politics hardens the boundaries and creates greater cleavages in the short run, with the aim of reducing them in the future in the name of equality and greater unity.*

The split in American feminism between White and Black women and in transnational feminism between feminists in developed and developing countries is repeated wherever there are differences in economic resources and political resources. Charges of invisibility and neglect of the issues of the most disadvantaged group have escalated to hostility and organizational and political separateness.

For example, in the last ten years, there has been a schism in Israeli feminism between Ashkenazi women (Jews of European or American origin) and Mizrahi women (Jews of North African origin). Henriette Dahan-Kalev's analysis describes the politics of class that are comparable to those that split African American, White American middle-class, and White American working-class feminists. Ashkenazi Jews tend to be middle and upper class and college-educated; Mizrahi Jews have been working class and have more recently entered academia and the professions. In the world of women, Ashkenazi women are social workers and employers of household labor; Mizrahi women are their clients and cleaning women. In 1994 at a feminist conference, a group of Mizrahi women accused Ashkenazi feminists of oppressing them, both in Israeli society in general and in the women's movement as well. They have since formed their own movement and continue to confront more established feminist organizations with accusations of exclusion.[26]

Longtime feminists who have urged diversity have experienced this divisive pattern in many national and international venues. The result has been that no one dares criticize the social practices of women in different cultures; one may criticize only those of one's own culture.[27] As Ranjana Khanna says:

Transnational feminism has allowed us to perceive the central-
ity of different relations to rules. This perception has initiated a
fracturing. Differences have been reified to such an extent that
separate ethical universes have been produced, with the over-
arching imperative being that one does not comment on another context.[28]

It is important to acknowledge that what seems like oppression
to one group may be liberating to another, as when strict dress
rules, gender-segregated schools, and a religiously oriented cur-
riculum provide a setting in which conservative parents can
sanction the education of their daughters.[29] But once the cleavages have produced distance and distrust on all sides, can the
differences be successfully diminished? And if they are not, can
a critical feminist politics prevail?

- *The fourth paradox is that if you want to be multicultural, you
  need to maintain distinct cultures.*

One effect of negative discrimination is that it preserves distinctiveness, because if the members of a group cannot be distinguished, how can they be discriminated against? Of course,
mainstreaming often produces what Urvashi Vaid calls virtual
equality, the erasure of differences without changes in the social
structure that make it possible to live together. But for the
group, the marks of differentness may help their members
identify one another as sources of help. As Suzanna Danuta
Walters says of the gay and lesbian community in the United
States, "One of the positive 'fallouts' of discrimination is the
forging of community and the development of a concern for
others, activism, a culture of responsibility. The response to

AIDS is only one example." However, Jane Ward's research on an AIDS service organization found that Latina lesbian women felt their health-care needs were neglected because most of the money went to gay Latino men.[30]

If boundaries are maintained, how can groups form coalitions with other groups for stronger political action?

- *The fifth paradox is that it is possible to bracket the question of differences in political action that ignores them while using those differences when it is necessary to counter invisibility.*

Feminist multidimensional political action has addressed the matrix of domination, going beyond the sources of oppression that are specific to women. Without giving up the fight against sexual exploitation and violence against women, feminists have had to search for ways to open access to economic resources, educational opportunities, and political power. Feminists have focused on gender when it is necessary, but have also had to recognize that women of different classes may not be interested in political action because their statuses are superior or because they feel they have too much to lose from changes in the status quo. In some situations, it has been necessary to reach out to subordinated men who are similarly oppressed and who want similar changes in the redistribution of resources and recognition of distinct cultures.[31] Thus, Rina Amiri, an adviser to UNESCO and the Ministry of Women's Affairs in Kabul, said after the fall of the Taliban in Afghanistan that "advocacy on behalf of Afghan women must be tied to support for all ethnic and religious groups that have lacked representation in Afghanistan."[32]

The Structure of Feminist Politics

These paradoxes of gender identity are minimized when we view feminist politics at different structural levels. There is a structure to feminist politics that goes from identity politics at the grassroots level to coalitions of people of diverse identities in organized NGOs. NGOs have the potential to work with feminists from different political groups who enter state, national, and international governments and bureaucracies.

At the grassroots level, political action centered on primary identities makes particular injustices visible and forms a basis for organizing around those identities.[33] Thus, poor women mobilize around their traditional roles as wives and mothers to fight for better living and working conditions and improved health care for their families. As Christine Bose and Edna Acosta-Belén note, in Latin America and the Caribbean, women organize

> collective meals, health cooperatives, mothers' clubs, neighborhood water-rights groups, or their own textile and craft collectives. . . . Thus, rather than *privatizing* their survival problems, these women *collectivize* them and form social-change groups based on social reproduction concerns. In these new terms, the political discourse and arena of struggle is . . . moral persuasion to place demands on the state for rights related to family survival.

In the process, women define their needs not as family or gender issues but as citizenship claims on states.[34]

At this level, identities are primary; problems and solutions are localized. But since social problems of subsistence, shelter, and work opportunities in the face of economic restructuring are global, the collective solutions can become the basis for transcommunity and transnational organizing and for a global redefinition of what it means to be a citizen.

At the next level, NGOs are formed to sustain the grassroots collective political-action and problem-solving tactics, to bring in people with varied skills, and to raise money. The central identities of gender or racial ethnic group or class may blur as middle-class administrators and credentialed professionals join in.[35] The central focus shifts from identity politics to specific political issues, such as legal protections and rights, or to specific social problems, such as battering, rape, and prostitution.

NGOs encourage data collection by feminist researchers and use feminist academics' theories and structural analyses. There may be a conflict between activist members of NGOs and feminist academics and researchers, with activism and the search for viable solutions to problems conflicting with the need for objectivity in research. There may also be conflicts between NGO political strategists and fund-raisers and the members of grassroots organizations, and these may result in reproducing the very inequalities the NGOs are trying to address. But when members of national NGOs work reciprocally with members of grassroots collectives and researchers, they often become bridges between them.[36]

Simultaneous membership in multiple groups brings groups together in what Nira Yuval-Davis calls transversal politics, where borders are crossed and boundaries are redrawn to create coalitions and bridge divides.[37] Thus, the most productive feminist work may occur at the NGO level, where problem solving and political action can be focused, but not so narrowly as to preclude useful coalitions.

At the next level, feminists start infiltrating governments and government agencies—local, state, national, and international—where they try to showcase feminist issues and exert pressure for equal representation of women. A positive outcome by feminists within a government has been South Africa's gender-egalitarian constitution.[38]

When feminists work within established governments and bureaucracies, the thrust of their feminism is necessarily diluted in the course of trying to gain allies to pass laws and promulgate policies. Any critique of the establishment has to be moderated, since they are now part of it. The searchlight focusing on practices and problems that need changing floats as events reorder priorities. Feminists within governments may not be as radical or critical as feminists at the grassroots or NGO levels, but they come in with a different perspective, and they can be reached by feminists on the outside.[39] Government-level involvement allows prominent women to showcase feminist causes in speeches and the media, such as Hillary Rodham Clinton's presentation at the 1995 Beijing UN Conference on Women, which sent around the world the slogan "Women's rights are human rights and human rights are women's rights."

Linking all the levels are transnational networks and coalitions. Some of the most powerful feminist organizations are described by Valentine Moghadam as "organizations linking women in developing and developed regions and addressing social, economic and foreign policy issues in supra-national terms." These networks and coalitions are, she says, "a new organizational . . . form of collective action in an era of globalization."[40] Their focus might be the needs of women in a particular area growing out of historic events, such as the Network of East-West

Women, a coalition of women in former Soviet republics and in the United States that focuses on legal issues, reproductive rights, and transnational prostitution. Women Living under Muslim Laws is an international informational and support network of women living in diverse Muslim communities. Through WLUML, women share knowledge of differing interpretations and applications of *shari'ah,* the Islamic rules of conduct and personal status laws. The goals are the exchange of knowledge and the formation of links to other women in similar situations in common projects as well as the creation of a base for political action.[41]

United Nations conferences, with their parallel NGO meetings, have provided an impetus for transnational and intergovernment organizing. Manisha Desai notes two parallel strategies of action:

> The more prominent national and international groups tended to caucus to influence the agenda setting of the world conferences and the UN bodies, while the vast majority of NGOs focused on sharing information and experiences and networking for collaborative action in the future.[42]

Ranjana Khanna argues that it is feminists' disidentification with their own nations' failures in addressing the problems of women that "allows for coalitions between women internationally where a concept of *justice* is forged in the full knowledge of the thorniness of spectres of colonial relations and 'local' abuse of women."[43]

Feminists recognize that universal slogans of "equality, freedom, and justice for all" and "women's rights are human rights" often conflict with local cultural traditions and politics. State policies and civil laws in any country reflect the dominant group's history, ideology, and political interests. Concepts of individual rights and gender equality are embedded in the history, ideology, and political struggles of Westernized nation-states and cannot be exported without accusations of cultural imperialism. What also must be factored in are the economic inequalities, within countries and globally, that underpin gendered, racial ethnic, and class-based dominance and subordination and undermine the free play of individualism and equality. These class and racial ethnic hierarchies may permeate the interactions of transnational NGOs and local grassroots organizations in an invidious "politics of virtue"—advantaged urban White middle-class women "helping" poor rural Black women.[44]

It is here that multiple identities become so valuable. Multiple identities encourage cross-fertilization of ideas, practices, and tactics. Multiple standpoints recognize differences but work with commonalities. For example, the Boston Women's Health Book Collective, the originators of *Our Bodies, Ourselves,* encouraged feminist collectives in non-Western countries to develop versions reflective of local needs rather than insisting on direct translation.[45] What seems like fragmentation becomes, with the pressure of coalition politics, a multivoiced, multibranched, intertwined, and dense feminist political movement growing in force.

DOING MULTIDIMENSIONAL FEMINIST POLITICS

So how do feminists live with diversity and still do political action? Globally minded feminists

- reach out to people who are similarly oppressed and want similar changes
- enlist subordinated and sympathetic men in feminist political action
- attack the whole matrix of domination, not just women's part of it
- work with the positive aspects of gender regimes and undermine the negative aspects

Such diverse feminist political action is evident throughout the world, even when it is not named feminism. As Mary Hawkesworth said in her criticism of the premature "burial" of feminism:

> Within the official institutions of state in Africa, Asia, Australia, Europe, Latin America, and North America, feminist projects are ongoing through gender mainstreaming and the creation of "national machinery" for women, such as ministries for women, women's bureaus, and gender equality commissions. The feminist arm of the United Nations, the United Nations Development Fund for Women (UNIFEM), is working with indigenous women's organizations on all continents to safeguard women's lives and livelihoods and to secure their economic, political, and civil rights. Several states, such as Sweden and the Netherlands, have included gender equity efforts among their major foreign policy initiatives. Femocrats work within public agencies in all but one or two nations to structure policy initiatives that address women's needs, concerns, and interests, however contested these concepts may be. . . . Feminist NGOs have proliferated, creating a vibrant feminist civil society.[46]

The future strength of the feminist movement lies in the variety of organizations and the density of the multiple identities of their members. The primary identity of feminists may be gender, racial ethnic group, religion, social class, or sexual orientation. The focus of feminist work may be peace, an end to sexual violence, political parity, economic opportunity, health care, reproductive rights, or one of many proliferating causes. The beneficiaries may be one specific oppressed group or many. Feminist identity may be way down on the list, implicit, or even masked, but as long as the goal is political, economic, and cultural equality for all and as long as the implementation is a structure of equality, then feminist work is being done—all over the world.

Chapter Six
A WORLD WITHOUT GENDER: MAKING THE REVOLUTION

But what is it that is impossible to think, and what kind of impossibility are we faced with here?
—Michel Foucault[1]

WITH ALL THE DIVERSITY AND DIVISIONS of gender identities and gender practices, the ultimate paradox is that gender systems are still binary. Societies in developed and developing countries with vastly different cultures, complex economies, and a variety of family groupings organize their members into categories of people who have different statuses, roles, access to economic resources and skills training, and opportunities for leadership and political power. Gender is only one of those sorting mechanisms, but it is virtually universal. The ubiquity of gender as an organizing principle of social life leads to the belief that the man-woman division is a male-female division. It is not. Societies are not divided into "penises" and "vaginas" or "wombs" and "nonwombs" or "ovaries" and "testes." Nor are most modern societies divided into child bearers and non–child bearers. When gender as a social institution organizes a society, the divisions are "women" and "men"—social identities whose breaches are possible but often punishable. The comparative social categories for "woman" and "man" are not body types but social divisions like "slave" and "free man," "peasant" and "aristocrat," "Black" and "White." In societies that do not have third genders, you pass at great peril as a person of the gender category opposite the one you are legally assigned, but it is done easily, especially when all it takes is a clothing change.[2]

The insidiousness of such deeply embedded social categories is that they control our lives.[3] They create differences between one group and its supposed opposite and designate the first group as primary, the norm, and the second as subordinate, the other. The differences are established through the contrast of socially created opposites. As Joan Wallach Scott notes, "Any unitary concept in fact contains repressed or negated material; it is established in explicit opposition to another term."[4] Because the categorical opposites contain elements of the other, similarities must be suppressed; if the similarities were allowed to emerge, they would blur the boundaries between the two groups and undermine the distinction of one as dominant.

The distinctions between women and men and the dominance of men are hard to justify in modern Western societies, but they persist. Tracing the rise in women's status in the United States in the last 150 years, Robert Max Jackson argues that thanks to increasing bureaucratization and rationalization of many areas of modern life, women have substantial equality with men in jobs, legal rights, education, and voting power. Despite these marks of formal equality, what he calls residual inequalities are still to be tackled—the rarity of women in high political office and at the top levels of prestigious and lucrative professions, the widespread imbalance in domestic labor, greater costs to women in divorce and staying unpartnered, sexual harassment, rape, physical violence, and the persistent belief that women and men are inherently different.[5]

Modern Western societies are comparatively less gender-divided and more gender-egalitarian than feudal, aristocratic, or eighteenth- and nineteenth-century bourgeois societies were. But the areas of inequality are stubbornly resistant to change. Most men living in households with adult women do not share equally in domestic work and child care, so most women have a double work shift, or they hire to do "their" work another woman from the supply of those disadvantaged by poor education or immigrant status.[6] This unequal domestic division of labor diminishes women's worth in the paid workplace and cuts into opportunities to wield political power. Yet with modern technology, women and men can do much of the same work in home maintenance, child care, and the paid marketplace, and the presence of women at the top echelons of governments is becoming routine.

Nonetheless, the gender schema of male-female differences and men's dominance bubbles away beneath the public rhetoric of respect for individual differences and legal equality.[7] The continued social endorsement of men's dominance over women spills out in sexual entitlement—harassment of subordinates for sexual favors, sly and overt groping, date rape, gang rape, rape as an instrument of war, prostitution. It is also manifest in population and abortion policies that give women little choice in when and whether to procreate. The continued belief in the biological origin of differences between women and men continues to justify the gender divisions of family and paid work and the resulting inequality of economic resources and political power.

The ambivalence over gender divisions and allocation of responsibilities for child care, household maintenance, and paid work characterizes a social order in transition. In many respects, women and men are so equal that the gender divisions seem unnecessary, and then, when they are ignored, major aspects of inequality thwart women's ambitions. The infamous glass ceiling that allows women to see the road to the top and then bump their heads on invisible barriers is a case of perennial gender inequality. Gender segregation in the workplace is another. Women and men more and more do similar work, but dominant men continue to monopolize the better jobs, and the work world continues to replicate occupational gender segregation even as women move into jobs formerly considered men's work. During the 1970s and 1980s, women who went into occupations where the employees were predominantly men soon found that their co-workers became predominantly women because the men left. The entry of women did not drive the men out; it was because the men were leaving increasingly unattractive work sectors that positions for women opened. Similarly, women's and men's wages have become more equal because men's wages have declined, not because women's wages have increased; men still get the highest-paying jobs.[8]

At the other end of the spectrum from the increase in formal equality in the Western world is the deepening of the gendered divisions of work in the global economy. Financed by capital from developed countries, work organizations around the world exploit the labor of poor, young, unmarried women under sweatshop-like conditions while reserving better-paid jobs and support for entrepreneurship for middle-class men. The policies of the International Monetary Fund and other financial restructuring agencies do not include gender desegregation or encouraging women's education and access to health resources, which would allow women to break into men's occupations. In many of these countries, violence and sexual exploitation, as well as the spread of AIDS heterosexually, seriously undermine efforts to upgrade the lives of women and girls. Population policies are embedded in gendered stratification systems. Feminist work here has all it can do to prevent women's lives from worsening and to influence the programs of development agencies to be attentive to the needs of women and girls.[9]

The persistence of gender inequality makes it necessary to have a gendered perspective on how work and family are organized, how resources are awarded, and how power is distributed. However, I think that we also have to include in this perspective the other major social statuses intertwined with gender—at a minimum, social class, racial ethnic group, and sexual orientation. For many purposes, age, parental and relational status, physical ability, education, and religion have to be included as well. This multiple perspective fragments gender and breaks the hold of binary categorization. I think that for feminists in modern Western civilizations, going beyond gender is a needed step toward gender equality, with the immediate target for change the legal rigidity of gender statuses, their constant use in the allocation of family work and paid jobs, and the embedded notion of men's entitlement to women's services and sexuality.

FEMINISM AND SOCIAL CHANGE

Feminists have described the history and changing content of gender categories—the fluidity of "masculinity" and "femininity," the switches of tasks and jobs, the turnabouts of beliefs about what is "natural." Many feminists have intensively documented the practices that sustain the gendered social order in an effort to change the processes, expectations, and value systems that blight women's lives. But few feminists are now challenging the binary divisions themselves, perhaps because they, too, believe in their ultimate biological underpinnings. As Christine Delphy says, "Feminists seem to want to abolish hierarchy and even sex roles, but not difference itself."[10] That is, while feminists want women and men to be equal, few talk now about doing away with gender divisions altogether. One who does is Sandra Lipsitz Bem, who advocates "a vision of utopia in which gender polarization . . . has been so completely dismantled that—except in narrowly biological contexts like reproduction—the distinction between male and female no longer organizes the culture and the psyche."[11]

Eradicating the social division of women and men is hardly a new idea for feminists. In 1971, Shulamith Firestone said that "the end goal of feminist revolution must be . . . not just the elimination of male *privilege* but of the sex *distinction* itself: genital differences between human beings would no longer matter culturally." In 1972, Lois Gould's classic tale of childhood degendering, "X: A Fabulous Child's Story," was published in *Ms.* magazine. In 1980, Monique Wittig challenged lesbians and gay men to deny the divisive power of heterosexuality by refusing to think of themselves as women and men. In 1986, I said we needed to dismantle "Noah's ark"—lockstep binary thinking. Since 1990, postmodernists and queer theorists, following Judith Butler's lead in *Gender Trouble,* have questioned the twofold divisions of gender, sexuality, and even sex, undermining the solidity of a world built on men/women, heterosexuals/homosexuals, and male/female. Currently, in *Undoing Gender,* Butler argues that gender is a fluid psychological and sexual category but that collective social norms sustain gender divisions and the power intrinsic in gender hierarchies.[12]

Yet feminism as a movement, in the fight for equal treatment within the present gender structure, has lost sight of the revolutionary goal of dismantling gender divisions. The present drive toward gender balance or mainstreaming gender continues the attempts to undo the effects of gender divisions, but it is these divisions that perpetuate gender inequality. The distinctions between women and men may be deceptive, as Cynthia Fuchs Epstein argues, but they are unlikely to wither away by themselves.[13]

Part of the reason the dismantling of gender divisions was abandoned was that some feminists began to focus on women's bodily, sexual, and emotional differences from men and to valorize those differences, taking joy and pride in being a woman. Moving away from the goal of liberal feminists—to gain equality in the public world of work and politics—difference feminists insisted that what women gave men and children, and each other, in nurturance and emotional sustenance should not be relegated to secondary labor but should be rewarded as a primary contribution to society. In the debate over gender theory and politics, difference feminists and gender feminists became opposing factions.[14]

GENDER, WOMEN, AND DIFFERENCE

Gender feminists argue for the value of the generality of the concept, contending that gender encompasses the social construction of masculinities as well as femininities, the interrelations of women and men, the division of labor in the economy and in the family, and the structural power imbalances of modern Western societies. Difference feminists argue that the concept of gender minimizes the body and sexuality, the significance of women's procreative and nurturing capacities, and the violent potentialities of men's control of women's bodies, sexuality, and emotions. Difference feminists, using psychoanalytic and linguistic analyses of bodies, sexualities, psyches, and cultural representations, have eschewed a concept of gender for a deconstruction of the symbolic social order as deeply divided between the dominant possessors of the phallus and oppressed others.[15]

Standpoint feminism, a theoretical perspective that links the gendered division of labor in the work world and in the home to gendered consciousness, incorporates marxist and psychoanalytic theories of difference.[16] Standpoint feminism locates the source of differences between women and men in the gendered structure of family work and paid work, as well as in bodies and sexualities. As physical and social reproducers of children, women use their bodies, emotions, thoughts, and physical labor, and so they are grounded in material reality in ways that men are not. Women are responsible for most of the everyday work, even if they are highly educated, while highly educated men concentrate on the abstract and the intellectual. Because women's lives connect them to their bodies and emotions, their unconscious, as well as their conscious, view of the world is unitary and concrete. If women produced knowledge, what we know would be much more in touch with the everyday material world, with bodies, procreative rhythms, and the connectedness among people, because that is what women experience in the gendered social world.

Standpoint feminism privileges women's viewpoint; multicultural feminism asks, Which women? Multicultural and postcolonial feminists, addressing the national and international sources of women's oppression, claim that they are enmeshed in complex systems of class and racial ethnic dominance and subordination, in which some men are subordinate to other men and to some women as well. Feminist studies of men show that all men may have a "patriarchal dividend" of privilege and entitlement to women's labor, sexuality, and emotions, but some men additionally have the privileges of whiteness, education, prosperity, and prestige. These analyses see gender hierarchies as inextricable from the hierarchies of class and racial ethnic statuses.[17]

In this sense, *difference* is expanded from men versus women to the multiplicities of sameness and difference among women and among men and within individuals as well. All these differences arise from different social locations or standpoints, and it is hard to justify privileging one over others. Joan Wallach Scott points out that within-gender differences are especially compatible with "an equality that rests on differences—differences that confound, disrupt, and render ambiguous the meaning of any fixed binary opposition."[18] Working with these differences, feminist philosophers and political scientists have developed gendered theories of justice and have located gender in the matrix of complex inequality.

Feminist theories of justice contend that gender is a different form of inequality from social class or racial ethnic disadvantage because of women's responsibility for family work. Gendering family work produces inequality in the home because of the imbalance of the division of domestic labor. It also produces inequality in the workforce because women workers carry the extra baggage of care for husband, home, and children. Where they don't, there are other forms of inequality similar to those for men—in social class, racial ethnic categorization, sexual orientation, education, occupation, immigration. Thus, women as a group suffer from both public and private forms of injustice. As Leslie McCall says, "The discussion of inequality must therefore be expanded from one revolving around a unitary term—the new inequality—to one involving an open question about the overlapping and conflicting manifestations of gender, race, and class inequality."[19]

Degendering and Feminist Theories

Many feminists have implicitly called for a gender-free society by urging the minimization of the effects of gender, to the point of gender's practical disappearance. I am arguing here for a gender-free society to be an *explicit and primary goal*. This goal is not incompatible with feminist theories of difference, standpoint feminism, psychoanalytic theories, or feminist theories of justice. In fact, in many ways it is the logical outcome of these theories.

Difference feminists argue that gender feminists neglect the valued qualities of women's lives that come from their bodies, sexualities, and intimate parenting—nurturance, interrelatedness, emotionality. The basis of standpoint feminism is that women live in a world in touch with bodies, children, and hands-on physical labor. Difference and standpoint feminists may argue that degendering will create a masculine world—objective, instrumental, and bureaucratic. However, men also do physical labor, for pay or as volunteers and do-it-yourselfers, so they are not all detached from the material world.

Men also do far more caring for others, including elderly parents and infants, than is recognized by gendered norms for masculine behavior. These norms expect men to look out for their buddies in times of war and danger, but men also care for elderly parents and sick spouses and partners.[20] Degendering policies would encourage men to routinely care for children, the elderly, and each other and not leave emotional sustenance for family and friends to women. Thus, men as well as women would develop the valued qualities of nurturance, relatedness, and emotional expression.

Work relations in the modern world are both formal in organization and informal in practice, rule-based and relational, rational and emotional at the same time, and so are women and men workers. Organizational bureaucracies necessitate objectivity, rationality, and adherence to rules. The parallel informal organization of work creates circles of colleagues built on trust and loyalty and networks of sponsors, mentors, and novices, the "families" that make work life so attractive to men and women.[21] Diminution of gender divisions as an organizing principle of workplaces would not turn warmhearted women into coldhearted men any more than it would turn warmhearted men into coldhearted women. It would, rather, degender the best—and the worst—qualities of people so that good and bad characteristics are no longer seen as "the way women are" or "the way men are."

Gender feminism has been accused of superficiality in that

it does not attend to unconscious desires and deeply embedded personality patterns. In psychoanalytic theories of parenting, those are the outcome of women's primary parenting. These theories argue that women's openness to others and child-care capabilities are produced by continued identification of daughters with their mothers to the point of blurred ego boundaries. Men's repression of emotionality emerges from their need to separate from their mothers and from their hostility toward women, which in turn emerges from their fears that they, too, will lose their penises, just as their mothers must have. Sons develop the ego boundaries encouraged by identification with an emotionally distant father and demanded by the competitiveness of the world of men they enter as his heir. Castration fears are sublimated into control of emotions and dominating relationships with women.

Degendering parenting is a way of cutting into this loop of the reproduction of gendered children by gendered parents. Boys close to fathers who "mother" would not have to repress emotions to be masculine, and girls could identify with fathers and mothers. Misogynist views of women as castrated inferiors and potential castrators would also be diminished by boys' not having to reject everything womanly to be masculine. Degendering parenting would undercut distinct personality structures—objective and rational men, relational and emotional women—allowing boys and girls to develop the characteristics to compete and be authoritative, as well as to cooperate and befriend.

Feminist multicultural, social-class, and racial ethnic studies, as well as feminist studies of men, have long called for a perspective that locates gender in stratification systems of multiple domination or intersectionality. Degendering places gender within the matrix of complex inequality and calls for erasure of all invidious divisions and open access to economic resources, educational opportunities, and political power. These multiviewed perspectives have to be translated into praxis by seeking solutions to problems in ways that do not rely on conventional categories and conventional assumptions. As Carol Lee Bacchi warns, when we ask, What is the problem? we need to challenge "deeply held cultural assumptions, given specific historical, economic and cultural locations."[22]

Gender balance—putting women's as well as men's needs and perspectives into public policies—perpetuates gender divisions and women's subordinate position, since women as a group are matched against dominant men. Since separate is never equal, we need gender "mainstreaming" policies built on the assumption that all groups are equally entitled to public resources but not in exactly the same way. The groups that are compensated in the fight for equality need to be carefully constructed to reflect multiple sources of disadvantage. Advantages only to women, just like a single-minded focus on the needs of disadvantaged racial ethnic or social-class groups, can too easily be undercut by protesters who invoke the needs of the other groups.

Iris Marion Young says that a just heterogeneous society would attend to the needs of different groups, not erase differences: "Justice in a group-differentiated society demands social equality of groups, and mutual recognition and affirmation of group differences."[23] A policy of degendering would recognize people of different social classes, racial ethnic categories, ages, sexual orientations, parental and relational statuses, and so on, as shifting groups, cooperating and conflicting, depending on the situation and the policy question.

There is a testable equation in degendering. I am arguing that it is only by undercutting the gender system of legal statuses, bureaucratic categories, and official and private allocation of tasks and roles that gender equality can be permanently achieved. In the countries that are the most degendered in the sense of treating women and men the same legally and bureaucratically, women and men have more equal statuses. They are more likely to be comparably educated, work in comparable occupations and professions, have comparable political power and economic resources, and have shared responsibility for the care of children.

Degendering is already common in many gender-equal societies, such as Sweden and Norway. The extent of degendering in those countries is in sharp contrast to the forcefulness of gendering in such countries as Saudi Arabia, where every aspect of women's and men's lives is controlled by gender, to women's marked disadvantage. The feminist task of gaining citizenship rights and economic equality for most of the world's women is undeniably of first priority, but a second task can be done where women are not so terribly unequal—challenging the binary structures just a little bit more by asking why they are necessary at all.

Degendering will not do away with wars and hunger and economic disparities. But I do think that degendering will undercut the patriarchal and oppressive structure of Western societies and social institutions and give all of us the space to use our energies to demilitarize, work for peaceable solutions to conflicts, grow and distribute food, and level the gaps between social classes.

A World without Gender

In an essay about why war is futile, Jonathan Schell, recalling Marx's "all that was solid melted into air," begins:

> There are moments in history when a crack in time seems to open and swallow the known world: solid-seeming institutions, rotted from within, collapse or are discarded, settled beliefs are unsettled; old truths are discovered to be provisional; acts that were forbidden are permitted or even required; boundaries thought impassable are passed without comment; and outrageous and unreal events . . . flood in profusion from some portal of future that no one was guarding or even watching.[24]

I think that in the not-too-far future, we will see this crumbling of gender divisions and statuses.

Throughout this book, I have suggested ways to think about families, work, political regimes, and political action from the perspective of multiple gendering. I have said that these multiplicities challenge the solidity of the binary gender order and provide examples of degendering practices. Now I would like to think beyond gender to the possibilities of a totally nongendered social order.[25]

In *Paradoxes of Gender,* I described two thought experiments that render gender irrelevant.[26] In the first, an imaginary society divided into two genders treats them strictly equally, with half of all jobs held by men and half by women, family work done half by women and half by men, men and women serving alternately as heads of governments, equal numbers of women and men in the officer corps and ranks of armed forces, on sports teams, in cultural productions, and so on throughout society. In the second imaginary society, all work is equally valued and recompensed, regardless of who does it, and families and work groups are structured for equality of control of resources and decisions. Either path would render gender irrelevant—strict parity by the interchangeability of women and men and strict equality by making no category of people more valuable than any other. Strict parity would make it pointless to construct and maintain gender differences; strict equality would contradict the purpose of gender divisions by undercutting the subordination of women by men. As Christine Delphy says:

> If we define men within a gender framework, they are first and foremost dominants with characteristics which enable them to remain dominants. To be like them would be also to be dominants, but this is a contradiction in terms. . . . To be dominant one must have someone to dominate.[27]

At the end of *Paradoxes of Gender,* I asked the reader to envisage a scrupulously gender-equal world. Here I am going further and trying to imagine a world without genders at all. Can we think the impossible and envisage societies where people come in all colors, shapes, and sizes and where body characteristics are not markers for status identification or for predetermined allocation to any kind of activity? Here is my vision of such a world:

LOVE AND SEXUALITY, friendships and intimacies revolve around people with a mutual attraction to each other's bodies, intellects, interests, and personalities. Males inseminate willing females through copulation or provide sperm for insemination. Females who want to, give birth to infants. These infants become part of families of different kinds of kinship groups and households composed of a variety of responsible adults. They are breast-fed by lactating females and cared for by competent child minders. They receive love and affection from the older children and adults in their circles of relationships. Their favorites and role models vary over time, but there is at least one legally responsible adult for every child.

Children are not sexed at birth—their genitalia are irrelevant in the choice of names, blankets, and clothing. "A child is born to . . . ," the announcements read. In play groups and schools, children are organized by age, size, talents, skills, reading ability, math competence—whatever the needs of the group. Children's talents, skills, and interests shape their choices of further education and job training.

If we can assume nonassortment by other invidious categories, such as racial ethnic group, people are hired on the basis of their credentials, experience, interviewing skills, and connections. The salary scales and prestige value of occupations and professions depend on various kinds of social assessments, just as they do now, but the positions that pay best and are valued most are not monopolized by any one type of person. Science is done by scientists, teaching by teachers, cultural productions by writers, artists, musicians, dancers, singers, actors, and media producers. The beliefs and values and technologies of the time and place govern the content.

Positions of public authority in corporations, bureaucracies, and governments are attained by competition, sponsorship and patronage, networking, and other familiar forms of mobility. Charity, honesty, and competence are as evident as corruption, double-dealing, and shoddy work—people are people.

So there are still murders, wars, and other forms of violence, although perhaps through an ethical evolution, societies might develop in which people are taught how to handle anger and conflict in positive ways. But rules are made to be broken, so there is still a need for police and soldiers, judges and prison guards.

Games and sports are played for fitness and fun. New games are devised that put less emphasis on body shapes and more on skill. In competitions, people of different levels of body functioning and abilities compete against one another in a variety of "Olympics."

In the major and minor religions, new liturgies and rituals are in use, but old ones are turned to for their historical cultural value, as are the old novels, plays, songs, and operas. Those who have the calling and the talent lead congregations and prayer services and speak for the god(s).

New language forms develop that do not mark or categorize the speaker or the spoken about.[28] The old forms of language and literature are studied for their archaic beauty and what they tell us about the way people used to live and behave and think.

People group and identify themselves on the basis of all sorts of similarities and disdain others on the basis of all sorts of differences. Sometimes those who identify with each other wear similar clothing or hair styles or jewelry or cosmetics. Sometimes these displays become fashions for all who consider themselves chic. Group and individual ways of speaking, dressing, and behaving serve as cues for interaction and distancing.

There are no women or men, boys or girls—just parents and children, siblings and cousins and other newly named kin, and partners and lovers, friends and enemies, managers and workers, rulers and ruled, conformers and rebels. People form social groups and have statuses and positions and rights and responsibilities—and no gender. The world goes on quite familiarly but is radically changed—gender no longer determines an infant's upbringing, a child's education, an adult's occupation, a parent's care, an economy's distribution of wealth, a country's politicians, the world's power brokers.

To go back to the kabbalistic metaphor of broken bowls, a commentator on kabbalah said of Miriam the prophet, who led the women in dance at the shore of the Red Sea after the Israelites' safe passage, "By making a circle dance, she drew down the supernal light [from the source] where the categories of masculine and feminine do not exist."[29] The goal of *tikkun olam*—repair of the world—is to gather the scattered points of light so all the world will be one. If we apply this metaphor of unification to degendering, at least one human division can be erased.

Epilogue
WHAT DEGENDERING DOES TO THE COMPONENTS OF GENDER

AN INSTITUTION is like a glass room. You may not realize the walls are there until you crash into them. One individual is not likely to make a crack in a wall, but many crashing at the same spot will. Unfortunately, on the other side are other glass rooms. Few revolutions bring the whole glass house down, and such houses are, unfortunately, easily rebuilt unless constantly dismantled. In *Paradoxes of Gender,* I laid out the components of gender as an institution and for individuals.[1] Here I show how they would—or would not—be changed by degendering.

AS A SOCIAL INSTITUTION, gender is composed of:

Gender statuses, the socially recognized genders in a society and the norms and expectations for their enactment behaviorally, gesturally, linguistically, emotionally, and physically. How gender statuses are evaluated depends on their historical development in any particular society.
   Degendering eliminates gender statuses—and the norms and expectations built into them. How people act will depend on the norms and expectations of other major social statuses and group identities.
Gendered division of labor, the assignment of productive and do-

mestic work to members of different gender statuses. The work assigned to those of different gender statuses depends on how the society evaluates those statuses—the higher the status, the more prestigious and valued the work and the greater its rewards.

Degendering eliminates allocation by gender. Barring the intervention of other statuses, allocation of jobs, tasks, and occupations and professions will be on the basis of credentials, experience, abilities. Rewards—economic and prestigious—accrue to the type of work, as they do today, but the distribution of people to work of different sorts will vary by capabilities. Superiors and subordinates in workplaces will relate to each other as people of the same gender do today.

Gendered kinship, the family rights and responsibilities for each gender status. Kinship statuses reflect and reinforce the prestige and power differences of the different genders.

Degendering kinship will necessitate some way in which to regularize responsibility for dependents—legalized civil unions, household contracts. It is hoped that a structure of equality for the adults involved and shared care for dependents will be part of these contracts.

Gendered sexual scripts, the normative patterns of sexual desire and sexual behavior, as prescribed for the different gender statuses. Members of the dominant gender have more sexual prerogatives; members of a subordinate gender may be sexually exploited.

With degendering, sexual scripts can be fluid and open, like those of many transgenders. Dominance and exploitation will not be eliminated if social-class, racial ethnic, or other stratified statuses permeate the structure of a relationship. Degendered marriage contracts or legal partnerships can help protect the rights of the weaker partner in long-term relationships.

Gendered personalities, the combinations of traits patterned by gender norms that prescribe how members of different gender statuses are supposed to feel and behave. Social expectations of others in face-to-face interaction constantly reinforce these norms.

With degendering, situational norms for work, classroom, and informal occasions among equals and behavioral rules for formal occasions governed by protocol will not be gendered, nor will expressions of emotion. Degendering means that expectations and assessment of others in interaction will not be influenced by assumptions of gendered traits or attributes. Other statuses may shape how people feel, identify, and interact.

Gendered social control, the formal and informal approval and reward of conforming behavior and the stigmatization, social isolation, punishment, and medical treatment of nonconforming behavior.

Degendering means no control by gender, no gender dysphoria, no differential treatment on the basis of gendered body types, gendered sexual preferences, gendered lifestyles. Other forms of valuation and control may still be in place.

Gender ideology, the justification of gender statuses, particularly their differential evaluation. The dominant ideology tends to suppress criticism by making these evaluations seem natural.

An ideology of degendering assumes that sex is biological, physiological, and procreative, not a basis for social categorization; that sexual desire is fluid, not bound by gendered opposites; and that gender is not a valid basis for organizing societies.

Gender imagery, the cultural representations of gender and embodiment of gender in symbolic language and artistic productions that reproduce and reinforce gender statuses. Culture is one of the main supports of the dominant gender ideology.

Without binary opposites, cultural representations of people will be much more varied and imaginative, as in some science fiction today. The process of degendering and resistance and rebellion will provide rich cultural material.

FOR AN INDIVIDUAL, gender is composed of:

Sex category, the category to which the infant is assigned at birth based on appearance of genitalia. With prenatal testing and sex-typing, categorization is prenatal. Sex category may be changed later through surgery or reinspection of ambiguous genitalia.

With degendering, genitalia, internal organs, chromosomes, and genes indicate potential for body shape and procreation. They may be altered surgically and/or hormonally for physiological reasons, but not to conform to markers of a gender category.

Gender identity, the individual's sense of gendered self as a worker and family member.

A degendered identity may be based on many characteristics and commitments, group memberships, and senses of self.

Gendered marital and procreative status, fulfillment or nonfulfillment of allowed or disallowed mating, impregnation, childbearing, kinship roles.

In a degendered society, partner, parent, child, sibling, and other kin relationships will be transformed by new family norms and expectations. Biological procreation may be more commonly separated from parenting.

Gendered sexual orientation, socially and individually patterned sexual desires, feelings, practices, and identification.

Degendering means that sexual desire, emotional relationships, and social scripts for intimacy will be far more fluid and flexible. Relationships will be formed on the basis of personality, interests, and other individual characteristics and, to a lesser extent, on genital preferences. Sexual choices will not be the basis for social identities.

Gendered personality, internalized patterns of socially normative emotions as organized by family structure and parenting.

New degendered theories of personality development will be needed.

Gender processes, the social practices of learning, being taught, picking up cues, enacting behavior already learned to be gender-appropriate (or inappropriate, if rebelling or testing), developing a gender identity, "doing gender" as a member of a gender status in relationships with gendered others, acting deferential or dominant.

We learn how we are expected to act in interaction with others in recurrent situations. Degendering eliminates only one form of appropriate behavior, but one that permeates all interaction today. Socialization of children will not reinforce a gender identity, no one will "do gender," deference and domination will have nongendered sources.

Gender beliefs, incorporation of or resistance to gender ideology.

A degendered society should not be rigid about continued gendering. Members of religious or other groups may choose to continue gendering. There may be individual resistance to degendering in the form of exaggerated masculinity or femininity by traditionalists and rebels.

Gender display, presentation of self as a certain kind of gendered person through dress, cosmetics, adornments, and permanent and reversible body markers.

Degendering will encourage varieties of self-display—multiple presentations for different occasions, communities, identities. Rebels may resuscitate extreme gender displays, somewhat like drag. Gender traditionalists will need to choose ways of displaying their beliefs to one another and to the degendered. There will be conflicts and crossovers and multiple levels of gendering and degendering within a society. Without the legality of gender statuses, presentations of self will depend on membership in a variety of groups. These may be loose or restrictive.

DEGENDERING MEANS FREEDOM from gender restrictions, but it does not mean anarchy. Gradual degendering would be preferable, until all taken-for-granted gender practices were replaced with degendered practices in bureaucracies and work organizations and in informal interaction in everyday life. But a period of self-conscious attention to gendering has to come first. You have to be aware of gendering to degender.

NOTES

INTRODUCTION

1. Doris Lessing, *The Golden Notebook* (New York: Simon & Schuster, 1962), p. 59.

2. Judith Lorber, *Paradoxes of Gender* (New Haven, Conn.: Yale University Press, 1994).

3. Judith Lorber, "It's the 21st Century—Do You Know What Gender You Are?" in *International Feminist Challenges to Theory,* Advances in Gender Research, vol. 5, ed. Vasilikie Demos and Marcia Texler Segal (Greenwich, Conn.: JAI Press, 2001); "Using Gender to Undo Gender: A Feminist Degendering Movement," *Feminist Theory* 1 (2000): 101–18; "Crossing Borders and Erasing Boundaries: Paradoxes of Identity Politics," *Sociological Focus* 32 (1999): 355–69; "Beyond the Binaries: Depolarizing the Categories of Sex, Sexuality, and Gender," *Sociological Inquiry* 66 (1996): 143–59.

4. See, for example, Patricia Hill Collins, *Fighting Words: Black Women and the Search for Justice* (Minneapolis: University of Minnesota Press, 1998), and Jane Flax, "Postmodernism and Gender Relations in Feminist Theory," *Signs: Journal of Women in Culture and Society* (hereafter *Signs*) 12 (1987): 621–43.

5. See in particular R. W. Connell, *Masculinities* (Berkeley: University of California Press, 1995).

6. On matrices of domination, see Patricia Hill Collins, *Black Feminist Thought: Knowledge, Consciousness, and the Politics of Empowerment* (Boston: Unwin Hyman, 1990). On gender and complex inequality, see Leslie McCall, *Complex Inequality: Gender, Class, and Race in the New Economy* (New York: Routledge, 2001).

7. Wendy Brown calls this contrapuntal gender: "the 'radical instability of gender' and the 'relentless power of gender.' " "Gender in Counterpoint," *Feminist Theory* 4 (2003): 365.

8. Selma Sevenhuijsen, "The Place of Care: The Relevance of the Feminist Ethic of Care for Social Policy," *Feminist Theory* 4 (2003): 194. See also Joan Tronto, "Time's Place," *Feminist Theory* 4 (2003): 121–125.

9. See Teresa de Lauretis, *Alice Doesn't: Feminism, Semiotics, Cinema* (Bloomington: Indiana University Press, 1984), and *Technologies of Gender* (Bloomington: Indiana University Press, 1987); E. Anne Kaplan, "Is the Gaze Male?" in *Powers of Desire: The Politics of Sexuality,* ed. Ann Snitow, Christine Stansell, and Sharon Thompson (New York: Monthly Review Press, 1983); Susan McClary, *Feminine Endings: Music, Gender, and Sexuality* (Minneapolis: University of Minnesota Press, 1991); Laura Mulvey, *Visual and Other Pleasures* (Bloomington: Indiana University Press, 1989); Linda Nochlin, *Women, Art, and Power and Other Essays* (New York: Harper & Row, 1988); Elaine Showalter, ed., *The New Feminist Criticism: Essays on Women, Literature, and Theory* (New York: Pantheon Books, 1985); and Suzanna Danuta Walters, "Sex, Text, and Context: (In) between Feminism and Cultural Studies," in *Revisioning Gender,* ed., Myra Marx Ferree, Judith Lorber, and Beth B. Hess (Thousand Oaks, Calif.: Sage, 1999).

10. On borderlands, see Gloria E. Anzaldúa, *Borderlands/La Frontera: The New Mestiza* (San Francisco: Spinsters/Aunt Lute, 1987). On panethnicity, see Yen Espiritu, *Asian American Panethnicity: Bridging Institutions and Identities* (Philadelphia: Temple University Press, 1992).

CHAPTER 1   FRAMING THE ISSUES: GENDER THEORY AND DEGENDERING

1. Jenny Holzer, in "The Age of Modernism: Art in the Twentieth Century" (exhibition, Martin-Gropius-Bau, Berlin, May 7–July 27, 1997).

2. For a well-documented description of how things have stayed the same in the past twenty-five years, see Ann Oakley, *Gender on Planet Earth* (New York: New Press, 2002), 48–72.

3. I reserve the use of *male* and *female* to refer to sex (biological) differences; thus, when I am referring to a status position, I use *woman* and *man* as adjectives.

4. The kabbalistic background is that during creation, ideal types of beings (angels) were contained in three bowls of light, and finite types of beings (human beings) in six. The earthlings broke their six bowls, and their light was scattered. Reunification of the sparks of light is the goal of *tikkun olam,* repair of the world. Philologos, "On Language: Those Are the Breaks," *Forward,* March 3, 1993; Gershon Scholem, *On the Kabbalah and Its Symbolism* (New York: Schocken, 1965), 112–13.

5. Judith Lorber, "Dismantling Noah's Ark," *Sex Roles* 14 (1986): 567–80, and *Paradoxes,* 302.

6. See Andrew Abbott, *Methods of Discovery: Heuristics for the Social Sciences* (New York: W. W. Norton, 2004), 158–61.

7. Orna Sasson-Levy and Sarit Amram, "Gender Chaos in the Officer Training School," trans. Nik John (paper presented at the annual meeting of the Israeli Sociological Society, Be'er Sheva, February 25–26, 2004). Women make up 32 percent of the regular Israeli army. See Stuart Cohen, "Towards a New Portrait of the (New) Israeli Soldier," *Israeli Affairs* 3 (1997): 77–117.

8. The military instituted one strict rule to prevent sexual harassment and sexual violence: no soldier was to touch another except in extreme circumstances of physical collapse or danger.

9. In theories of complex inequality, the invidious effects of gender spill into social class and racial ethnic discrimination. Chris Armstrong, "Complex Equality: Beyond Equality and Difference," *Feminist Theory* 3 (2002): 67–82; McCall, *Complex Inequality*. The source of complex inequality theory is Michael Walzer, *Spheres of Justice: A Defense of Pluralism and Equality* (New York: Basic Books, 1983).

10. For information on government quotas, see International Institute for Democracy and Electoral Assistance, "Global Database of Quotas for Women," International IDEA and Stockholm University, http://www.idea.int/quota/index.cfm.

11. Marek Fuchs, "Women's Colleges Learning How to Get a Man," *New York Times,* December 4, 2002, B10.

12. Jane Gross, "Dividing the Sexes, for the Tough Years," *New York Times,* May 31, 2004, B1, 4.

13. Hill Collins, *Black Feminist Thought;* bell hooks, *Talking Back: Thinking Feminist, Talking Black* (Boston: South End Press, 1989); Gloria T. Hull, Patricia Bell Scott, and Barbara Smith, eds., *All the Women Are White, All the Blacks Are Men, but Some of Us Are Brave: Black Women's Studies* (Old Westbury, N.Y.: Feminist Press, 1982); Gloria I. Joseph and Jill Lewis, eds., *Common Differences: Conflicts in Black and White Feminist Perspectives* (Garden City, N.Y.: Anchor Press / Doubleday, 1989); Deborah King, "Multiple Jeopardy, Multiple Consciousness: The Context of a Black Feminist Ideology," *Signs,* 14 (1988): 42–72; Elizabeth Spelman, *Inessential Woman: Problems of Exclusion in Feminist Thought* (Boston: Beacon Press, 1988); Becky Thompson, "Multiracial Feminism: Recasting the Chronology of Second Wave Feminism," *Feminist Studies* 28 (2002): 337–55.

14. Ki Namaste, " 'Tragic Misreadings': Queer Theory's Erasure of Transgender Subjectivity," in *Queer Studies: A Lesbian, Gay, Bisexual, and Transgender Anthology,* ed. Brett Beemyn and Mickey Eliason (New York: New York University Press, 1996).

15. Kate Bornstein, *Gender Outlaw: On Men, Women, and the Rest of Us* (New York: Vintage, 1995); Leslie Feinberg, *Transgender Warriors: Making History from Joan of Arc to Dennis Rodham* (Boston: Beacon Press, 1996).

16. For an excellent discussion of the concept of gender as a social institution, see Patricia Yancey Martin, "Gender as Social Institution," *Social Forces* 82 (2004): 1249–75.

17. Robert Max Jackson, *Destined for Equality: The Inevitable Rise of Women's Status* (Cambridge, Mass.: Harvard University Press, 1998).

18. The major sources for this perspective are Sandra Lipsitz Bem, *The Lenses of Gender: Transforming the Debate on Sexual Inequality* (New Haven, Conn.: Yale University Press, 1993); Judith Butler, *Gender Trouble: Feminism and the Subversion of Identity* (New York: Routledge, 1990); R. W. Connell, *Gender and Power* (Palo Alto, Calif.: Stanford University Press, 1987); and Lorber, *Paradoxes*.

19. The concept of "doing gender" was first articulated in Candace West and Don Zimmerman, "Doing Gender," *Gender & Society* 1 (1987): 125–51. On the lack of reflection, see Patricia Yancey Martin, " 'Said and Done' versus 'Saying and Doing': Gendering Practices, Practicing Gender at Work," *Gender & Society* 17 (2003): 342–66. On undoing gender, see Judith Butler, *Undoing Gender* (New York: Routledge, 2004); Lorber, "Using Gender to Undo Gender," and Barbara J. Risman, "Gender as Social Structure: Theory Wrestling with Activism," *Gender & Society* 18 (2004): 429–50.

20. There are societies that have third genders—in some Native American tribes, biological males have the gender status of a woman; in some African societies, females have the gender status of sons or husbands, and males have the status of wives. See Ifi Amadiume, *Male Daughters, Female Husbands: Gender and Sex in an African Society* (London: Zed Books, 1987); Stephen O. Murray and Will Roscoe, eds., *Boy-Wives and Female Husbands: Studies of African Homosexualities* (New York: St. Martin's Press, 1998); and Walter L. Williams, *The Spirit and the Flesh: Sexual Diversity in American Indian Culture* (Boston: Beacon Press, 1986).

21. Bonnie S. Anderson and Judith P. Zinsser, *A History of Their Own: Women in Europe from Prehistory to the Present* (New York: Harper & Row, 1988), 1:297–331.

22. Bonnie S. Anderson and Judith P. Zinsser, *A History of Their Own: Women in Europe from Prehistory to the Present* (New York: Harper & Row, 1989), 2:41–61.

23. Oyèrónké Oyěwùmí, *The Invention of Women: Making an African Sense of Western Gender Discourses* (Minneapolis: University of Minnesota Press, 1997); Denise Riley, *Am I That Name? Feminism and the Category of Women in History* (Minneapolis: University of Minnesota Press, 1988); Joan Wallach Scott, *Gender and the Politics of History* (New York: Columbia University Press, 1988).

24. Michel Marriott, "For Venus and Mars, a Midpoint in Design," *New York Times,* October 9, 2003, G1, 6; Penelope Green, "Books of Style: For Men from Venus," review of *The Metrosexual Guide to Style: A Handbook for the Modern Man* by Michael Flocker, Sunday

Styles, *New York Times,* October 19, 2003, 11. From Green's review: "A metrosexual is a straight urban male with enough feminine affinities, like a knowledge of hair products and how to use them, to make him attractive to both sexes—and to just about every marketer on the planet."

25. Andrew Sum, Neeta Fogg, Paul Harrington, et al., *The Growing Gender Gaps in College Enrollment and Degree Attainment in the U.S. and Their Potential Economic and Social Consequences* (Washington, D.C.: Business Roundtable, 2003).

26. "Women in National Parliaments," Inter-Parliamentary Union, http://www.ipu.org/wmn-e/classif.htm. See also Lisa D. Brush, *Gender and Governance* (Walnut Creek, Calif.: AltaMira Press, 2003).

27. Denise Bielby and William T. Bielby, "She Works Hard for the Money: Household Responsibilities and the Allocation of Work Effort," *American Journal of Sociology* 93 (1988): 1031–59.

28. Michelle J. Budig and Paula England, "The Wage Penalty for Motherhood," *American Sociological Review* 66 (2001): 204–25; Ann Crittenden, *The Price of Motherhood: Why the Most Important Job in the World Is Still the Least Valued* (New York: Metropolitan Books, 2001).

29. For recent research, see Verta Taylor and Nancy Whittier, eds., "Gender and Social Movements," special issue, *Gender & Society* 12 (Dec. 1998) and 13 (Feb. 1999).

30. Barbara F. Reskin, "Bringing the Men Back In: Sex Differentiation and the Devaluation of Women's Work," *Gender & Society* 2 (1988): 58–81.

31. For an overview and critique of the sex/gender discourse, see Wendy Cealey Harrison and John Hood-Williams, *Beyond Sex and Gender* (London: Sage, 2002).

32. For the history and critique of the so-called sex hormones and "brain sex," see Anne Fausto-Sterling, *Sexing the Body: Gender Politics and the Construction of Sexuality* (New York: Basic Books, 2000); Nelly Oudshoorn, *Beyond the Natural Body: An Archeology of Sex Hormones* (New York: Routledge, 1994); and Marianne Van den Wijngaard, *Reinventing the Sexes: The Biomedical Construction of Femininity and Masculinity* (Bloomington: Indiana University Press, 1997). On the persistence of binary biology in popular thought, see Celia Roberts, " 'A Matter of Embodied Fact': Sex Hormones and the History of Bodies," *Feminist Theory* 3 (2002): 7–26. For a challenge to biological and sexual binarism in animals and fish, see Joan Roughgarden, *Evolution's Rainbow: Diversity, Gender, and Sexuality in Nature and People* (Berkeley: University of California Press, 2004).

33. See Raphael Carter's science fiction speculation, "Congenital Agenesis of Gender Ideation, by K. N. Sirsi and Sandra Botkin," on what it would be like to have the ability to

classify people by hormonal, chromosomal, and genital variations or rather the inability to sort twenty-two physiological types into two social genders. In *Starlight 2,* ed. Patrick Nielsen Hayden (New York: Tor Books/Tom Doherty Associates, 1998).

34. Suzanne J. Kessler, *Lessons from the Intersexed* (New Brunswick, N.J.: Rutgers University Press, 1998).

35. Suzanne J. Kessler and Wendy McKenna, *Gender: An Ethnomethodological Approach* (Chicago: University of Chicago Press, 1978). In Kessler and McKenna's view, genitals as gender markers are not physical but cultural.

36. Judith Butler, *Bodies That Matter: On the Discursive Limits of "Sex"* (New York: Routledge, 1993); Momim Rahman and Anne Witz, "What Really Matters: The Elusive Quality of the Material in Feminist Thought," *Feminist Theory* 4 (2003): 243–61.

37. For an overview of gender and epidemiology, see Judith Lorber and Lisa Jean Moore, *Gender and the Social Construction of Illness,* 2nd ed. (Walnut Creek, Calif.: AltaMira Press, 2002), chap. 2.

38. See Catherine B. Silver, "Gendered Identities in Old Age: Toward (De)gendering?" *Journal of Aging Studies* 17 (2003): 379–97.

39. Thomas Laqueur, *Making Sex: Body and Gender from the Greeks to Freud* (Cambridge, Mass.: Harvard University Press, 1990).

40. Oyèrónké Oyěwùmí, "De-confounding Gender: Feminist Theorizing and Western Culture, a Comment on Hawkesworth's 'Confounding Gender,' " *Signs* 23 (1998): 1049–62.

41. Oyěwùmí, *The Invention of Women,* 42.

42. Marjorie Garber, *Vice Versa: Bisexuality and the Eroticism of Everyday Life* (New York: Simon & Schuster, 1995); Paula C. Rodríguez Rust, ed., *Bisexuality in the United States* (New York: Columbia University Press, 2000); Merl Storr, ed., *Bisexuality: A Critical Reader* (New York: Routledge, 1999); Martin S. Weinberg, Colin J. Williams, and Douglas W. Pryor, *Dual Attraction: Understanding Bisexuality* (New York: Oxford University Press, 1994).

43. Weinberg, Williams, and Pryor, *Dual Attraction,* 49–58.

44. Germaine Greer, *The Change: Women, Aging, and the Menopause* (New York: Fawcett Columbine, 1991); Susan Wendell, *The Rejected Body: Feminist Philosophical Reflections on Disability* (New York: Routledge, 1996).

45. Gayle Rubin, "Thinking Sex: Notes for a Radical Theory of the Politics of Sexuality," in *Pleasure and Danger: Exploring Female Sexuality,* ed. Carol S. Vance (Boston: Routledge & Kegan Paul, 1984).

46. Butler, *Gender Trouble*.

47. See Steven P. Schacht, "Lesbian Drag Kings and the Feminine Embodiment of the Masculine," in *The Drag King Anthology*, ed. Donna Troka, Kathleen Lebesco, and Jean Noble (New York: Harrington Park Press, 2002), and "Four Renditions of Doing Female Drag: Feminine Appearing Conceptual Variations of a Masculine Theme," in *Gendered Sexualities*, Advances in Gender Research, vol. 6, ed. Patricia Gagné and Richard Tewksbury (Greenwich, Conn.: JAI Press, 2002). On drag as social protest, see Leila J. Rupp and Verta Taylor, *Drag Queens at the 801 Cabaret* (Chicago: University of Chicago Press, 2003), 212–21.

48. See Patricia Gagné, Richard Tewksbury, and Deanna McGaughey, "Coming Out and Crossing Over: Identity Formation and Proclamation in a Transgender Community," *Gender & Society* 11 (1997): 478–508, and Patricia Gagné and Richard Tewksbury, "Conformity Pressures and Gender Resistance among Transgendered Individuals," *Social Problems* 45 (1998): 81–101.

49. Marjorie Garber, *Vested Interests: Cross-Dressing and Cultural Anxiety* (New York: Routledge, 1992).

50. Justine Nicholas, "Changing Gender without Changing Jobs," *Women's Enews*, October 23, 2003, http://www.womensenews.org/article.cfm?aid=1575; Carol Kaesuk Yoon, "Scientist at Work: Joan Roughgarden; A Theorist with Personal Experience of the Divide between the Sexes," Science Times, *New York Times*, October 17, 2000, F1; Deirdre McCloskey, *Crossing: A Memoir* (Chicago: University of Chicago Press, 1999); Jan Morris, *Conundrum* (New York: Signet Books, 1975); Andrew Newman, "Back on the Beat in Her Hoboken an Identity Later," *New York Times*, January 13, 1996, 25–26; Jennifer Finney Boylan, *She's Not There: A Life in Two Genders* (New York: Broadway Books, 2003); Renée Richards with Jack Ames, *Second Serve* (New York: Stein & Day, 1983). Professions are in the order mentioned in the text. Richards was an ophthalmologist and competitive tennis player who successfully sued for the right to play women's tennis.

51. Louis Uchitelle, "A Transsexual Economist's 2d Transition: She Says Gender Determines One's Approach to Her Field," Arts & Ideas, *New York Times*, June 19, 1999, B7.

52. Janice G. Raymond, *The Transsexual Empire: The Making of the She-male* (Boston: Beacon Press, 1979); Sandy Stone, "The *Empire* Strikes Back: A Posttranssexual Manifesto," in *Body Guards: The Cultural Politics of Gender Ambiguity*, ed. Julia Epstein and Kristina Straus (New York: Routledge, 1991), 298.

53. Fred A. Bernstein, "On Campus, Rethinking Biology 101," Sunday Styles, *New York Times*, March 7, 2004, 1, 6.

54. According to Dreger, maintaining clear sex/gender boundaries is usually the reason for intensive medical and legal interest in intersexuals. Alice Domurat Dreger, *Hermaphrodites*

and the Medical Invention of Sex (Cambridge, Mass.: Harvard University Press, 1998), 1–14.

55. Kessler, *Lessons from the Intersexed.*

56. On intersexual politics, see Cheryl Chase, "Hermaphrodites with Attitude: Mapping the Emergence of Intersex Political Activism," *GLQ: A Journal of Gay and Lesbian Studies* 4 (1998): 189–211; Sharon E. Preves, *Intersex and Identity: The Contested Self* (New Brunswick, N.J.: Rutgers University Press, 2003); and Stephanie S. Turner, "Intersex Identities: Locating New Intersections of Sex and Gender," *Gender & Society* 13 (1999): 457–79.

57. Julie Butler, "X Marks the Spot for Intersex Alex," *West Australian,* January 11, 2003, retrieved from http://www.bodieslikeours.org/intersexalex.html. For a comprehensive discussion of the legal issues, see Stephen Whittle, *Respect and Equality: Transsexual and Transgender Rights* (London: Cavendish, 2002). For a science fiction version of the politics of categories, see Melissa Scott, *Shadow Man* (New York: Tom Doherty Associates, 1995).

58. "Individuals with this mental disorder are uncomfortable with their apparent or assigned gender and demonstrate persistent identification with the opposite sex." American Psychiatric Association, *Diagnostic and Statistical Manual of Mental Disorders,* 4th ed., text rev. (Washington, D.C.: American Psychiatric Association, 2000); quotation retrieved from http://www.behavenet.com/capsules/disorders/genderiddis.htm.

59. The problem is the same as that faced by the American Sociological Association in framing a statement on race that would recognize both its social constructedness and the necessity of using current bureaucratic categories to collect certain kinds of data, such as demographic changes and crime statistics. Roberta Spalter-Roth, "ASA Issues Official Statement on Importance of Collecting Data on Race," *Footnotes* 30 (September–October 2002): 1, 7, and Council of the American Sociological Association, "Statement of the American Sociological Association on the Importance of Collecting Data and Doing Scientific Research on Race," http://www.asanet.org/governance/racestm.html.

60. Michael Kimmel, e-mail to Sociologists for Women in Society (SWS) list, July 18, 2002, listserve.uconn.edu/sws=1.html, used with permission. Given the strength of the gender schema, Zachary is unfortunately likely to be much more conventional in his gender categorizations as he encounters peers and teachers. See Susan A. Gelman, Pamela Collman, and Eleanor E. Maccoby, "Inferring Properties from Categories versus Inferring Categories from Properties: The Case of Gender," *Child Development* 57 (1986): 396–404.

61. David Knoke and James H. Kuklinski, *Network Analysis* (Newbury Park, Calif.: Sage, 1982); Shulamit Reinharz, *Feminist Methods in Social Research* (New York: Oxford University Press, 1992), 145–63; Anselm L. Straus and Juliet Corbin, *Basics of Qualitative Research: Grounded Theory Procedures and Techniques* (Newbury Park, Calif.: Sage, 1990).

62. Richard Ekins, "On Male Femaling: A Grounded Theory Approach to Cross-Dressing and Sex-Changing," *Sociological Review* 41 (1993): 1–29.

63. Mary Clare Lennon and Sarah Rosenfeld, "Relative Fairness and the Division of Housework: The Importance of Options," *American Journal of Sociology* 100 (1994): 506–31.

64. A recent quantitative comparison of U.S. and Japanese women and men on values and identity found limited gender differences and significant national differences. Tania Levey and Catherine B. Silver, "Gender and Value Orientations: What's the Difference?! The Case of U.S. and Japan" (unpublished manuscript, 2004).

65. Joshua Gamson, "Sexualities, Queer Theory, and Qualitative Research," in *The Handbook of Qualitative Research*, ed. Norman K. Denzin and Yvonna S. Lincoln (Thousand Oaks, Calif.: Sage, 2000); David Valentine, "We're 'Not about Gender'; The Uses of Transgender," in *Out in Theory: The Emergence of Lesbian and Gay Anthropology*, ed. Ellen Lewin and William L. Leap (Urbana: University of Illinois Press, 2002), and " 'I Went to Bed with My Own Kind Once': The Erasure of Desire in the Name of Identity," *Language & Communication* 23 (2003): 123–38; Salvador Vidal-Ortiz, "Queering Sexuality and Doing Gender: Transgender Men's Identification with Gender and Sexuality," in *Gendered Sexualities,* ed. Gagné and Tewksbury.

66. Donna Haraway, *Modest_Witness@Second_Millennium. FemaleMan©.Meets OncoMouse™: Feminism and Technoscience* (New York: Routledge, 1997), 161.

67. On the effective use of new language by feminist and inadvertent activists, see Jane Mansbridge and Katherine Flaster, "The Cultural Politics of Everyday Discourse: The Case of 'Male Chavinism,' " unpublished manuscript (2004). The use of *Ms.* for "Miss" or "Mrs." is a case in point.

68. Cf. Oyěwùmí's contention that

> in the conceptual framework on Yorùbá, there are neither concepts/words connoting son, daughter, brother, or sister, nor are there any corresponding social roles. . . . Concepts of power and authority are not gendered, and no exclusive male or female social roles or identities exist.

The Invention of Women, 105.

69. See Michael S. Kimmel: "Saving the Males: The Sociological Implications of the Virginia Military Institute and the Citadel," *Gender & Society* 14 (2000): 494–516.

70. Judith Halberstam, *Female Masculinity* (Durham, N.C.: Duke University Press, 1998), 20–29.

71. Harvey Molotch, "The Restroom and Equal Opportunity," *Sociological Forum* 3 (1988): 128–32.

72. Lynn P. Freedman, "Shifting Visions: 'Delegation' Policies and the Building of a 'Rights-Based' Approach to Maternal Mortality," *Journal of the American Medical Women's Association* 57 (2002): 154–58; Gita Sen, Asha George, and Priosko Ostlin, *Engendering International Health: The Challenge of Equity* (Cambridge, Mass.: MIT Press, 2002); Theresa M. Wizemann and Mary-Lou Pardue, eds., *Exploring the Biological Contributions to Human Health: Does Sex Matter?* (Washington, D.C.: National Academy Press, 2001).

73. For an overview of gender and AIDS, see Lorber and Moore, *Gender and the Social Construction of Illness*, chap. 7.

74. Butler, *Gender Trouble*, 148–49.

CHAPTER 2   NO MORE MOTHERS AND FATHERS: DEGENDERING PARENTING

1. Grace Paley, "Fathers," *New Yorker,* February 17 and 24, 2003, 175. The idea of no more mothers and fathers comes from Sara Ruddick, *Maternal Thinking: Toward a Politics of Peace* (Boston: Beacon Press, 1995).

2. Twenty-five years ago, the pressures of managerial careers were the rationale for why men executives couldn't do quality fathering; today, the target of study is women executives. See Charles Handy, "Going against the Grain: Working Couples and Greedy Occupations," in *Working Couples,* ed. Robert Rapoport and Rhona Rapoport (New York: Harper & Row, 1978), and Mary Blair-Loy, *Competing Devotions: Career and Family among Women Executives* (Cambridge, Mass.: Harvard University Press, 2003).

3. Calvin D. Smith, " 'Men Don't Do This Sort of Thing': A Case Study of the Social Isolation of Househusbands," *Men and Masculinities* 1 (1998): 138–72.

4. James A. Levine, "The Other Working Parent," Op-Ed, *New York Times,* March 4, 1999, A25. For alternative language frames in redefining work and family structures, see Julia C. Nentwich, "Doing Difference and Equality in a Swiss Organization" (paper presented at the Third International Interdisciplinary Conference, Gender, Work, and Organization, Keele University, Staffordshire, U.K. June 25–27, 2003).

5. Thomas Laqueur, "The Facts of Fatherhood," in *Conflicts in Feminism,* ed. Marianne Hirsch and Evelyn Fox Keller (New York: Routledge, 1990), 209.

6. Budig and England, "The Wage Penalty for Motherhood," 205; see also Crittenden, *The Price of Motherhood.* Paid care is also poorly recompensed; see Paula England, Michelle Budig, and Nancy Folbre, "Wages of Virtue: The Relative Pay of Care Work," *Social Problems* 49 (2002): 455–73.

7. Nancy Folbre, *Who Pays for the Kids? Gender and the Structures of Constraint* (London: Routledge, 1994).

8. See Jean L. Potuchek, *Who Supports the Family? Gender and Breadwinning in Dual-Earner Marriages* (Palo Alto, Calif.: Stanford University Press, 1997).

9. Heidi I. Hartmann, "Capitalism, Patriarchy, and Job Segregation by Sex," *Signs* 1, no. 3, pt. 2 (1976): 139.

10. Myra Marx Ferree, "Patriarchies and Feminisms: The Two Women's Movements of Unified Germany," *Social Politics* 2 (1995): 10–24.

11. Hill Collins, *Black Feminist Thought*, 115–37; Silvia Domínguez and Celeste Watkins, "Creating Networks for Survival and Mobility: Social Capital among African-American and Latin-American Low-Income Mothers," *Social Problems* 50 (2003): 111–35; Lynne Haney and Miranda March, "Married Fathers and Caring Daddies: Welfare Reform and the Discursive Politics of Paternity," *Social Problems* 50 (2003): 461–81; Bart Landry, *Black Working Wives: Pioneers of the American Family Revolution* (Berkeley: University of California Press, 2000); Jeffrey Weeks, Catherine Donovan, and Brian Heaphy, *Same Sex Intimacies: Families of Choice and Other Life Experiments* (New York: Routledge, 2001); Kathleen Gerson, *No Man's Land: Men's Changing Commitments to Family and Work* (New York: Basic Books, 1993).

12. Alice S. Rossi, "Equality between the Sexes: An Immodest Proposal," *Daedalus* 93 (1964): 607–52, "A Biosocial Perspective on Parenting," *Daedalus* 106 (1977): 1–31, and "Gender and Parenthood," *American Sociological Review* 49 (1984): 1–19.

13. Fausto-Sterling, *Sexing the Body*, 195–232; Wijngaard, *Reinventing the Sexes*.

14. Frans B. M. de Waal, "Peace Lessons from an Unlikely Source," *PloS Biology* 2 (April 2004), http://www.plosbiology.org/plosonline/?request=get-document&doi=10.1371/journal.pbio.002010]; Robert M. Sapolsky and Lisa J. Share, "A Pacific Culture among Wild Baboons: Its Emergence and Transmission," *PLoS Biology* 2 (April 2004), http://www.plosbiology.org/plosonline/?request=get-document&doi=10.1371%2Fjoural.pbio.0020106.

15. Shelley E. Taylor et al., "Biobehavioral Responses to Stress in Females: Tend-and-Befriend, Not Fight-or-Flight," *Psychological Review* 107 (2000): 411–29; Theodore D. Kemper, *Social Structure and Testosterone: Explorations of the Socio-Bio-Social Chain* (New Brunswick, N.J.: Rutgers University Press, 1990).

16. For feminist critiques of the male biases in these theories, see Donna J. Haraway, *Primate Visions* (New York: Routledge, 1989), and Margaret Ehrenberg, *Women in Prehistory* (Norman: University of Oklahoma Press, 1989). On the feminist view of women's evolution, see Sarah Blaffer Hrdy, *The Woman That Never Evolved* (Cambridge, Mass.: Harvard University Press, 1981, repr., 1999), and *Mother Nature: A History of Mothers, Infants, and Natural Selection* (New York: Pantheon Books, 1999).

17. Adrienne Zihlman, "The Paleolithic Glass Ceiling: Women in Human Evolution," in *Women in Human Evolution,* ed. Lori D. Hager (New York: Routledge, 1997).

18. Judith Stacey, *Brave New Families: Stories of Domestic Upheaval in Late-Twentieth-Century America* (New York: Basic Books, 1991); Immanuel Wallerstein and Joan Smith, "Households as an Institution of the World-Economy," in *Gender, Family, and Economy: The Triple Overlap,* ed. Rae Lesser Blumberg (Newbury Park, Calif.: Sage, 1991).

19. In the United States in 2002, there were 1,038,000 mothers with children under one year working full-time in the civilian labor force. U.S. Department of Labor, Bureau of Labor Statistics, Current Population Survey, Employment Characteristics of Families, Table 4, "Families with Own Children: Employment Status of Parents by Age of Youngest Child and Family Type, 2001–02 Annual Averages," http://www.bls.gov/news.release/ famee.t04.htm.

20. Linda M. Blum notes that German and French women factory workers between the world wars demanded on-site breast-feeding facilities and time to nurse. "Mothers, Babies, and Breastfeeding in Late Capitalist America: The Shifting Contexts of Feminist Theory," *Feminist Studies* 19 (1993): 309–31.

21. Lizette Alvarez, "Norway Leads Industrial Nations Back to Breast-Feeding," *New York Times,* October 21, 2003, A3. The six-month rate for the United States is 32 percent; for Britain, 20 percent.

22. See Margot Slade, "Have Pump, Will Travel: Combining Breast-Feeding and a Career," *New York Times,* December 14, 1997, sec. 3, p. 12. The *New York Times Magazine* reported on a surrogate mother who ships three hundred ounces of her pumped breast milk once a week to the parents of the twins she birthed for them. They pay the seventy-five-dollar shipping costs for this updated wet-nursing. "Two Lives to Give," *New York Times Magazine,* October 19, 2003, 138.

23. Barbara Katz Rothman, *Recreating Motherhood: Ideology and Technology in a Patriarchal Society* (New Brunswick, N.J.: Rutgers University Press, 2000), 154.

24. Jules Law, "The Politics of Breastfeeding: Assessing Risk, Dividing Labor," *Signs* 25 (2000): 442.

25. Nancy J. Chodorow, *The Reproduction of Mothering: Psychoanalysis and the Sociology of Gender* (Berkeley: University of California Press, 1978).

26. Feminists have transposed the mother-daughter duo into lesbian intimacy. See Luce Irigaray, *This Sex Which Is Not One,* trans. Catherine Porter with Carolyn Burke (Ithaca, N.Y.: Cornell University Press, 1977, repr., 1985), and Adrienne Rich, "Compulsory Heterosexuality and Lesbian Existence," *Signs* 5 (1977): 631–60.

27. On masculinity, fatherhood, and the structure of men's power, see Jeff Hearn, "Men, Fathers, and the State: National and Global Relations," in *Making Men into Fathers: Men, Masculinities, and the Social Politics of Fatherhood,* ed. Barbara Hobson (Cambridge: Cambridge University Press, 2002).

28. bell hooks, *Feminist Theory: From Margin to Center* (Boston: South End Press, 1984), 137.

29. On custody conflicts and gender-neutral custody law reform, see Scott Coltrane, *Gender and Families* (Thousand Oaks, Calif.: Pine Forge Press, 1998), 153–59. On *couvade* as a claiming ritual, see Karen Ericksen Paige and Jeffrey M. Paige, *The Politics of Reproductive Ritual* (Berkeley: University of California Press, 1981), 189–90.

30. Michael E. Lamb, "Introduction: The Emergent American Father," in *The Father's Role: Cross-Cultural Perspectives,* ed. Michael E. Lamb (Hillsdale, N.J.: Lawrence Erlbaum Associates, 1987). A well-publicized slogan of one of Israel's women's organizations was "Be a man, give her a hand."

31. Scott Coltrane, *Family Man: Fatherhood, Housework, and Gender Equity* (New York: Oxford University Press, 1996), 56–83, 116–117. On working out father-son issues, see also Leonard Pitts, Jr., *Becoming Dad: Black Men and the Journey to Fatherhood* (Atlanta: Longstreet Press, 1999).

32. Diane Ehrensaft, *Parenting Together: Men and Women Sharing the Care of Their Children* (Urbana: University of Illinois Press, 1987).

33. Scott Coltrane, "Household Labor and the Routine Production of Gender," *Social Problems* 36 (1989), 483, 485; Barbara J. Risman, "Intimate Relationships from a Microstructural Perspective: Men Who Mother," *Gender & Society* 1 (1987): 6–32. See also Geoffrey L. Greif, *Single Fathers* (Lexington, Mass.: Lexington Books, 1985).

34. Pitts, *Becoming Dad,* 198, 205.

35. Barbara Hobson and David Morgan, introduction to *Making Men into Fathers,* ed. Barbara Hobson.

36. Livia Sz. Oláh, Eva M. Bernhardt, and Frances K. Goldscheider, "Coresidential Paternal Roles in Industrialized Countries: Sweden, Hungary, and the United States," Ann Shola Orloff and Renee Monson, "Citizens, Workers, or Fathers? Men in the History of U.S. Social Policy," and Helena Bergman and Barbara Hobson, "Compulsory Fatherhood: The Coding of Fatherhood in the Swedish Welfare State," all in *Making Men into Fathers,* ed. Hobson. Sweden's parental-leave policy compensates either parent at 80 to 90 percent of wages with high maximum limits for a year. The leave can be divided between the parents, except for a reserved "daddy month" and a reserved "mommy month." The time does not have to be taken in chunks but can be spread out up to the child's eighth birthday.

37. Questionnaires answered by 1,360 Norwegian fathers and interviews with 30 couples found that the benefits of the month-long father-designated parental leave in bonding and in shaping fathering practices depended on the men's having full responsibility for the child without the wife's presence. Berit Brandth and Elin Kvande, " 'Home Alone' Fathers," *Nikk magasin* (Nordic Institute for Women's Studies and Gender Research, Oslo), no. 3 (2003): 22–25.

38. On shared parenting in heterosexual couples, see Sandra Lipsitz Bem, *An Unconventional Family* (New Haven, Conn.: Yale University Press, 1998); Scott Coltrane, *Family Man;* Francine M. Deutsch, *Halving It All: How Equally Shared Parenting Works* (Cambridge, Mass.: Harvard University Press, 1999); Anna Dienhart, *Reshaping Fatherhood: The Social Construction of Shared Parenting* (Thousand Oaks, Calif.: Sage, 1998); Diane Ehrensaft, *Parenting Together;* and Barbara J. Risman, *Gender Vertigo: American Families in Transition* (New Haven, Conn.: Yale University Press, 1998).

39. On gay parents, see John C. Miller, " 'My Daddy Loves Your Daddy': A Gay Father Encounters a Social Movement," and Maureen Sullivan, "Alma Mater: Family 'Outings' and the Making of the Modern Other Mother (MOM)," both in *Queer Families, Queer Politics: Challenging Culture and the State,* ed. Mary Bernstein and Renate Reimann (New York: Columbia University Press, 2001); Gillian A. Dunne, "Opting into Motherhood: Lesbians Blurring the Boundaries and Transforming the Meaning of Parenthood and Kinship," *Gender & Society* 14 (2000): 11–35; and Susan E. Dalton and Denise D. Bielby, " 'That's Our Kind of Constellation': Lesbian Mothers Negotiate Institutionalized Understandings of Gender within the Family," *Gender & Society* 14 (2000): 36–61.

40. Kareen Malone and Rose Cleary, "(De)Sexing the Family: Theorizing the Social Science of Lesbian Families," *Feminist Theory* 3 (2002): 271–93.

41. Christopher Carrington, *No Place like Home: Relationships and Family Life among Lesbians and Gay Men* (Chicago: University of Chicago Press, 1999).

42. A random sampling from the U.S. Census found that of 9,328 same-gender couples, 26 percent of the homosexual couples and 22 percent of the lesbian couples had a stay-at-home parent; 25 percent of comparable heterosexual couples had such a parent, and of those, few were the father. Ginia Bellafante, "Two Fathers, with One Happy to Stay at Home," *New York Times,* January 12, 2004, A1, 12.

43. Coltrane found similar patterns in Hispanic couples. *Family Man,* 84–115. Hochschild coined the phrase "economy of gratitude" to explain the leverage women have over men who are reluctant to share in domestic work. A woman who earns more than her husband is not necessarily in a better bargaining position than one who makes a lot less than her husband: the "economy of gratitude" may let her use his failed aspirations against him, or it may make her feel that she owes it to her low-earning husband not to ask him to do

domestic work since her greater success has already lowered his status. Arlie Russell Hochschild with Anne Machung, *The Second Shift: Working Parents and the Revolution at Home* (New York: Viking Press, 1989).

44. Risman, *Gender Vertigo,* 93–127.

45. Dienhart, *Reshaping Fatherhood.*

46. As I was writing this chapter, in the fall of 2003, there was a thread on the SWS e-mail list on academic mothers' guilt over taking time away from their children. At my request, fathers wrote of very similar work and family pressures. The concepts of "good enough mother" (or father) and "good enough career" were invoked as sensible standards for self-assessment.

47. Laura Sanchez and Elizabeth Thomson, "Becoming Mothers and Fathers: Parenthood, Gender, and the Division of Labor," *Gender & Society* 11 (1997): 767; Susan Sanderson and Vetta L. Sanders Thompson, "Factors Associated with Perceived Paternal Involvement in Childrearing," *Sex Roles* 46 (2002): 99–111.

48. Susan Moller Okin, *Justice, Gender, and the Family* (New York: Basic Books, 1989), 185; Deutsch, *Halving It All.*

49. Risman, *Gender Vertigo,* 140, 149.

50. Judith Stacey and Timothy Biblarz, "(How) Does the Sexual Orientation of Parents Matter?" *American Sociological Review* 66 (2001): 177. See also Mike Allen and Nancy Burrell, "Comparing the Impact of Homosexual and Heterosexual Parents on Children: Meta-Analysis of Existing Research," *Journal of Homosexuality* 32 (1996): 19–35, and Susan Golombok and Fiona Tasker, "Do Parents Influence the Sexual Orientation of Their Children? Findings from a Longitudinal Study of Lesbian Families," *Developmental Psychology* 32 (1996): 3–11.

51. Kathleen Gerson, "Moral Dilemmas, Moral Strategies, and the Transformation of Gender: Lessons from Two Generations of Work and Family Change," *Gender & Society* 16 (2002): 8–28.

52. Deutsch, *Halving It All,* 11, 61, 65. See also Diane Ehrensaft, "The Kinderdult: The New Child Born to Conflict between Work and Family," and Arlie Russell Hochschild, "Eavesdropping Children, Adult Deals, and Cultures of Care," both in *Working Families: The Transformation of the American Home,* ed. Rosanna Hertz and Nancy L. Marshall (Berkeley: University of California Press, 2001).

53. Judith Stacey, *In the Name of the Family: Rethinking Family Values in the Postmodern Age* (Boston: Beacon Press, 1996), 18, 37.

54. See Weeks, Donovan, and Heaphy, *Same Sex Intimacies.* On second-parent adoption, see Susan E. Dalton, "Protecting Our Parent-Child Relationships: Understanding the

Strengths and Weaknesses of Second-Parent Adoption," in *Queer Families, Queer Politics,* ed. Bernstein and Reimann. On arguments for gay marriage, compare David L. Chambers, " 'What If?' The Legal Consequences of Marriage and the Legal Needs of Lesbian and Gay Male Couples," with Suzanna Danuta Walters, "Take My Domestic Partner, Please: Gays and Marriage in the Era of the Visible," both in *Queer Families, Queer Politics,* ed. Bernstein and Reimann. In February and March 2004, the issue of gay marriages was in U.S. newspapers every day as some mayors issued licenses for them and President George W. Bush called for a constitutional amendment forbidding them. For a short summary, see "The Road to Gay Marriage," editorial, Week in Review, *New York Times,* March 7, 2004, 12.

55. Martha Albertson Fineman, *The Neutered Mother, the Sexual Family, and Other Twentieth Century Tragedies* (New York: Routledge, 1995), 234–35.

56. On proposals for "delegalizing" marriage, see Lisa Duggan, "Holy Matrimony!" *Nation,* March 15, 2004, http://www.thenation.com/doc.mhtml?i=20040315&s=duggan, and Richard Kim, "The Descent of Marriage?" *Nation,* March 15, 2004, http://www.the nation.com/doc.mhtml?i=20040315&s=kim.

57. Moller Okin advocates that employers split a worker's wages between the job holder and the home worker in recognition that each is supporting the household. *Justice, Gender, and the Family,* 181.

58. Sandra Lipsitz Bem, who called for eradicating gender divisions in *The Lenses of Gender,* said that her own family, as described in *An Unconventional Family,* was the feminist practice of her feminist theory of degendering.

CHAPTER 3   WORKERS HAVE FAMILIES: DEGENDERING THE WORKPLACE

1. Yancey Martin, " 'Said and Done' versus 'Saying and Doing,' " 345.

2. Stanislaw Lem, "The Twenty-fourth Voyage," in *Memoirs of a Space Traveler: Further Reminiscences of Ijon Tichy* (New York: Harcourt Brace Jovanovich, 1981), 17–31.

3. Lisa Belkin, "When Caring for the Family Becomes the Job," *New York Times,* May 9, 2004, sec. 10, p. 1.

4. See, among others, Lourdes Benería, *Gender, Development, and Globalization: Economics as If All People Mattered* (New York: Routledge, 2003), 131–60, and Nancy Folbre, *The Invisible Heart: Economics and Family Values* (New York: New Press, 2001). Folbre notes that Amartya Sen critiqued rational-man theory a generation ago in "Rational Fools: A Critique of the Behavioral Foundations of Economic Theory," *Philosophy & Public Affairs* 6 (1977): 317–44; see 236 n6.

5. Lena M. Lundgren, Jennifer Fleischer-Cooperman, Robert Schneider, and Therese Fitzgerald, "Work, Family, and Gender in Medicine: How Do Dual-Earners Decide Who Should Work Less?" in *Working Families,* ed. Hertz and Marshall.

6. For recent overviews, see Hertz and Marshall, eds., *Working Families;* Jody Heymann, *The Widening Gap: Why America's Working Families Are in Jeopardy and What Can Be Done About It* (New York: Basic Books, 2000); Arlie Russell Hochschild, *The Time Bind: When Work Becomes Home and Home Becomes Work* (New York: Metropolitan Books, 1997); Jerry A. Jacobs and Kathleen Gerson, *The Time Divide: Work, Family, and Gender Inequality* (Cambridge, Mass.: Harvard University Press, 2004); Phyllis Moen, ed., *It's about Time: Couples and Careers* (Ithaca, N.Y.: ILR Press, 2003); Marcie Pitt-Catsouphes and Bradley K. Googins, eds., *The Evolving World of Work and Family: New Stakeholders, New Voices,* Annals of the American Academy of Political and Social Science, vol. 562 (Thousand Oaks, Calif.: Sage, 1999); and Joan Williams, *Unbending Gender: Why Family and Work Conflict and What to Do about It* (New York: Oxford University Press, 2000).

7. Eileen Appelbaum, Thomas Bailey, Peter Berg, and Arne L. Kalleberg, *Shared Work, Valued Care: New Norms for Organizing Market Work and Unpaid Care Work* (Washington, D.C.: Economic Policy Institute, 2002); Selma Sevenhuijsen, "The Place of Care"; Patricia Spakes, "Women, Work, and Babies: Family-Labor Market Policies in Three European Countries," *Affilia* 10 (1995): 369–97.

8. Blair-Loy, *Competing Devotions,* 31.

9. Hochschild, *The Time Bind.*

10. Phyllis Moen, "Integrative Careers: Time In, Time Out, and Second Acts" (presidential address, Eastern Sociological Society, New York, February 2004); Phyllis Moen and Shin-Kap Han, "Gendered Careers: A Life-Course Perspective," in *Working Families,* ed. Hertz and Marshall; Sonya Williams and Shin-Kap Hap, "Career Clocks: Forked Roads," in *It's About Time,* ed. Moen.

11. When women leave a high-prestige position "for the sake of their family," they are usually believed; when men do, it's seen as polite window dressing for the "real reason."

12. Blair-Loy, *Competing Devotions;* Dafna N. Izraeli, "Culture, Policy, and Women in Dual-Earner Families in Israel," in *Dual-Earner Families: International Perspectives,* ed. Susan Lewis, Dafna N. Izraeli, and Helen Hootsmans (London: Sage, 1992); Lisa Rantalaiho and T. Heiskanen, eds., *Gendered Practices in Working Life* (New York: St. Martin's Press, 1997); Barbara J. Risman, Maxine P. Atkinson, and Stephen P. Blackwelder, "Understanding the Juggling Act: Gendered Preferences and Social Structural Constraints," *Sociological Forum* 14 (1999): 319–44.

13. Sue Falter Mennino and April Brayfield, "Job-Family Trade-offs: The Multidimensional Effects of Gender," *Work & Occupations* 29 (2002): 226–56.

14. Michal Frenkel, "Women in Hi-Tech: Has the 'Motherhood Wall' Collapsed?" (research report submitted to the Israel Women's Network and the Hadassah Foundation, 2004). The report was based on a study done in collaboration with Dafna Izraeli. The information on divorced fathers came from focus groups. See also Nina Toren and Dahlia Moore, "Family and Work Go Well Together: Changes in the Perceptions and Preferences of Working Women in Israel," unpublished manuscript (2004).

15. Heymann, *The Widening Gap.*

16. Lise Vogel, *Mothers on the Job: Maternity Policy in the United States* (New Brunswick, N.J.: Rutgers University Press, 1993).

17. Crittenden, *The Price of Motherhood,* 39.

18. On the gendered structure and culture of organizations, see Joan Acker, "Hierarchies, Jobs, and Bodies: A Theory of Gendered Organizations," *Gender & Society* 4 (1990): 139–58; Lisa Adkins, "Cultural Feminization: 'Money, Sex, and Power' for Women," *Signs* 26 (2001): 669–95; Dana M. Britton, "The Epistemology of the Gendered Organization," *Gender & Society* 14 (2000): 418–34; Kathy E. Ferguson, *The Feminist Case against Bureaucracy* (Philadelphia: Temple University Press, 1984); Silvia Gherardi, *Gender, Symbolism, and Organizational Cultures* (Thousand Oaks, Calif.: Sage, 1995); Jeff R. Hearn and Wendy Parkin, *Gender, Sexuality, and Violence in Organizations: The Unspoken Forces of Organization Violations* (Thousand Oaks, Calif.: Sage, 2002); Winifred R. Poster, "Dangerous Places and Nimble Fingers: Discourses of Gender Discrimination and Rights in Global Corporations," *International Journal of Politics, Culture, & Society* 15 (2001): 77–105; Barbara Reskin and Catherine Ross, "Jobs, Authority, and Earnings among Managers: The Continuing Significance of Sex," *Work & Occupations* 19 (1992): 342–65; and Celia Ridgeway, "Interaction and the Conservation of Gender Inequality: Considering Employment," *American Sociological Review* 62 (1997): 218–35.

19. In 2002, the median weekly earnings of U.S. full-time women workers with children under six were 91 percent of what they were for women without children and 96 percent if the women had children between six and seventeen years old. The comparable figures for men showed an increase of 15 percent with children under six and 25 percent for older children. U.S. Department of Labor, Bureau of Labor Statistics, Report 972, "Highlights of Women's Earnings in 2002," September 2003, Tables 9 and 15, http://www.bls.gov/cps/cpswom2002.pdf.

20. Gherardi, *Gender, Symbolism, and Organizational Cultures,* 7–37.

21. David L. Collinson, David Knights, and Margaret Collinson, *Managing to Discriminate* (New York: Routledge, 1990), 193–94.

22. Yancey Martin, " 'Said and Done' versus 'Saying and Doing.' "

23. Neela Banerjee, "Some 'Bullies' Seek Ways to Soften Up: Toughness Has Risks for Women Executives," *New York Times*, August 10, 2001, C1, 2.

24. Ridgeway, "Interaction and the Conservation of Gender Inequality," 230. See also Patricia Yancey Martin and Shirley Harkreader, "Multiple Gender Contexts and Employee Rewards," *Work & Occupations* 20 (1993): 296–336, and Celia L. Ridgeway and Shelley J. Correll, "Unpacking the Gender System: A Theoretical Perspective on Gender Beliefs and Social Relations," *Gender & Society* 18 (2004): 510–31.

25. On gatekeeping in the informal organization of work, see Sharon R. Bird, "Welcome to the Men's Club: Homosociality and the Maintenance of Hegemonic Masculinity," *Gender & Society* 10 (1996): 117–32; Cynthia Cockburn, *In the Way of Women: Men's Resistance to Sex Equality in Organizations* (Ithaca, N.Y.: ILR Press, 1991); Judith Lorber, "Guarding the Gates: The Micropolitics of Gender," in *Paradoxes;* Patricia Yancey Martin, " 'Mobilizing Masculinities': Women's Experiences of Men at Work," *Organization* 8 (2001): 587–618; Linda McDowell, *Capital Culture: Gender at Work in the City* (Oxford: Basil Blackwell, 1997); and Judy Wajcman, *Managing like a Man: Women and Men in Corporate Management* (University Park: Pennsylvania State University Press, 1998).

26. On the advancement of men in women-dominated occupations, see Michelle J. Budig, "Male Advantage and the Gender Composition of Jobs: Who Rides the Glass Escalator?" *Social Problems* 49 (2002): 258–77, and Christine L. Williams, "The Glass Escalator: Hidden Advantages for Men in the 'Female' Professions," *Social Problems* 39 (1992): 253–67.

27. Everett C. Hughes, *The Sociological Eye* (Chicago: Aldine-Atherton, 1971), 146.

28. *Time*, December 30, 2002/January 6, 2003, 30–60. *Time*'s names for the women in the profile headlines reflect their outsider status: Rowley is "the Special Agent," Cooper is "the Night Detective," and Watkins is "the Party Crasher." For a follow-up on Watkins, see Deborah Solomon, "Life after Whistle-Blowing," *New York Times Magazine*, June 6, 2004, 25. For accounts of other recent women whistle-blowers, see Riva D. Atlas, "Fund Inquiry Informant Discloses Her Identity," *New York Times,* December 9, 2003, C1, 4; Joyce Purnick, "A Whistle Still Ringing in Wall St. Ears," *New York Times,* December 11, 2003, B1; and Eric Lichtblau, "Whistle-Blowing Said to Be Factor in F.B.I. Firing," *New York Times,* July 29, 2004, A1, 14.

29. Bielby and Bielby, "She Works Hard for the Money."

30. For U.S. data, see Linda J. Waite and Mark Nielsen, "The Rise of the Dual-Earner Family, 1963–1997," in *Working Families,* ed. Hertz and Marshall.

31. Janis E. Blair and Julia A. Files, "In Search of Balance: Medicine, Motherhood, and Madness," *Journal of the American Medical Women's Association* 58 (2003): 212–16. See also

Robert M. Orrange, Francille M. Firebaugh, and Ramona K. Z. Heck, "Managing House-holds," in *It's about Time,* ed. Moen.

32. Jacobs and Gerson, *The Time Divide,* 41–55, 221 n4.

33. Jacobs and Gerson, *The Time Divide,* 119–147, 216, table A7; Janet Gornick was an additional author on this chapter.

34. Jacobs and Gerson, *The Time Divide,* 59–79.

35. Jacobs and Gerson, *The Time Divide,* 80–98. Data are from 1997.

36. Jeremy Reynolds, "When Too Much Is Not Enough: Actual and Preferred Work Hours in the United States and Abroad," *Sociological Forum* 19 (2004): 89–120.

37. Jacobs and Gerson, *The Time Divide,* 55.

38. Cynthia Fuchs Epstein and Arne L. Kalleberg, "Time and the Sociology of Work," *Work & Occupations* 28 (2001): 5–16; Julia Kristeva, "Women's Time," trans. Alice Jardine and Harry Blake, *Signs* 7 (1981): 13–35; Tronto, "Time's Place"; Eviatar Zerubavel, *Hidden Rhythms: Schedules and Calendars in Social Life* (Chicago: University of Chicago Press, 1981).

39. A classic study is Maria Mies, *The Lace Makers of Narsapur: Indian Housewives Produce for the World Market* (London: Zed Books, 1982).

40. For the discriminatory aspects of these gendered rules in international corporations to-day, see Poster, "Dangerous Places and Nimble Fingers," and Winifred R. Poster, "Global-ization, Gender, and the Workplace: Women and Men in an American Multinational Corporation in India," *Journal of Developing Societies* 14 (1998): 40–65.

41. The technology includes laptops, cell phones and pagers, fax machines, e-mail, and data transport. See Noelle Chesley, Phyllis Moen, and Richard P. Shore, "The New Tech-nology Climate," in *It's about Time,* ed. Moen.

42. Jerry A. Jacobs, "The Faculty Time Divide," *Sociological Forum* 19 (2004): 3–27.

43. Oriel Sullivan, "Changing Gender Practices within the Household," *Gender & Society* 18 (2004): 215–16.

44. Karin Knorr Cetina and Urs Bruegger, "Global Microstructure: The Virtual Societies of Financial Markets," *American Journal of Sociology* 107 (2002): 905–50. See also Michele Gregory, "Women on the Line: A Qualitative Study of Gender and Sexuality in the Adver-tising and Computing Industries" (Ph.D. diss., University of London, Institute of Educa-tion, London, 2003).

45. Mary Blair-Loy and Jerry A. Jacobs, "Globalization, Work Hours, and the Care Deficit among Stockbrokers," *Gender & Society* 17 (2003): 230–49.

46. Jacobs and Gerson, *The Time Divide*, 177–78.

47. Appelbaum, Bailey, Berg, and Kalleberg, *Shared Work, Valued Care*.

48. Cynthia Fuchs Epstein, Carroll Seron, Bonnie Oglensky, and Robert Sauté, *The Part-Time Paradox: Time Norms, Professional Lives, Family, and Gender* (New York: Routledge, 1999).

49. Williams, *Unbending Gender*, 65.

50. Williams, *Unbending Gender*, 84–100. On new "language games," see also Nentwich, "Doing Difference and Equality in a Swiss Organization."

51. Cynthia Fuchs Epstein, "Border Crossings: The Constraints of Time Norms in Transgressions of Gender and Professional Roles," in *Fighting for Time: Shifting Boundaries of Work and Social Life*, ed. Cynthia Fuchs Epstein and Arne L. Kalleberg (New York: Russell Sage Foundation, 2004).

52. Patricia V. Roehling, Phyllis Moen, and Rosemary Batt, "Spillover," and Phyllis Moen, Ronit Waismel-Manor, and Stephen Sweet, "Success," both in *It's about Time*, ed. Moen, quote on p. 149.

53. Erving Goffman, *Frame Analysis: An Essay on the Organization of Experience* (New York: Harper Colophon, 1974), 22. See also William A. Gamson, *Talking Politics* (Cambridge: Cambridge University Press, 1992).

54. Appelbaum, Bailey, Berg, and Kalleberg, *Shared Work, Valued Care*, 6–7.

55. Nancy Folbre calls this view children as pets. *The Invisible Heart*, 109–35.

56. Rosalind C. Barnett, "A New Work-Life Model for the Twenty-First Century," in *The Evolving World of Work and Family*, ed. Pitt-Catsouphes and Googins.

57. Michal Frenkel, personal communication, March 2004. European countries are similar to Israel; the proportion of children aged three to five years old in full-time publicly financed child care ranges from 53 percent (Finland) to 99 percent (France). In the United States, 54 percent of children that age are in part-time day care (Jacobs and Gerson, *The Time Divide*, table 6.3, 144).

58. See Jacobs and Gerson, *The Time Divide*, 217 n3, which cites Anita Garey, *Weaving Work and Motherhood* (Philadelphia: Temple University Press, 1999).

Chapter 4   Heroes, Warriors and Burqas: Gender after September 11

1. Frank Rich, "How Kerry Became a Girlie-Man," *New York Times*, September 5, 2004, http://www.nytimes.com/2004/09/05/arts/05RICH.html. Many commentators on the 2004

Democratic and Republican national conventions noted the speakers' constant invocation of their candidate's masculinity and the opposing party's candidate's wimpiness.

2. For feminist perspectives on September 11, see Judith Butler, *Precarious Life: The Power of Mourning and Violence* (New York: Verso, 2004); Amy Caiazza, "Why Gender Matters in Understanding September 11: Women, Militarism, and Violence," Institute for Women's Policy Research, Publication 1908, November 2001, http://www.iwpr.org/pdf/terrorism.pdf; Susan Hawthorne and Bronwyn Winter, eds., *September 11, 2001: Feminist Perspectives* (North Melbourne, Australia: Spinifex, 2002); Michael S. Kimmel, "Globalization and Its Mal(e)contents: The Gendered Moral and Political Economy of Terrorism," *International Sociology* 18 (2003): 603–20; Iris Marion Young, "The Logic of Masculinist Protection: Reflections on the Current Security State," *Signs* 29 (2003): 1–25; "Roundtable: Gender and September 11," *Signs* 28 (2002): 432–79; "Roundtable: September 11 and Its Aftermath: Voices from Australia, Canada, and Africa," *Signs* 29 (2004): 575–617; and "Forum: The Events of 11 September 2001 and Beyond," *International Feminist Journal of Politics* 4 (2002): 95–113.

3. Most of the media examples that follow were taken from the *New York Times,* which covered the events of September 11 extensively, with a separate section, A Nation Challenged, that ran until December 31, 2001.

4. William Langewiesche, *American Ground: Unbuilding the World Trade Center* (New York: North Point Press, 2002), 7.

5. Langewiesche, *American Ground,* 10. For reports of women rescuers and ground zero personnel, see Maya Dollarhide, "Women at Ground Zero: Rescuers, Rebuilders," *Women's Enews*, October 14, 2001, http://www.womensenews.org/article.cfm/dyn/aid/685/context/archive; Peggy F. Drexler, "This Time, the Brother Is a Sister," *Women's Enews*, April 3, 2002, http://www.womensenews.org/article.cfm/dyn/aid/820/context/archive; and Susan Hagen and Mary Carouba, *Women at Ground Zero: Stories of Courage and Compassion* (Indianapolis: Alpha Books, 2002). According to Hagen and Carouba, in 2001, there were 25 women firefighters out of 11,500 in the New York Fire Department, more than 6,000 women police officers out of 38,000 in the New York Police Department, and 99 women Port Authority police officers out of 1,350. *Women at Ground Zero,* xi–xviii.

6. Maureen Dowd, "Hunks and Brutes," Op-Ed, *New York Times,* November 28, 2001, 25.

7. Leslie J. Calman, "The Heroic Women of Sept. 11," letter to the editor, *New York Times,* December 3, 2001, A18.

8. Richard Lezin Jones, "Day of Honor and of Pain for 40,000," *New York Times*, December 5, 2001, B8. Smith's identifiable remains were found in the spring: "Policewoman's Remains Found at Trade Center," *New York Times*, March 21, 2002, B4.

9. Drexler, "This Time, the Brother Is a Sister." In commenting on its choice of three women whistle-blowers for its 2002 Persons of the Year, *Time* said, "These women were for the 12 months just ending what New York City firefighters were in 2001: Heroes at the scene, anointed by circumstances." December 30, 2002/January 6, 2003, 32.

10. Hagen and Carouba, *Women at Ground Zero,* xii.

11. Dan Barry, "As Sept. 11 Widows Unite, Grief Finds Political Voice," *New York Times,* November 25, 2001, A1. The group's official name is the 9/11 Widows and Victims' Families Association. They are mostly firefighters' widows, but there are other widows' groups among the ten thousand to fifteen thousand family members of the victims of the World Trade Center terrorism. See Kirk Johnson, "In Bereavement, Pioneers on a Lonely Trail," *New York Times,* September 8, 2002, 1, 28, 29. The "widows" nomenclature invokes a powerful gendered imagery that enchances the legitimacy of the group and its actions, so it is not used accidentally. See Rachel L. Einwohner, Jocelyn A. Hollander, and Toska Olson, "Engendering Social Movements: Cultural Images and Movement Dynamics," *Gender & Society* 14 (2000): 679–99.

12. On the widows' political power, see Langewiesche, *American Ground,* 164–70. On their waning influence, see Edward Wyatt, "Victims' Families Sense Influence on Ground Zero Plans Is Waning," *New York Times,* November 16, 2002, A1, B2. On their influence with the 9/11 Commission, see Lydia Polgreen, "Families Savor Their Victory over Grief and a Reluctant Government," *New York Times,* July 23, 2004. *The 9/11 Commission Report: Final Report of the National Commission on Terrorist Attacks upon the United States* was published on July 22, 2004 (New York: W. W. Norton).

13. Jane Gross, "U.S. Fund for Tower Victims Will Aid Some Gay Partners," *New York Times,* May 30, 2002, A1. The ruling covered all domestic partners. Domestic partners were covered for compensation in New York State by Governor George Pataki's executive order, but they were not covered in Virginia. By the second anniversary, feminists had grouped together two of the neglected groups—women rescuers and gay victims. See Asjylyn Loder, "Female First Responders, Gays Push for 9-11 Equity," *Women's Enews,* September 11, 2003, http://www.womensenews.org/article.cfm?aid=1522. For an early comment on the neglect of gays and lesbians as victims of the World Trade Center and Pentagon attacks, see Judith Butler, "Violence, Mourning, Politics" (Tenth Annual David Kessler Lecture in Lesbian and Gay Studies, Graduate Center, City University of New York, December 7, 2001).

14. Elaine Enarson and Betty Hearn Morrow, "Why Gender? Why Women? An Introduction to Women and Disaster," in *The Gendered Terrain of Disaster: Through Women's Eyes,* ed. Elaine Enarson and Betty Hearn Morrow (Westport, Conn.: Praeger, 1998), 6.

15. See Maureen Fordham and Anne-Michelle Ketteridge, " 'Men Must Work and Women Must Weep': Examining Gender Stereotypes in Disasters," in *The Gendered Terrain of Disas-*

ter, ed. Enarson and Morrow, and Jane Gross, "Grandma Helps to Fill the Void Left by Sept. 11," *New York Times,* February 1, 2002, A1, B2.

16. Steve Fishman, "The Dead Wives' Club, or Char in Love," *New York,* May 31, 2004, 22. Fishman estimates that a fireman's widow would receive between two or three million dollars, much of it tax free, from the Victim Compensation Fund, charity donations earmarked for firefighters' families, and the continuation of their husbands' salaries, plus life insurance payments. "The Dead Wives' Club," 26. On the love affairs, see also Susan Dominus, "One Very Tangled Post-9/11 Affair," *New York Times Magazine,* May 23, 2004, 36–41.

17. For some of the reports on a series of suicide bombings in Israel by women in the spring of 2002, see James Bennet, "Arab Woman's Path to Unlikely 'Martyrdom,' " *New York Times,* January 31, 2002, A1, 10, and "Arab Press Glorifies Bomber as Heroine," *New York Times,* February 11, 2002, A8; and Joel Greenberg, "Portrait of an Angry Young Arab Woman," *New York Times,* March 1, 2002, A10, and "2 Girls, Divided by War, Joined in Carnage," *New York Times,* April 5, 2002, A1, 12. Suicide bombings by women continued throughout the world but were not major news until a mother of two young children killed herself and four Israeli security personnel at an important Gaza checkpoint. Greg Myre, "Gaza Mother, 22, Kills Four Israelis in Suicide Bombing," *New York Times,* January 15, 2004, A3. The topic was on the front pages again when Chechnyan women— "black widows"—were implicated in bombings and terrorist attacks in Russia. Steven Lee Myers, "From Dismal Chechnya, Women Turn to Bombs," *New York Times,* September 10, 2004, A1, A6.

18. It may have been the first time for women suicide bombers, but it was hardly the first time there were women terrorists in the Middle East, as well as in the Far East, Northern Ireland, Britain, and Germany. See Eileen MacDonald, *Shoot the Women First* (London: Arrow Books, 1991).

19. "Facing Combat," *New York Times,* March 21, 2003, B1. Despite the semblance of gender equality, the number of military women who had died by September 6, 2004, when the count of American deaths in Iraq reached one thousand, was twenty-four, less than 3 percent but more than in any other conflict since World War II. Monica Davey, "For 1,000 Troops, There Is No Going Home," *New York Times,* September 9, 2004, A1, A20–21.

20. Nicholas Kristof, "A Woman's Place," Op-Ed, *New York Times,* April 25, 2003, A31. On U.S. military women during the war, see Jodi Wilgoren, "A New War Brings New Role for Women," *New York Times,* March 28, 2003, B1, 11, and Shauna Curphey, "1 in 7 U.S. Military Personnel in Iraq Is Female," *Women's Enews,* March 22, 2003, http://www. womensenews.org/article.cfm?aid=1265.

21. See Rick Bragg, *I Am a Soldier, Too: The Jessica Lynch Story* (New York: Alfred A. Knopf, 2003); Alessandra Stanley, "In Hoopla over a P.O.W., a Mirror of U.S. Society," *New*

York Times, April 18, 2003, B9; Alan Feuer, "Rescued Soldier's Iraqi Doctors Doubled as Her Guardians," *New York Times*, April 21, 2003, A12; Mark Bowden, "Sometimes Heroism Is a Moving Target," *New York Times,* Week in Review, June 8, 2003, 1; Nicholas Kristof, "Saving Private Jessica," *New York Times,* Op-Ed, June 20, 2003, A23; David D. Kirkpatrick, "Jessica Lynch Criticizes U.S. Accounts of Her Ordeal," *New York Times*, November 7, 2003, A25; and Frank Rich, "Pfc. Jessica Lynch Isn't Rambo Anymore," *New York Times,* November 9, 2003, sec. 2, p. 1. On the narrative of rescuing women from savages, see Melani McAlister, "Saving Private Lynch," *New York Times*, Op-Ed, Week in Review, April 6, 2003, 13. And perhaps the final story was "Ex–P.O.W. Lynch to Marry," *New York Times*, November 3, 2003, A15.

22. Charles Krauthammer, "Abu Ghraib as Symbol," *Washington Post*, May 7, 2004, A33. See also James Dao, "From a Picture of Pride to a Symbol of Abuse in Iraq," *New York Times*, May 7, 2004, A1, 13; Barbara Ehrenreich, "Feminism's Assumptions Upended," *Los Angeles Times,* May 16, 2004; and Jodi Enda, "Female Face of Abuse Provokes Shock," *Women's Enews*, May 10, 2004, http://www.womensenews.org/article.cfm?aid=1828.

23. Frank Rich, "Saving Private England," *New York Times,* Arts & Leisure, May 16, 2004, 1, 8.

24. Kimmel, "Globalization and Its Mal(e)contents."

25. Michael S. Kimmel, "Declarations of War," *Chronicle of Higher Education*, October 26, 2001, B18.

26. "A Fire Captain's Eulogy," *New York Times,* Week in Review, December 23, 2001, 9.

27. See C. J. Chivers and David Rohde, "The Jihad Files: Life in bin Laden's Army," *New York Times,* March 17, 2002, sec. 1, pp. 1, 18–20, and "Training the Troops," March 18, 2002, Al, 14–15.

28. Niza Yanay, "Understanding Collective Hatred," *ASAP* (*Analyses of Social Issues and Public Policy*) 2, no. 1 (2002): 53–60, http://www.asap-spssi.org/pdf/asap024.pdf.

29. Evelyn Nieves, "Passenger on Jet: Gay Hero or Hero Who Was Gay?" *New York Times,* January 16, 2002, A12.

30. Jon Lee Anderson, "Letter from Afghanistan: After the Revolution," *New Yorker,* January 28, 2002, 65.

31. Shahin Gerami, personal communication, February 24, 2002.

32. David F. Greenberg, *The Construction of Homosexuality* (Chicago: University of Chicago Press, 1988), 25–40.

33. See Thomas Eriksen Hylland, "The Sexual Life of Nations: Notes on Gender and Nationhood," *Kvinder, køn, & forskning* 11, no. 2 (2002): 52–65.

34. Connell, *Masculinities,* 37.

35. Langewiesche, *American Ground,* 131.

36. Langewiesche, *American Ground,* 154–58.

37. Langewiesche, *American Ground,* 34. On the class origins of those who died at the World Trade Center, see Eric Lipton, "In Cold Numbers, a Census of the Sept. 11 Victims," *New York Times,* April 19, 2002, A14.

38. Langewiesche, *American Ground*, 9–11, 184–92.

39. I thank Dafna Izraeli for pointing out the instability of the firefighters' elevated position.

40. Shahin Gerami, "Mullahs, Martyrs, and *men:* Conceptualizing Masculinity in the Islamic Republic of Iran," *Men & Masculinities* 5 (2003): 257–74.

41. Thomas L. Friedman, "The 2 Domes of Belgium," Week in Review, *New York Times,* January 27, 2002, 13. See also Scott Atran, "Who Wants to Be a Martyr?" Op-Ed, *New York Times,* May 5, 2003, A23, and Tariq Modood, "Muslims and the Politics of Multiculturalism in Britain," in *Critical Views of September 11: Analyses from Around the World,* ed. Eric Hershberg and Kevin W. Moore (New York: New Press, 2002).

42. Lakshmi Bandlamudi, "Alienated Muslims and the West," letter to the editor, *New York Times,* January 29, 2002, A20.

43. Michael S. Kimmel, "Gender, Class, and Terrorism," *Chronicle of Higher Education*, February 8, 2002, B12.

44. Shahin Gerami and Melodye Lehnerer, "Women's Agency and Household Diplomacy: Negotiating Fundamentalism," *Gender & Society* 15 (2001): 556–73.

45. Mounira Maya Charrad, *States and Women's Rights: The Making of Postcolonial Tunisia, Algeria, and Morocco* (Berkeley: University of California Press, 2001).

46. Valentine M. Moghadam, "Revolution, Religion, and Gender Politics: Iran and Afghanistan Compared," *Journal of Women's History* 10 (1999): 172–95.

47. Elaine Sciolino, "A Prize, Laureate Says, 'Good for Democracy,' " *New York Times,* October 11, 2003, A6; Craig S. Smith, "In Speech, Nobel Winner Rebukes the U.S.," *New York Times,* December 11, 2003, A20.

48. On Afghanistan, see Sharon Groves, "Afghan Women Speak Out," *Feminist Studies* 27 (2001): 753–59; Sabul Gul Khattak, "Violence and Home: Afghan Women's Experience of Displacement," in *Understanding September 11,* ed. Craig Calhoon, Paul Price, and Ashley Timmer (New York: New Press, 2002); and Noeleen Heyzer, "Making a Nation More Equal," *New York Times,* December 3, 2003, A31. On Iran, see Elham Gheytanchi, "Civil

Society in Iran: Politics of Motherhood and the Public Sphere," *International Sociology* 16 (2001): 557–76. On the value of the participation of women in civil society and government in Iraq, see Nicholas Kristof, "Iraq's Little Secret," Op-Ed, *New York Times*, October 1, 2002, A31, and Raja Habib Khuzai and Songul Chapouk, "Iraq's Hidden Treasure," Op-Ed, *New York Times*, December 3, 2003, A31.

49. See Leila Ahmed, *Women and Gender in Islam* (New Haven, Conn.: Yale University Press, 1992); Amal Amireh, "Framing Nawal El Saadawi: Arab Feminism in a Transnational World," *Signs* 26 (2000): 215–49; Margot Badran, "Islamic Feminism: What's in a Name?" *Al-Ahram Weekly On-line*, no. 569, January 17–23, 2002, http://weekly.ahram. org.eg/2002/569/cu1.htm; Deniz Kandiyoti, ed., *Women, Islam, and the State* (Philadelphia: Temple University Press, 1991); Fatima Mernissi, *Beyond the Veil: Male-Female Dynamics in Modern Muslim Society* (Bloomington: Indiana University Press, 1987), and *The Veil and the Male Elite: A Feminist Interpretation of Women's Rights in Islam,* trans. Mary Jo Lakeland (Cambridge, Mass.: Perseus Books, 1991); Valentine M. Moghadam, "Islamic Feminism and Its Discontents: Towards a Resolution of the Debate," *Signs* 27 (2002): 1135–71; and Amina Wadud, *Qur'an and Woman: Rereading the Sacred Text from a Woman's Perspective* (New York: Oxford University Press, 1999).

50. Badran, "Islamic Feminism."

51. Farida Shaheed, "Controlled or Autonomous: Identity and the Experience of the Network, Women Living under Muslim Laws," *Signs* 19 (1994): 997–1019.

52. See Yesim Arat, "One Ban and Many Headscarves: Islamist Women and Democracy in Turkey," *Hagar: International Social Science Review* 2 (2001): 47–60; Caitlin Killian, "The Other Side of the Veil: North African Women in France Respond to the Headscarf Affair," *Gender & Society* 17 (2003): 567–90; Jen'nan Ghazal Read and John P. Bartkowski, "To Veil or Not to Veil? A Case Study of Identity Negotiation among Muslim Women in Austin, Texas," *Gender & Society* 14 (2000): 395–417.

53. Elizabeth Bumiller, "The Bawler in Chief: Real Men Can Cry," Week in Review, *New York Times*, November 30, 2003, 2.

54. Shirin Ebadi, Nobel Lecture by the Nobel Peace Prize Laureate, Oslo, December 10, 2003, http://www.nobel.se/peace/laureates/2003/ebadi-lecture- e.html.

55. Ebadi, Nobel Lecture.

CHAPTER 5 PARADOXES OF GENDER IDENTITY: STRATEGIES OF FEMINIST POLITICS

1. Chandra Talpade Mohanty, *Feminism without Borders: Decolonizing Theory, Practicing Solidarity* (Durham, N.C.: Duke University Press, 2003), 2.

2. Nira Yuval-Davis, "The 'Multi-Layered Citizen': Citizenship in the Age of 'Glocalization,' " *International Feminist Journal of Politics* 1 (1999): 119–36.

3. Barbara Katz Rothman, "Existential Orphanhood and Identity Politics: On Jews, Dwarfs, and Gays," in *Genetic Maps and Human Imaginations* (New York: W. W. Norton, 1998), 237.

4. Enrique Laraña, Hank Johnson, and Joseph R. Gusfield, *New Social Movements: From Ideology to Identity* (Philadelphia: Temple University Press, 1994); Alberto Melucci, *Nomads of the Present: Social Movements and Individual Needs in Contemporary Society* (Philadelphia: Temple University Press, 1989).

5. Rabab Abdulhadi, "The Palestinian Women's Autonomous Movement: Emergence, Dynamics, Challenges," *Gender & Society* 12 (1998): 649–73; Hanna Herzog, "A Space of Their Own: Social-Civil Discourses among Palestinian-Israeli Women in Peace Organizations," *Social Politics: International Studies of Gender, State, and Society* 6 (1999): 344–69; Simone Sharoni, "Gender in Conflict: The Palestinian-Israeli Conflict through Feminist Lenses," *Signs* 24 (1999): 487–99.

6. Iris Marion Young, "Gender as Seriality: Thinking about Women as a Social Collective," *Signs* 19 (1994): 713–38.

7. Carol Schachet, "Talking Politics with Barbara Smith." *RESIST Newsletter* 11, no. 5 (June 2002): 1.

8. Judith Squires, "Representing Groups, Deconstructing Identities," *Feminist Theory* 2 (2001): 7–27; Hill Collins, *Fighting Words,* 201–28.

9. Leila J. Rupp and Verta Taylor, "Forging Feminist Identity in an International Movement: A Collective Identity Approach to Twentieth-Century Feminism," *Signs* 24 (1999): 363–86.

10. Maxine Baca Zinn and Bonnie Thornton Dill, "Theorizing Difference from Multiracial Feminism," *Feminist Studies* 22 (1996): 321–31; King, "Multiple Jeopardy, Multiple Consciousness"; Alma M. Garcia, "The Development of Chicana Feminist Discourse, 1970–1980," *Gender & Society* 3 (1989): 217–38; Esther Ngan-Ling Chow, "The Development of Feminist Consciousness among Asian American Women," *Gender & Society* 1 (1987): 284–99.

11. Mary Field Belenky, Blythe McVicker Clinchy, Nancy Rule Goldberger, and Jill Mattuck Tarule, *Women's Ways of Knowing: The Development of Self, Voice, and Mind* (New York: Basic Books, 1986).

12. Donna Haraway, "Situated Knowledges: The Science Question in Feminism and the Privilege of Partial Perspective," *Feminist Studies* 14 (1988): 575–99; Sandra Harding, *The*

Science Question in Feminism (Ithaca, N.Y.: Cornell University Press, 1986), *Whose Science? Whose Knowledge? Thinking from Women's Lives* (Ithaca, N.Y.: Cornell University Press, 1991), and *Is Science Multicultural? Postcolonialisms, Feminisms, and Epistemologies* (Bloomington: Indiana University Press, 1998).

13. Bandana Purkayastha and Rosalie Torres Stone, "Ethnicity, Gender, Place, and Earnings: The Case of Asian Indian, Filipino, and White Women" (paper presented at the annual meeting of the Eastern Sociological Society, Boston, 1999).

14. Dafna Nundi Izraeli, "The Zionist Women's Movement in Palestine, 1911–1927: A Sociological Analysis," *Signs* 7 (1981): 97.

15. Bernice McNair Barnett, "Invisible Southern Black Women Leaders in the Civil Rights Movement: The Triple Constraints of Gender, Race, and Class," *Gender & Society* 7 (1993): 162–82; Doug McAdam, "Gender as a Mediator of the Activist Experience: The Case of Freedom Summer," *American Journal of Sociology* 97 (1992): 1211–49.

16. Lynn Chancer, "New Bedford, Massachusetts, March 6, 1983–March 22, 1984: The 'Before and After' of a Group Rape," *Gender & Society* 1 (1987): 239–60.

17. Drucilla Cornell, *At the Heart of Freedom: Feminism, Sex, and Equality* (Princeton, N.J.: Princeton University Press, 1998), 21–22; Sum, Fogg, Harrington, et al., *The Growing Gender Gaps in College Enrollment and Degree Attainment in the U.S.*

18. Sylvia Walby, "Beyond the Politics of Location: The Power of Argument in a Global Era," *Feminist Theory* 1 (2000): 195.

19. Butler, *Bodies That Matter*, 29.

20. Susan Hekman, "Beyond Identity: Feminism, Identity, and Identity Politics," *Feminist Theory* 1 (2000): 289–308.

21. Dale M. Bauer and Priscilla Wald, "Complaining, Conversing, Coalescing," *Signs* 25 (2000): 1300. For case histories of successful and unsuccessful coalitions and radical alliances that bring together "seemingly diverse persons and groups around shared ideological beliefs, values, and principles," see Jill M. Bystydzienski and Steven P. Schacht, eds., *Forging Radical Alliances across Difference: Coalition Politics for the New Millennium* (Lanham, Md.: Rowman & Littlefield, 2001), 7.

22. William E. Connelly, *Identity/Difference: Democratic Negotiations of Political Paradox* (New York: Cornell University Press, 1991), 64. For a similar critique of the repression of heterogeneity by "the logic of identity," see Iris Marion Young, *Justice and the Politics of Difference* (Princeton, N.J.: Princeton University Press, 1990), 96–121; in particular, see p. 99:

> The irony of the logic of identity is that by seeking to reduce the differently similar to the same, it turns the merely different into the absolutely other. It inevitably

generates dichotomy instead of unity, because the move to bring particulars under a universal category creates a distinction between inside and outside.

23. Joan Wallach Scott, *Only Paradoxes to Offer: French Feminists and the Rights of Man* (Cambridge, Mass.: Harvard University Press, 1996), 3–4.

24. Maxine Baca Zinn, "Family, Feminism, and Race in America," *Gender & Society* 4 (1990): 68–82.

25. Jan Wickman, *Transgender Politics: The Construction and Deconstruction of Binary Gender in the Finnish Transgender Community* (Åbo, Finland: Åbo Akademi University Press, 2001).

26. Henriette Dahan-Kalev, "The Oppression of Women by Other Women: Relations and Struggle between Mizrahi and Ashkenazi Women in Israel," *Israel Social Science Research* 12 (1997): 31–44, and "Tensions in Israeli Feminism: The Mizrahi-Ashkenazi Rift," *Women Studies International Forum* 24 (2001): 669–84.

27. A case in point is the issue of female genital cutting. See Carla Mahklouf Obermeyer, "Female Genital Surgeries: The Known, the Unknown, and the Unknowable," *Medical Anthropology Quarterly* 13 (1999): 79–106.

28. Ranjana Khanna, "Ethical Ambiguities and Specters of Colonialism," in *Feminist Consequences: Theory for a New Century,* ed. Elisabeth Bronfen and Misha Kavka (New York: Columbia University Press, 2001), 102.

29. Jane Mary Howard, *Inside Iran: Women's Lives* (Washington, D.C.: Mage, 2002), 84–85.

30. Urvashi Vaid, *Virtual Equality: The Mainstreaming of Gay and Lesbian Liberation* (New York: Anchor Press / Doubleday, 1995); Suzanna Danuta Walters, *All the Rage: The Story of Gay Visibility in America* (Chicago: University of Chicago Press, 2001), 19; Jane Ward, " 'Not All Differences Are Created Equal': Multiple Jeopardy in a Gendered Organization," *Gender & Society* 18 (2004): 82–102.

31. On the dual politics of redistribution and recognition, see Nancy Fraser, *Justice Interruptus: Critical Reflections on the "Postsocialist" Condition* (New York: Routledge, 1997), and Nancy Fraser and Axel Honneth, *Redistribution or Recognition? A Political-Philosophical Exchange,* trans. Joel Golb, James Ingram, and Christine Wilke (London: Verso, 2003).

32. Rina Amiri, "Muslim Women as Symbols—and Pawns," Op-Ed, *New York Times,* November 27, 2001.

33. Ayala Emmett, "Sex and Gender as Raw Political Material: Local Women Negotiate Globalization," *Sex Roles* 39 (1998): 503–13; Nancy A. Naples, *Grassroots Warriors: Activist Mothering, Community Work, and the War on Poverty* (New York: Routledge, 1998).

34. Christine E. Bose and Edna Acosta-Belén, "Colonialism, Structural Subordination, and Empowerment: Women in the Development Process in Latin America and the Caribbean," in *Women in the Latin American Development Process,* ed. Christine E. Bose and Edna Acosta-Belén (Philadelphia: Temple University Press, 1995), 28. See also Nancy A. Naples and Manisha Desai, eds., *Women's Activism and Globalization: Linking Local Struggles and Transnational Politics* (New York: Routledge, 2002).

35. Lisa Markowitz and Karen W. Tice, "Paradoxes of Professionalization: Parallel Dilemmas in Women's Organizations in the Americas," *Gender & Society* 16 (2002): 941–58.

36. Jackie Smith, "Bridging Global Divides? Strategic Framing and Solidarity in Transnational Social Movement Organizations," *International Sociology* 17 (2002): 509–28; Valerie Sperling, Myra Marx Ferree, and Barbara Risman, "Constructing Global Feminism: Transnational Advocacy Networks and Russian Women's Activism," *Signs* 26 (2001): 1155–86.

37. Nira Yuval-Davis, *Gender & Nation* (Thousand Oaks, Calif.: Sage, 1997), 116–33.

38. Hester Eisenstein, *Inside Agitators: Australian Femocrats and the State* (Philadelphia: Temple University Press, 1996); Gay W. Seidman, "Gendered Citizenship: South Africa's Democratic Transition and the Construction of a Gendered State," *Gender & Society* 13 (1999): 287–307.

39. Dafna Nundi Izraeli, "Gender Politics in Israel: The Case of Affirmative Action for Women Directors," *Women's Studies International Forum* 26 (2003): 109–28.

40. Valentine M. Moghadam, "Transnational Feminist Networks: Collective Action in an Era of Globalization," *International Sociology* 15 (2000): 58, 59.

41. Shaheed, "Controlled or Autonomous: Identity and the Experience of the Network, Women Living under Muslim Laws."

42. Manisha Desai, "Transnational Solidarity: Women's Agency, Structural Adjustment, and Globalization" in *Women's Activism and Globalization,* ed. Naples and Desai, 31.

43. Khanna, "Ethical Ambiguities and Specters of Colonialism," 121. Grewal and Kaplan use the term *scattered hegemonies* in their critique of global feminism. Inderpal Grewal and Caren Kaplan, *Scattered Hegemonies: Postmodernity and Transnational Feminist Practice* (Minneapolis: University of Minnesota Press, 1994).

44. Deborah Mindry, "Nongovernmental Organizations, 'Grassroots,' and the Politics of Virtue," *Signs* 26 (2001): 1187–1211.

45. Kathy Davis, "Feminist Body/Politics as World Traveler: Translating *Our Bodies, Ourselves,*" *European Journal of Women's Studies* 9 (2002): 233–47.

46. Mary Hawkesworth, "The Semiotics of Premature Burial: Feminism in a Postfeminist Age," *Signs* 29 (2004): 961–62.

Chapter 6 A World without Gender: Making the Revolution

1. Michel Foucault, *The Birth of the Clinic: An Archeology of Medical Perception* (London: Tavistock, 1973), xv.

2. That is why some societies and religions forbid wearing the clothes of the opposite gender and ensure that men's and women's clothing looks markedly and identifiably different. In the United States, women in pants don't get a second glance, but men in skirts are still sanctioned, as a reporter paid to spend a day in a skirt and a rebellious student found. See Michael Brick, "Guy in Skirt Seeks Sensitivity in Brooklyn," Sunday Styles, *New York Times*, November 2, 2003, 1, 11, and Alison Leigh Cowan, "So a Guy Walks into a School in a Skirt . . . ," *New York Times*, November 13, 2003, B5. However, evening skirts on fashionable men are not so new or outlandish, according to a report from the *New York Times* Styles section of February 19, 1985 ("About Town: Skirts for Men"). A museum exhibition, "Bravehearts: Men in Skirts," showed that modern men wear many forms of skirts besides kilts: dressing gowns, caftans, pareus, and long, swinging trench coats. See Herbert Muschamp, "In the Land of the Free, Who Wears the Skirts?" *New York Times*, November 7, 2003, E27, 35.

3. The idea of control by categorization is Michel Foucault's. His analyses of the processes and effects of categorization on how we think appear in *The Order of Things: An Archeology of the Human Sciences* (London: Tavistock, 1966) and *The Archeology of Knowledge and the Discourse on Language* (London: Tavistock, 1972). He applied these ideas to clinical medicine in *The Birth of the Clinic* and to sexuality in *The History of Sexuality*, vol. 1, *An Introduction* (New York: Pantheon, 1978), and *The History of Sexuality, vol. 2, The Use of Pleasure* (New York: Random House, 1985).

4. Joan Wallach Scott, "Deconstructing Equality-versus-Difference: Or, the Uses of Post-Structuralist Theory for Feminism," *Feminist Studies* 14 (1988): 37.

5. Jackson, *Destined for Equality*, 8.

6. Evelyn Nakano Glenn, "From Servitude to Service Work: Historical Continuities in the Racial Division of Paid Reproductive Labor," *Signs* 18 (1992): 1–43; Hochschild, *The Second Shift*.

7. Lipsitz Bem, *The Lenses of Gender;* Virginia Valian, *Why So Slow? The Advancement of Women* (Cambridge, Mass.: MIT Press, 1998).

8. On occupational gender segregation, see Jerry A. Jacobs, *Revolving Doors: Sex Segregation and Women's Careers* (Palo Alto, Calif.: Stanford University Press, 1989), and Barbara F. Reskin and Patricia A. Roos, *Job Queues, Gender Queues: Explaining Women's Inroads into Male Occupations* (Philadelphia: Temple University Press, 1990). On wage discrepancies, see Annette Bernhardt, Martina Morris, and Mark S. Handcock, "Women's Gains or Men's Losses? A Closer Look at the Shrinking Gender Gap in Earnings," *American Journal of Sociology* 101 (1995): 302–28, and U.S. Department of Labor, Report 972.

9. Benería, *Gender, Development, and Globalization;* Esther Ngan-Ling Chow, ed., *Transforming Gender and Development in East Asia* (New York: Routledge, 2001); Naila Kabeer and Ramya Subrahmanian, *Institutions, Relations, and Outcomes: A Framework and Case Studies for Gender-Aware Planning* (London: Zed Books, 2000); M. Bahati Kuumba, "A Cross-Cultural Race/Class/Gender Critique of Contemporary Population Policy: The Impact of Globalization," *Sociological Forum* 14 (1999): 447–63; Maria Mies, Veronika Bennholdt-Thomsen, and Claudia von Werlhof, *Women: The Last Colony* (London: Zed Books, 1988); Valentine M. Moghadam, ed., *Patriarchy and Development: Women's Positions at the End of the Twentieth Century* (Oxford: Clarendon Press, 1996); Pamela Sparr, ed., *Mortgaging Women's Lives: Feminist Critiques of Structural Adjustment* (London: Zed Books, 1994); World Health Organization, "Women's Health: Improve Our Health, Improve the World" (position paper, Fourth World Conference on Women, Beijing, 1995).

10. Christine Delphy, "Rethinking Sex and Gender," *Women's Studies International Forum* 16 (1993): 6.

11. Lipsitz Bem, *The Lenses of Gender,* 192.

12. Shulamith Firestone, *The Dialectic of Sex: The Case for Feminist Revolution* (New York: Bantam Books, 1971), 11; Lois Gould, "X: A Fabulous Child's Story," *Ms.*, December 1972, 74–76, 105–06; Monique Wittig, "The Straight Mind," *Feminist Issues* (Summer 1980): 103–11; Lorber, "Dismantling Noah's Ark"; Butler, *Gender Trouble* and *Undoing Gender.*

13. Cynthia Fuchs Epstein, *Deceptive Distinctions: Sex, Gender, and the Social Order* (New Haven, Conn.: Yale University Press, 1988).

14. Johanna Foster, "An Invitation to Dialogue: Clarifying the Position of Feminist Gender Theory in Relation to Sexual Difference Theory," *Gender & Society* 13 (1999): 431–56.

15. For gender theory feminism, see Lipsitz Bem, *The Lenses of Gender;* Connell, *Gender and Power;* and Lorber, *Paradoxes*. For difference feminism, see Catherine A. MacKinnon, *Toward a Feminist Theory of the State* (Cambridge, Mass.: Harvard University Press, 1989), and Deborah L. Rhode, ed., *Theoretical Perspectives on Sexual Difference* (New Haven, Conn.: Yale University Press, 1990). Difference feminism is sometimes called cultural feminism, for its focus on the qualities of women's worlds. See Jessie Bernard, *The Female World* (New York:

Free Press, 1981), and Verta Taylor and Leila Rupp, "Women's Culture and Lesbian Feminist Activism: A Reconsideration of Cultural Feminism," *Signs* 19 (1993): 150–61. On psychoanalytic feminism, see Nancy J. Chodorow, *The Reproduction of Mothering* and *Femininities, Masculinities, Sexualities: Freud and Beyond* (Lexington: University Press of Kentucky, 1994); Jane Gallop, *The Daughter's Seduction: Feminism and Psychoanalysis* (Ithaca, N.Y.: Cornell University Press, 1982); and Juliet Mitchell, *Psychoanalysis and Feminism* (New York: Vintage, 1975). French feminists were particularly influential in developing feminist psychoanalytic and linguistic theory. See Hélène Cixous and Catherine Clément, *The Newly Born Woman*, trans. Betsy Wing (Minneapolis: University of Minnesota Press, 1975, repr., 1986); and Luce Irigaray, *Speculum of the Other Woman*, trans. Gillian C. Gill (Ithaca, N.Y.: Cornell University Press, 1974, repr., 1985) and *This Sex Which Is Not One*.

16. See in particular, Nancy C. M. Hartsock, *Money, Sex, and Power: Toward a Feminist Historical Materialism* (New York: Longman, 1983), and *The Feminist Standpoint Revisited and Other Essays* (Boulder, Colo.: Westview Press, 1998).

17. On multicultural and postcolonial feminism, see Baca Zinn and Thornton Dill, "Theorizing Difference from Multiracial Feminism"; bell hooks, *Ain't I a Woman: Black Women and Feminism* (Boston: South End Press, 1981) and *Feminist Theory*; Gayatri Chakravorty Spivak, *In Other Worlds: Essays in Cultural Politics* (New York: Routledge, 1988); and T. Minh-ha Trinh, *Woman, Native, Other: Writing Postcoloniality and Feminism* (Bloomington: Indiana University Press, 1989). On men, see Connell, *Masculinities;* Michael S. Kimmel and Michael A. Messner, eds., *Men's Lives*, 6th ed. (Boston: Allyn & Bacon, 2004), and Richard Majors and Janet Mancini Billson, *Cool Pose: The Dilemmas of Black Manhood in America* (New York: Lexington Books, 1992). On feminist views of social class, see Joan Acker, "Rewriting Class, Race, and Gender: Problems in Feminist Rethinking," in *Revisioning Gender,* ed. Ferree, Lorber, and Hess; Johanna Brenner, *Women and the Politics of Class* (New York: Monthly Review Press, 2000); and McCall, *Complex Inequality*.

18. Rosi Braidotti, *Nomadic Subjects: Embodiment and Sexual Difference in Feminist Theory* (New York: Columbia University Press, 1994); Rita Felski, "The Doxa of Difference," *Signs* 23 (1997): 1–21; Marilyn Frye, "The Necessity of Differences: Constructing a Positive Category of Women," *Signs* 21 (1996): 991–1010; Haraway, "Situated Knowledges"; Wallach Scott, "Deconstructing Equality-versus-Difference," 48.

19. Armstrong, "Complex Equality"; Cornell, *At the Heart of Freedom;* Moller Okin, *Justice, Gender, and the Family;* Young, *Justice and the Politics of Difference;* McCall, *Complex Inequality*, 90.

20. See Francesca Cancian and Stacey Oliker, *Caring and Gender* (Thousand Oaks, Calif.: Pine Forge Press, 2000), 131–34, 149–59; Lenard W. Kaye and Jeffrey S. Applegate, *Men as Caregivers to the Elderly: Understanding and Aiding Unrecognized Family Support* (Lexington, Mass.: Lexington Books, 1990); and Heather A. Turner, Robert B. Hays, and Thomas J.

Coates, "Determinants of Social Support among Gay Men: The Context of AIDS," *Social Problems* 34 (1993): 37–53.

21. Hochschild, *The Time Bind*.

22. Carol Lee Bacchi, *Women, Policy, and Politics: The Construction of Policy Problems* (Thousand Oaks, Calif.: Sage, 1999), 205.

23. Young, *Justice and the Politics of Difference*, 191.

24. Jonathan Schell, "No More into the Breach," *Harper's*, March 2003, 33.

25. In Pierre Bourdieu's progression (doxa, orthodoxy, heterodoxy), this is thinking heterodoxically:

> Orthodoxy, straight, or rather *straightened*, opinion, which aims, without ever entirely succeeding, at restoring the primal state of innocence of doxa, exists only in the objective relationship which opposes it to heterodoxy, that is, by reference to the choice—*hairesis,* heresy—made possible by the existence of *competing possibilities* and to the explicit critique of the sum total of the alternatives not chosen that the established order implies.

Pierre Bourdieu, *Outline of a Theory of Practice,* trans. Richard Nice (Cambridge: Cambridge University Press, 1977), 169; the entire discussion appears on pp. 159–71.

26. Lorber, *Paradoxes,* 294–302.

27. Delphy, "Rethinking Sex and Gender," 8.

28. Oyěwùmí, commenting on the genderization of Yorùbá by English colonials, says, "Genderlessness in language is not necessarily a futuristic undertaking; sadly, it could well be passé." *The Invention of Women,* 175.

29. Norman Lamm, *The Religious Thought of Hasidism: Text and Commentary* (New York: Yeshiva University Press, 1999), 603. On unifications of male and female principles in kabbalah, see Raphael Patai, *The Hebrew Goddess*, 3rd ed. (Detroit: Wayne State University Press, 1990), 112–211.

EPILOGUE   WHAT DEGENDERING DOES TO THE COMPONENTS OF GENDER

1. Lorber, *Paradoxes,* 30–31.

INDEX

abortion, 36, 122, 153
  of female fetuses, xiii
Abbott, Andrew (*Methods of Discovery: Heuristics for the Social Sciences*), 178 (n6)
Abdulhadi, Rabab ("The Palestinian Woman's Autonomous Movement: Emergence, Dynamics, Challenges"), 204 (n5)
Abu Ghraib prison abuse, 111
Acker, Joan ("Hierarchies, Jobs, and Bodies: A Theory of Gendered Organizations"), 194 (n18); (Rewriting Class, Race, and Gender: Problems in Feminist Rethinking"), 210 (n17)
Acosta-Belén, Edna, 144
Adkins, Lisa ("Cultural Feminization: 'Money, Sex, and Power' for Women"), 194 (n18)
adoption, second-parent, 65
affirmative action, 11, 83
Afghanistan
  advocacy for women of, 143
  status of women in, 122, 123–24, 128
  Taliban, 115, 123, 143
  war in, 102, 108
African American men, shared parenting by, 61
African American women, 12, 44–45, 141
aggression, 34, 46, 47
Ahmed, Leila (*Women and Gender in Islam*), 203 (n49)
AIDS, 37, 143, 154–55
Albright, Madeline, 12

Allen, Mike, and Nancy Burrell ("Comparing the Impact of Homosexual and Heterosexual Parents on Children: Meta-Analysis of Existing Research"), 191 (n50)
Alvarez, Lizette ("Norway Leads Industrial Nations Back to Breast Feeding"), 188 (n21)
Amadiume, Ifi (*Male Daughters, Female Husbands: Gender and Sex in an African Society*), 180 (n20)
American Ground: Unbuilding the World Trade Center (Langewiesche), 104
American Psychiatric Association (*Diagnostic and Statistical Manual of Mental Disorders*, 4th ed., text rev.), 184 (n58)
Amireh, Amal ("Framing Nawal El Saadawi: Arab Feminism in a Transnational World"), 203 (n49)
Amiri, Rina, xii, 143; ("Muslim Women as Symbols—and Pawns"), 206 (n31)
Anderson, Bonnie S., and Judith P. Zinsser (*A History of Their Own: Women in Europe from Prehistory to the Present*), 180 (n21, n22)
Anderson, Jon Lee, 115 ("Letter from Afghanistan: After the Revolution"), 201 (n30)
Anzaldúa, Gloria E. (*Borderlands/La Frontera: The New Mestiza*), 178 (n10)
Applebaum, Eileen, Thomas Bailey, Peter Berg, and Arne L. Kalleberg (*Shared Work, Valued Care: New Norms for Organizing Market Work and Unpaid*

Applebaum, Eileen (*cont.*)
  Care Work), 193 (n7), 197 (n47, n54)
Arat, Yesim ("One Ban and Many Head-
  scarves: Islamist Women and Democ-
  racy in Turkey"), 203 (n52)
Armstrong, Chris ("Complex Equality:
  Beyond Equality and Difference"),
  179 (n9), 210 (n19)
Atlas, Riva D. ("Fund Inquiry Informant
  Discloses Her Identity"), 195 (n28)
Atran, Scott ("Who Wants to Be a Mar-
  tyr?"), 202 (n41)
Atta, Mohammed, 120
Australia, passport to X, 29

Bacchi, Carol Lee, 163; (*Women, Policy, and
  Politics: The Construction of Policy
  Problems*), 211 (n22)
Badran, Margot, 125–26; ("Islamic Femi-
  nism: What's in a Name?"), 203
  (n49, n50)
Bandlamudi, Lakshmi, 119–20; ("Alien-
  ated Muslims and the West"), 202
  (n42)
Banerjee, Neela ("Some 'Bullies' Seek
  Ways to Soften Up: Toughness Has
  Risks for Women Executives"), 195
  (n23)
Barnett, Bernice McNair ("Invisible
  Southern Black Women Leaders in
  the Civil Rights Movement: The
  Triple Constraints of Gender, Race,
  and Class"), 205 (n15)
Barnett, Rosalind C. ("A New Work-Life
  Model for the Twenty-First Cen-
  tury"), 197 (n56)
Barry, Dan ("As Sept. 11 Widows Unite,
  Grief Finds Political Voice"), 199
  (n11)
bathrooms, 28, 35–36
Bauer, Dale M., 138
Bauer, Dale M., and Priscilla Wald, 138
  ("Complaining, Conversing, Coalesc-
  ing"), 205 (n21)
Beijing UN Conference on Women, 146
Belenky, Mary Field, Blythe McVicker

Clinchy, Nancy Rule Goldberger,
  and Jill Mattuck (*Women's Ways of
  Knowing: The Development of Self, Voice,
  and Mind*), 204 (n11)
Belgium, dual-career couples in, 87
Belkin, Lisa, 70 ("When Caring for the
  Family Becomes the Job"), 192 (n3)
Bellafante, Ginia ("Two Fathers, with One
  Happy to Stay at Home"), 190 (n42)
Bem, Sandra Lipsitz, 156; (*The Lenses of
  Gender: Transforming the Debate on Sex-
  ual Inequality*), 180 (n18), 192 (n58),
  208 (n7), 209 (n11), 209 (n15); (*An
  Unconventional Family*), 190 (n38),
  192 (n58)
Benería, Lourdes (*Gender, Development, and
  Globalization: Economics As If All
  People Mattered*), 192 (n4); 209
  (n9)
Benner, James ("Arab Woman's Path to
  Unlikely 'Martyrdom' "), 200 (n17);
  ("Arab Press Glorifies Bomber as
  Heroine"), 200 (n17)
Bergman, Helena, and Barbara Hobson
  ("Compulsory Fatherhood: The Cod-
  ing of Fatherhood in the Swedish
  Welfare State"), 189 (n36)
Bernard, Jessie (*The Female World*), 210
  (n15)
Bernhardt, Annette, Martina Morris, and
  Mark S. Handcock ("Women's Gains
  or Men's Losses? A Closer Look at
  the Shrinking Gender Gap in Earn-
  ings"), 209 (n8)
Bernstein, Fred A. ("On Campus, Re-
  thinking Biology 101"), 183 (n53)
Biblarz, Timothy, 63
Bielby, Denise, and William T. Bielby
  ("She Works Hard for the Money:
  Household Responsibilities and the
  Allocation of Work Effort"), 181
  (n27), 195 (n29)
binary system, gender as, 7, 15, 17, 151,
  155–57, 165
  ubiquity of, 151
Bingham, Mark, 114–15

biological sex differences
  belief in binary nature of, 22–24, 153
  gendered division of labor and, 45
  hurdles to degendered parenting, 45–48
Bird, Sharon R. ("Welcome to the Men's Club: Homosociality and the Maintenance of Hegemonic Masculinity"), 195 (n25)
bisexuals, 25
  gender freedom and, 12
Blair, Janis E., and Julia A. Files ("In Search of Balance: Medicine, Motherhood, and Madness"), 195 (n31)
Blair-Loy, Mary, 73; (Competing Devotions: Career and Family among Women Executives), 186 (n2), 193 (n8, n12)
Blair-Loy, Mary, and Jerry A. Jacobs ("Globalization, Work Hours, and the Care Deficit among Stockbrokers"), 196 (n45)
Blum, Linda M. ("Mothers, Babies, and Breastfeeding in Late Capitalist America: The Shifting Contexts of Feminist Theory"), 188 (n20)
body characteristics, 6, 22–24
Borstein, Kate (Gender Outlaw: On Men, Women, and the Rest of Us), 179 (n14)
Bose, Christine E., 144
Bose, Christine E., and Edna Acosta-Belén ("Colonialism, Structural Subordination, and Empowerment: Women in the Development Process in Latin America and the Caribbean"), 207 (n34)
Boston Women's Health Book Collective, 148
Bourdieu, Pierre (Outline of a Theory of Practice), 211 (n25)
Bowden, Mark ("Sometimes Heroism Is a Moving Target"), 201 (n21)
Boylan, Jennifer Finney ("She's Not There": A Life in Two Genders), 183 (n50)
Bragg, Rick (I Am a Soldier, Too: The Jessica Lynch Story), 201 (n21)
Braidotti, Rosi (Nomadic Subjects: Embodi-

ment and Sexual Difference in Feminist Theory), 210 (n18)
brain research, gender differences and, 46
Brandth, Berit, and Elin Kvande (" 'Home Alone' Fathers"), 190 (n37)
breaking the bowls, 5, 169
breast-feeding and shared parenting, 48–50
breast pumps, 49
Brenner, Johanna (Women and the Politics of Class), 210 (n17)
Brick, Michael ("Guy in Skirt Seeks Sensitivity in Brooklyn"), 208 (n2)
Britton, Dana M. ("The Epistemology of the Gendered Organization"), 194 (n18)
Brown, Wendy ("Gender in Counterpoint"), 177 (n7)
Bruegger, Urs, 91
Brush, Lisa D. (Gender and Governance), 181 (n26)
Budig, Michelle J., 42 ("Male Advantage and the Gender Composition of Jobs: Who Rides the Glass Elevator?"), 195 (n26)
Budig, Michelle J., and Paula England ("The Wage Penalty for Motherhood"), 181 (n28), 186 (n6)
Bumiller, Elizabeth ("The Bawler in Chief: Real Men Can Cry"), 203 (n53)
burnout, 73
Bush, George W., 127–28
Butler, Judith, 26–29, 37–38, 137–38, 156; (Bodies That Matter: On the Discursive Limits of "Sex"), 182 (n36), 205 (n19); (Gender Trouble: Feminism and the Subversion of Identity), 180 (n18), 182 (n46), 186 (n74), 209 (n12); (Precarious Life: The Power of Mourning and Violence), 198 (n2); (Undoing Gender), 180 (n19), 209 (n12); ("Violence, Mourning, Politics"), 199 (n13); ("X Marks the Spot for Intersex Alex"), 184 (n57)
Bystydzienski, Jill M., and Steven P. Schacht (Forging Radical Alliances

Bystydzienski, Jill M. (*cont.*)
  across Difference: Coalition Politics for the New Millennium), 205 (n21)

Caiazza, Amy ("Why Gender Matters in Understanding September 11: Women, Militarism, and Violence"), 198 (n2)
Calman, Leslie J., 105; ("The Heroic Women of Sept. 11"), 198 (n7)
Canada, dual-earner couples in, 87
Cancian, Francesca, and Stacey Oliker (*Caring and Gender*), 210 (n20)
Cantor Fitzgerald, widows of, 106–7
Carrington, Christopher (*No Place Like Home: Relationships and Family Life among Lesbians and Gay Men*), 190 (n41)
Carter, Raphael ("Congenital Agenesis of Gender Ideation, by K. N. Sirsi and Sandra Botkin"), 181 (n33)
Catherine the Great, 18
Cetina, Karin Knorr, 91
Cetina, Karin Knorr, and Urs Bruegger ("Global Microstructure: The Virtual Societies of Financial Markets"), 196 (n44)
Chambers, David L. (" 'What If?' The Legal Consequences of Marriage and the Legal Needs of Lesbian and Gay Male Couples"), 192 (n54)
Chambers, David L., and Suzanna Danuta Walters ("Take My Domestic Partner, Please: Gays and Marriage in the Era of the Visible"), 192 (n54)
Chancer, Lynn, 135 ("New Bedford, Massachusetts, March 6, 1983–March 22, 1984: The 'Before and After' of a Group Rape"), 205 (n16)
Charrad, Mounira Maya, 122; (*States and Women's Rights: The Making of Postcolonial Tunisia, Algeria, and Morocco*), 202 (n45)
Chase, Cheryl ("Hermaphrodites with Attitude: Mapping the Emergence of Intersex Political Activism"), 184 (n56)

Chesley, Noelle, Phyllis Moen, and Richard P. Shore ("The New Technology Climate"), 196 (n41)
childbirth, 23
  prenatal care and, 36
child care
  day care, 42, 72, 99, 100
  government subsidized, 42, 74, 75
  parenting, *see* parenting, degendering as women's unpaid work, 6–7, 19, 71
child-labor laws, 90
Chivers, C. J., and David Rohde ("The Jihad Files: Life in bin Laden's Army"), 201 (n27); ("Training the Troops"), 201 (n27)
Chodorow, Nancy J. (*The Reproduction of Mothering: Psychoanalysis and the Sociology of Gender*), 188 (n25), 210 (n15); (*Femininities, Masculinities, Sexualities: Freud and Beyond*), 210 (n15)
Chow, Esther Ngan-Ling ("The Development of Feminist Consciousness among Asian American Women"), 204 (n10)
Citadel, 35
civil rights movement, U.S., 135
civil unions, 65, 66
Cixous, Hélène, and Catherine Clément (*The Newly Born Woman*), 210 (n15)
Clinton, Hillary Rodham, 146
Cockburn, Cynthia (*In the Way of Women: Men's Resistance to Sex Equality in Organizations*), 195 (n25)
Cohen, Stuart ("Towards a New Portrait of the (New) Israeli Soldier"), 179 (n7)
Collins, Patricia Hill (*Black Feminist Thought*), 187 (n11); (*Fighting Words: Black Women and the Search for Justice*), 177 (n4); ("Black Feminist Thought: Knowledge, Consciousness, and the Politics of Empowerment"), 177 (n6), 179 (n13)
Collinson, David L., David Knights, and Margaret Collinson (*Managing to Discriminate*), 194 (n21)

Coltrane, Scott, 54, 55; (*Family Man: Fatherhood, Housework, and Gender Equity*), 189 (n31), 190 (n38); (*Gender and Families*), 189 (n29); ("Household Labor and the Routine Production to Gender"), 189 (n33)
complex inequality, matrix of, xii, 159
comradeship, 113–14
Connell, R. W., 116, 118; (*Gender and Power*), 180 (n18), 209 (n15); (*Masculinities*), 177 (n5), 202 (n34), 210 (n17)
Connelly, William E., 139; (*Identity/Difference: Democratic Negotiations of Political Paradox*), 205 (n22)
Cooper, Cynthia, 84–85
Cornell, Drucilla, 136; (*At the Heart of Freedom: Feminism, Sex, and Equality*), 205 (n17), 210 (n19)
Cornell Couples and Career Study, 96
coronary heart disease, gendered eating patterns and, 23
"cottage industries," 90
Council of the American Sociological Association ("Statement of the American Sociological Association on the Importance of Collecting Data and Doing Scientific Research on Race"), 184 (n59)
Cowan, Alison Leigh ("So a Guy Walks into a School in a Skirt . . . ,"), 208 (n2)
crèches, 49
Crittenden, Ann, 42; ("The Price of Motherhood: Why the Most Important Job in the World Is Still the Least Valued"), 181 (n28), 194 (n17)
cross-dressing, 26–27
cultural imperialism, 148
Curphey, Shauna ("1 in 7 U.S. Military Personnel in Iraq Is Female"), 200 (n20)
custody conflicts, 53

Dahan-Kalev, Henriette, 141; ("The Oppression of Women by Other Women: Relations and Struggle between Mizrahi and Ashkenazi Women in Israel"), 206 (n26); ("Tensions in Israeli Feminism: The Mizrahi-Ashkenazi Rift"), 206 (n26)
Dalton, Susan E. ("Protecting Our Parent-Child Relationships: Understanding the Strengths and Weaknesses of Second-Parent Adoption"), 192 (n54)
Dalton, Susan E., and Denise D. Bielby (" 'That's Our Kind of Constellation': Lesbian Mothers Negotiate Institutionalized Understandings of Gender within the Family"), 190 (n39)
Dao, James ("From a Picture of Pride to a Symbol of Abuse in Iraq"), 201 (n21)
Davey, Monica ("For 1,000 Troops, There Is No Going Home"), 200 (n19)
Davis, Kathy ("Feminist Body/Politics as World Traveler: Translating *Our Bodies, Ourselves*"), 208 (n45)
day care, 72, 99, 100
government subsidized, 42
"Declaration of War," 113
degendering
components of gender, effects on, 171–76
envisioning a totally nongendered social order, 165–69
explanation of concept of, xiii–xiv
feminist politics, strategies of, *see* feminist politics, strategies of
feminist theories and, 160–65
gender-equal societies, 164
gender theory and, *see* gender theory and degendering
goals of, 38
making the revolution, 151–69
of parenting, *see* parenting, degendering
practicing, 33–38
workplace, *see* work, workplace
de Lauretis, Teresa (*Alice Doesn't Feminism, Semiotics, Cinema*), 178 (n9); (*Technologies of Gender*), 178 (n9)
Delphy, Christine, 156, 166; ("Rethinking Sex and Gender), 209 (n10), 211 (n27)

Desai, Manisha, 147; ("Transnational Solidarity: Women's Agency, Structural Adjustment, and Globalization"), 207 (n42)

Deutsch, Francine, 59–60, 62, 64; (*Halving It All: How Equally Shared Parenting Works*), 190 (n38), 191 (n52)

developing countries, feminists in, 134–35, 141

de Waal, Frans B. M. ("Peace Lessons from an Unlikely Source"), 187 (n14)

Dienhart, Anna, 60–61; (*Reshaping Fatherhood: The Social Construction of Shared Parenting*), 190 (n38), 191 (n45)

difference feminists, 158, 160–61

Disheh, Darin Abu, 108–9

"Dismantling Noah's Ark," 5, 156

division of labor
  biological differences and, 45
  effects of degendering on, 171–72
  between gay and lesbian parents, 45, 58–59
  in the global economy, 154–55
  parenting and assumptions about gender, 39–40, 43, 71, 77, 98
  in the workplace, 20, 71, 74, 78, 153, 154–55, 171–72

doing gender, 16–20, 175

Dollarhide, Maya ("Women at Ground Zero: Rescuers, Rebuilders"), 198 (n5)

dominance, 34, 153, 166
  matrices of, xii, 143

Domínguez, Silvia, and Celeste Watkins ("Creating Networks for Survival and Mobility: Social Capital among African-American and Latin-American Low-Income Mothers"), 187 (n11)

Dominus, Susan ("One Very Tangled Post-9/11 Affair"), 200 (n16)

Dowd, Maureen, 104, 105; ("Hunks and Brutes"), 198 (n6)

drag, 26–29

Dreger, Alcie Domurat (*Hermaphrodites and the Medical Invention of Sex*), 183 (n54)

Drexler, Peggy F., 105; ("This Time, the Brother Is a Sister"), 198 (n5), 199 (n9)

Duggan, Lisa ("Holy Matrimony!"), 192 (n56)

Dunne, Gillian A. ("Opting into Motherhood: Lesbians Blurring the Boundaries and Transforming the Meaning of Parenthood and Kinship"), 190 (n39)

eating patterns, gendered, 23

Ebadi, Shirin, 123; (Nobel Lecture by the Nobel Peace Prize Laureate, Oslo, December 10, 2003), 203 (n54, n55)

Economic Policy Institute, 93

Ehrenberg, Margaret (*Women in Prehistory*), 187 (n16)

Ehrensaft, Diane, 54; ("Feminism's Assumptions Upended"), 201 (n21); ("The Kinderdult: The New Child Born to Conflict between Work and Family"), 191 (n52); (*Parenting Together: Men and Women Sharing the Care of Their Children*), 189 (n32)

Einwohner, Rachel L., Jocelyn A. Hollander, and Toska Olson ("Engendering Social Movements: Cultural Images and Movement Dynamics"), 199 (n11)

Eisenstein, Hester (*Inside Agitators: Australian Femocrats and the State*), 207 (n38)

Ekins, Richard, 31; ("On Male Femaling: A Grounded Theory Approach to Cross-Dressing and Sex-Changing"), 184 (n62)

elderly, care of the, 98, 99, 100, 161

Eleanor of Aquitane, 18

Elizabeth I, Queen of England, 18

Emmet, Ayala ("Sex and Gender as Raw Political Material: Local Women Negotiate Globalization"), 207 (n33)

"Empire Strikes Back, The," 27

Enarson, Elaine, 107

Enarson, Elaine, and Betty Hearn Morrow ("Why Gender? Why Women? An Introduction to Women and Disaster"), 199 (14)

Enda, Jodi ("Female Face of Abuse Provokes Shock"), 201 (n21)

England, Pfc. Lynndie R., 111, 112

England, Paula, 42

England, Paula, Michele Budig, and Nancy Folbre ("Wages of Virtue: The Relative Pay of Care Work"), 186 (n6)

Enron, 84–85

Epstein, Cynthia Fuchs, 96, 157; ("Border Crossings: The Constraints of Time Norms in Transgressions of Gender and Professional Roles"), 197 (n51); (Deceptive Distinctions: Sex, Gender, and the Social Order), 209 (n13)

Epstein, Cynthia Fuchs, and Arne L. Kalleberg ("Time and the Sociology of Work"), 196 (n38)

Epstein, Cynthia Fuchs, Carroll Seron, Bonnie Oglensky, and Robert Sauté (The Part-Time Paradox: Time Norms, Professional Lives, Family, and Gender), 197 (n48)

Espiritu, Yen (Asian American Panethnicity: Bridging Institutions and Identities), 178 (n10)

estrogen, 22

evolutionary theorists, 47

extended families, 48, 64–65

family, see parenting, degendering

Family and Medical Leave Act of 1993, 76

Farida, Shaheed ("Controlled or Autonomous: Identity and the Experience of the Network, Women Living under Muslim Laws"), 207 (n41)

Fatherhood Project, Families and Work Institute, 40

Faulkner, Shannon, 35

Fausto-Sterling, Anne (Sexing the Body: Gender Politics and the Construction of Sexuality), 181 (n32), 187 (n13)

Federal Bureau of Investigation (FBI), 84

Feinberg, Leslie (Transgender Warriors: Making History from Joan of Arc to Dennis Rodman), 179 (n15)

Felski, Rita ("The Doxa of Difference"), 210 (n18)

female genitalia
  ritual genital cutting, 126
  surgical transformation of, 23, 26, 28

feminist politics, strategies of, 130–50
  dismantling gender divisions, 155–57
  doing multidimensional feminist politics, 148–50
  identity politics, 136–38
  multiple identities, 131–33, 138
  multiple systems of domination and, 133–34
  paradoxes of gender identity, 139–43
  standpoint feminism, 134–36, 158–59
  structural levels of feminist politics, 144–48

Ferguson, Kathy E. (The Feminist Case against Bureaucracy), 194 (n18)

Ferree Myra Marx ("Patriarchies and Feminisms: The Two Women's Movements of Unified Germany"), 187 (n10)

Feuer, Alan ("Rescued Soldier's Iraqi Doctors Doubled as Her Guardians"), 201 (n21)

fight-or-flight response, 47

Fineman, Martha Albertson, 65–66; (The Neutered Mother, the Sexual Family, and Other Twentieth Century Tragedies), 192 (n55)

Finland
  dual-career couples in, 87
  factions within transgender community in, 140
  women in politics in, 19

firefighters after September 11, 113, 119
  bonding of, 116–17
  as heroes, 104–106, 127

Firestone, Shulamith, 156; (The Dialectic of Sex: The Case for Feminist Revolution), 209 (n12)

Fishman, Steve ("The Dead Wives' Club, or Char in Love"), 200 (n16)

Flax, Jane ("Postmodernism and Gender Relations in Feminist Theory"), 177 (n4)

flextime, 45, 75, 92, 93–96, 99, 100

Folbre, Nancy (*The Invisible Heart: Economics and Family Values*), 192 (n4), 197 (n55); (*Who Pays for the Kids? Gender and the Structures of Constraint*), 186 (n7)

Fordham, Maureen, and Anne-Michellè Ketteridge (" 'Men Must Work and Women Must Weep': Examining Gender Stereotypes in Disasters"), 199 (n15)

Foster, Johanna ("An Invitation to Dialogue: Clarifying the Position of Feminist Gender Theory in Relation to Sexual Difference Theory"), 290 (n14)

Foucault, Michel, 151; (*The Archeology of the Knowledge and the Discourse on Language*), 208 (n3); (*The Birth of the Clinic: An Archeology of Medical Perception*), 208 (n1, n3); (*The History of Sexuality*, vol. 1, *An Introduction*), 208 (n3); (*The History of Sexuality*, vol. 2, *The Use of Pleasure*), 208 (n3); (*The Order of Things: An Archeology of the Human Sciences*), 208 (n3)

Frame Analysis (Goffman), 97

France, dual-earner couples in, 87

Fraser, Nancy (*Justice Interruptus: Critical Reflections on the "Postsocialist" Condition*), 206 (n32)

Fraser, Nancy, and Axel Honneth (*Redistribution or Recognition? A Political-Philosophical Exchange*), 206 (n32)

Freedman, Lynn P. ("Shifting Visions: 'Delegation' Policies and the Building of a 'Rights-Based' Approach to Maternal Mortality"), 186 (n72)

Frenkel, Michal ("Woman in Hi-Tech: Has the 'Motherhood Wall' Collapsed?"), 194 (n14)

Friedman, Thomas L., 119; ("The 2 Domes of Belgium"), 202 (n41)

Frye, Marilyn ("The Necessity of Differences: Constructing a Positive Category of Women"), 210 (n18)

Fuchs, Marek ("Women's Colleges Learning How to Get a Man"), 179 (n11)

Gagné, Patricia, and Richard Tewksbury ("Conformity Pressures and Gender Resistance among Transgendered Individuals"), 183 (n48)

Gagné, Patricia, Richard Tewksbury, and Deanna McGaughey ("Coming Out and Crossing Over: Identity Formation and Proclamation in a Transgender Society"), 183 (n48)

Gallop, Jane (*The Daughter's Seduction: Feminism and Psychoanalysis*), 210 (n15)

Gamson, Joshua ("Sexualities, Queer Theory, and Qualitative Research"), 185 (n65)

Gamson, William A. (*Talking Politics*), 197 (n53)

Garber, Marjorie (*Vested Interests: Cross-Dressing and Cultural Anxiety*), 183 (n49); (*Vice Versa: Bisexuality and the Eroticism of Everyday Life*), 182 (n42)

Garcia, Alma M. ("The Development of Chicana Feminist Discourse, 1970–1980"), 204 (n10)

garnishment of wages of fathers, 56

gay marriage, xiii

gay men, September 11 and, 107, 114–15

gay parents, 58
   division of labor between, 45, 58–59
   studies of children of, 63

Gelman, Susan A., Pamela Collman, and Eleanor E. Macoby ("Inferring Properties from Categories versus Inferring Categories from Properties: The Case of Gender"), 184 (n60)

gender balance, 11–12, 157

gender beliefs, 175

gender complexity, recognizing, 7–8

gender differences, studies of inborn, 21
gender display, 175–76
gender diversity, 12, 132
Gendered Terrain of Disaster, The (Enarson and Morrow), 107
gender equality
  parenting to achieve, 41–45
  path to degendering, 165–66
gender feminists, 157–58
gender freedom, 12–13
gender identity, paradoxes of, 139–43
gender identity disorder, 29
gender inequality, acceptance of, 7
gender neutrality, degendering distinguished from, xiv
gender parity, 9–10, 166
gender processes, effect of degendering on, 175
gender statuses, effect of degendering on, 171
gender theory and degendering, 3–38
  abolition of gender boundaries and categories, 4–5
  binary system, gender as, 7, 15, 17, 151, 155–57, 165
  deliberate degendering, 6
  doing gender and creating structure, 16–20
  gender balance, 11–12, 157
  gender complexity, recognizing, 7–8
  gender diversity, 12
  gender freedom, 12–13
  gender visibility, 10–11
  multidimensional research, 30–33
  practicing degendering, 33–38
  social institution, gender as, *see* social institution, gender as
  social statuses intersecting gender categories, 7–8, 12
  transgendering, 26–29
  undoing gender, attempts at, xiii, 8–10
  undoing the gender structure, 20–22
Gender Trouble (Butler), 37–38, 156
gender visibility, 10–11, 132
genitalia, 6
  of intersexuals, 23, 28–29

ritual female genital cutting, 126
surgical transformation of, 23, 26, 28
in a world without gender, 167, 174
Gerami, Shahin, 119; ("Mullahs, Martyrs, and *men*: Conceptualizing Masculinity in the Islamic Republic of Iran"), 202 (n40)
Gerami, Shahin, and Melodye Lehnerer ("Women's Agency and Household Diplomacy: Negotiating Fundamentalism"), 202 (n44)
Germany
  dual-earner couples in, 87
  family and work policies in, 88–89
Gerson, Kathleen, 63–64, 87, 89, 92–93; ("Moral Dilemmas, Moral Strategies, and the Transformation of Gender: Lessons from Two Generations of Work and Family Change"), 191 (n51); (*No Man's Land: Man's Changing Commitments to Family and Work*), 187 (n11)
Gherardi, Silvia (*Gender, Symbolism, and Organizational Cultures*), 194 (n18, n20)
Gheytanchi, Elham ("Civil Society in Iran: Politics of Motherhood and the Public Sphere"), 203 (n48)
glass ceiling, 154
Glenn, Evelyn Nakano ("From Servitude to Service Work: Historical Continuities in the Racial Division of Paid Reproductive Labor"), 208 (n6)
global economy, gendered divisions of work in, 154–55
global time, 92
goals of degendering, 38
Goffman, Erving, 97 (*Fame Analysis: An Essay on the Organization of Experience*), 197 (n53)
Golombok, Susan, and Fiona Tasker ("Do Parents Influence the Sexual Orientation of Their Children? Findings from a Longitudinal Study of Lesbian Families"), 191 (n50)
Gormley, Capt. James, 113, 117

Gould Lois, 156 ("X: A Fabulous Child's Story"), 209 (n12)
government policy
cash-versus-care dimensions of fatherhood and, 56
for families, 42, 74–75, 100
night work for women, 90
recognizing family caretaking as work, 72
women's career choices and, 74–75
government positions, women in, 18, 19, 146
grassroots level of feminist politics, 144–45
Green, Penelope ("Books of Style: For Men from Venus"), 180 (n24)
Greenberg, David F. (*The Construction of Homosexuality*), 201 (n32)
Greenberg, Joel ("Portrait of an Angry Young Arab Woman"), 200 (n17); ("2 Girls Divided by War, Joined in Carnage"), 200 (n17)
Greer, Germaine (*The Change: Women, Aging, and the Menopause*), 182 (n44)
Gregory, Michele ("Women on the Line: A Qualitative Study of Gender and Sexuality in the Advertising and Computing Industries"), 196 (n44)
Greif, Geoffrey L. (*Single Fathers*), 189 (n33)
Grewal, Inderpal, and Caren Kaplan (*Scattered Hegemonies: Postmodernity and Transnational Feminist Practice*), 207 (n43)
Gross, Jane ("Dividing the Sexes, for the Tough Years"), 179 (n12); ("U.S. Fund for Tower Victims Will Aid Some Gay Partners"), 199 (n13)
grounded theory, 31
Groves, Sharon ("Afghan Women Speak Out"), 202 (n48)

Hagen, Susan, and Mary Carouba (*Women at Ground Zero: Stories of Courage and Compassion*), 198 (n5), 199 (n10)

Halberstam, Judith (*Female Masculinity*), 185 (n70)
Halving It All (Deutsch), 59–60
Handy, Charles ("Going against the Grain: Working Couples and Greedy Occupations"), 186 (n2)
Haney, Lynne, and Miranda March ("Married Fathers and Caring Daddies: Welfare Reform and the Discursive Politics of Paternity"), 187 (n11)
Haraway, Donna J., 33, 134; (*Modest_ Witness©Second_Millenium. Female Man;cW.MeetsOncoMouse™: Feminism and Technoscience*), 185 (n66); (*Primate Visions*), 187 (n16); ("Situated Knowledges: The Science Question in Feminism and the Privilege of Partial Perspective"), 205 (n12), 210 (n18)
Harding, Sandra, 134; (*Is Science Multicultural? Postcolonialisms, Feminisms, and Epistemologies*), 205 (n12); (*The Science Question in Feminism*), 205 (n 12); (*Whose Science? Whose Knowledge? Thinking from Women's Lives*), 205 (n12)
Harrison, Wendy Cealey, and John Hood-Williams (*Beyond Sex and Gender*), 181 (n31)
Hartmann, Heidi I. ("Capitalism, Patriarchy, and Job Segregation by Sex"), 187 (n9)
Hartsock, Nancy C. M. (*The Feminist Standpoint Revisited and Other Essays*), 210 (n15); (*Money, Sex, and Power: Toward a Feminist Historical Materialism*), 210 (n16)
Hawkesworth, Mary, 149; ("The Semiotics of Premature Burial: Feminism in a Postfeminist Age"), 208 (n46)
health care system, 36
government programs for children, 42
Hearn, Jeff R. ("Men, Fathers, and the State: National and Global Relations"), 189 (n27)

Hearn, Jeff R., and Wendy Parkin (*Gender, Sexuality, and Violence in Organizations: The Unspoken Forces of Organization Violations*), 194 (n18)

hegemonic men, 116, 117–18

Hekman, Susan, 138 ("Beyond Identity: Feminism, Identity, and Identity Politics"), 205 (n20)

Hertz, Rosanna, and Nancy L. Marshall (*Working Families: The Transformation of the American Home*), 193 (n6)

Herzog, Hanna ("A Space of Their Own: Social-Civil Discourse among Palestinian-Israeli Women in Peace Organizations"), 204 (n5)

heterosexuality, 25

Heyman, Jody (*The Widening Gap: Why America's Working Families Are in Jeopardy and What Can Be Done About It*), 193 (n6), 194 (n15)

Heyzer, Noeleen ("Making a Nation More Equal"), 203 (n48)

hiring practices, 42, 78–79, 83
    in a world without gender, 167

Hobson, Barbara, 56

Hobson, Barbara, and David Morgan (introduction to *Making Men into Fathers*), 189 (n35)

Hochschild, Arlie Russell, 32, 73; ("Eavesdropping Children, Adult Deals, and Cultures of Care"), 191 (n52); (*The Time Bind: When Work Becomes Home and Home Becomes Work*), 193 (n6, n8), 211 (n21)

Hochschild, Arlie Russell, and Anne Machung (*The Second Shift: Working Parents and the Revolution at Home*), 191 (n 43), 208 (n6)

Holzer, Jenny, 3; ("The Age of Modernism: Art in the Twentieth Century"), 178 (n1)

homosexuality, 25, 123
    post-September uses of, 114–16

homosexuals
    female-to-male (FTM), 12

Hood-Williams, John (*Beyond Sex and Gender*), 181 (n31)

hooks, bell, 52; (*Ain't I a Woman: Black Women and Feminism*), 210 (n17); (*Feminist Theory: From Margin to Center*), 189 (n28), 210 (n17); (*Talking Back: Thinking Feminist, Talking Black*), 179 (n13)

housework as women's unpaid work, 6–7, 19, 42–43, 71, 91, 153

Howard, Jane Mary (*Inside Iran: Women's Lives*), 206 (n29)

Hrdy, Sarah Blaffer (Mother Nature: A History of Mothers, Infants, and Natural Selection), 187 (n16); (*The Woman That Never Evolved*), 187 (n16)

Hughes, Everett, 83–84; (*The Sociological Eye*), 195 (n27)

Hull, Gloria T., Patricia Bell Scott, and Barbara Smith (*All the Women are White, All the Blacks Are Men, but Some of Us Are Brave: Black Women's Studies*), 179 (n13)

"Hunks and Brutes," 104

hunting-gathering societies, 48

Hylland, Thomas Eriksen ("The Sexual Life of Nations: Notes on Gender and Nationhood"), 202 (n33)

Ibadi, Shirin, 128–29

identities, multiple, *see* multiple identities

Identity/Difference (Connelly), 139

ideology of degendering, 173

Idris, Wafa, 108–9

imagery, degendered, 173–74

individual, components of gender for the, 174–76

infants
    gendering of, 6, 29, 174
    in world without gender, 167, 174

inheritance, rules of, 18

"In Search of Balance: Medicine, Motherhood, and Madness," 86

International Monetary Fund, 154–55

Intersex Society of North America, 28

intersexuals, 13, 22–23, 28–29
Iran
 masculine prototypes in, 119
 status of women in, 122–23
Iraq
 invasion of 2003, 102, 108, 109–10, 127
 status of women in, 124, 128
Irigaray, Luce (*This Sex Which Is Not One*), 188 (n26); (*Speculum of the Other Woman*), 210 (n15)
Islamic women
 feminists, 124–27
 statuses of, 121–24
 suicide bombers, 108–9
Israel, 108
 family-work balance in, 75
 schism in Israeli feminism, 141
 Zionist feminists of prestate, 135
Israeli army, 9–10
Italy, dual-earner couples in, 87
Izraeli, Dafna Nundi, 135; ("Culture, Policy, and Women in Dual-Earner Families in Israel"), 193 (n12); ("Gender Politics in Israel: The Case of Affirmative Action for Women Directors"), 207 (n39); ("The Zionist Women's Movement in Palestine, 1911–1927"), 205 (n14)

Jackson, Robert Max, 152 (*Destined for Equality: The Inevitable Rise of Women's Status*), 180 (n17), 208 (n5)
Jacobs, Jerry A., 87, 89, 92–93; ("The Faculty Time Divide"), 196 (n42); (*Revolving Doors: Sex Segregation and Women's Careers*), 209 (n8)
Jacobs, Jerry A., and Kathleen Gerson; (*The Time Divide: Work, Family, and Gender Inequality*), 193 (n6), 196 (n32–35, n37), 197 (n46, n 57, n58)
Japan, hours of work in, 89
Johnson, Kirk ("In Bereavement, Pioneers on a Lonely Trail"), 199 (n11)
Jones, Richard Lezin ("Day of Honor and of Pain for 40,000"), 198 (n8)

Joseph, Gloria I., and Jill Lewis (*Common Differences: Conflicts in Black and White Feminist Perspectives*), 179 (n13)
Journal of the American Medical Women's Association, 86
justice, feminist theories of, 159–60, 160, 163

kaballah, 5, 168
Kabeer, Naila, and Ramya Subrahmanian (*Institutions, Relations, and Outcomes: A Framework and Case Studies for Gender-Aware Planning*), 209 (n9)
Kandiyoti, Deniz (*Women, Islam, and the State*), 203 (n49)
Kaplan, E. Anne ("Is the Gaze Male?"), 178 (n9)
Karpinski, Brig. Gen. Janis, 111
Kaye, Lenard W., and Jeffrey S. Applegate (*Men as Caregivers to the Elderly: Understanding and Aiding Unrecognized Family Support*), 210 (n20)
Kemper, Theodore D. (*Social Structure and Testosterone: Explorations of the Socio-Bio-Social Chain*), 187 (n15)
Kessler, Suzanne J. (*Lessons from the Intersexed*), 182 (n34), 185 (n55)
Kessler, Suzanne J., and Wendy McKenna (*Gender: An Ethnomethodological Approach*), 182 (n35)
Khanna, Ranjana, 141–42, 147; ("Ethical Ambiguities and Specters of Colonialism"), 206 (n28), 207 (n43)
Khattak, Sabul Gul ("Violence and Home: Afghan Women's Experience of Displacement"), 203 (n48)
Khuzai, Raja Habib, and Songul Chapouk ("Iraq's Hidden Treasure"), 203 (n48)
Killian, Caitlan ("The Other Side of the Veil: North African Women in France Respond to the Headscarf Affair"), 203 (n52)
Kim, Richard ("The Descent of Marriage?"), 192 (n56)
Kimmel, Michael S., 30–31, 112–13, 120; ("Declarations of War"), 201

(n21); (Gender, Class, and Terrorism"), 202 (n43); ("Globalization and its Mal(e)contents: The Gendered Moral and Political Economy of Terrorism"), 198 (n2), 201 (n21); ("Saving the Males: The Sociological Implications of the Virginia Military Institute and the Citadel"), 185 (n69)

Kimmel, Michael S., and Michael A Messner (*Men's Lives*), 210 (n17)

King, Deborah ("Multiple Jeopardy, Multiple Consciousness: The Context of a Black Feminist Ideology"), 179 (n13), 204 (n10)

kinship, degendered, 172

Kirkpatrick, David D. ("Jessica Lynch Criticizes U.S. Accounts of Her Ordeal"), 201 (n21)

Knoke, David, and James H. Kulinski (*Network Analysis*), 184 (n61)

Kristof, Nicholas, 110; ("A Woman's Place"), 200 (n20); ("Saving Private Jessica"), 201 (n21); ("Iraq's Little Secret"), 203 (n48)

Kristeva, Julia (""Women's Time"), 196 (n38)

Kuumba, M. Bahati ("A Cross-Cultural Race/Class/Gender Critique of Contemporary Population Policy: The Impact of Globalization"), 209 (n9)

labor unions, 76

LaGuardia Community College, 119–20

Lamb, Michael E., 53; ("Introduction: The Emergent American Father"), 189 (n30)

Lamm, Norman (*The Religious Thought of Hasidism: Text and Commentary*), 211 (n29)

Landry, Bart (*Black Working Wives: Pioneers of the American Family Revolution*), 187 (n11)

Langewiesche, William, 104, 117, 118; (*American Ground: Unbuilding the World Trade Center*), 198 (n4, n5), 199 (n12), 202 (n35–38)

language
  gender and, 16, 33–34
  of parenting, 40–41
  in a world without gender, 168

Laqueur, Thomas, 41; ("The Facts of Fatherhood"), 186 (n5); (*Making Sex: Body and Gender from the Greeks to Freud*), 182 (n39)

Laraña, Enrique, Hank Johnson, and Joseph R. Gusfield (*New Social Movements: From Ideology to Identity*), 204 (n4)

Law, Jules, 50; ("The Politics of Breastfeeding: Assessing Risk, Dividing Labor"), 188 (n24)

Lem, Stanislaw, 69; ("The Twenty-fourth Voyage"), 192 (n2)

Lennon, Mary Clare, 32

Lennon, Mary Clare, and Sarah Rosenfeld ("Relative Fairness and the Division of Housework: The Importance of Options"), 185 (n63)

lesbian parents, 58
  division of labor between, 45, 58–59
  studies of children of, 63

lesbians
  male-to-female (MTF), 12
  September 11 and, 107

Lessing, Doris (*The Golden Notebook*), 177 (n1)

Levey, Tania, and Catherine B. Silver ("Gender and Value Orientations: What's the Difference?! The Case of U.S. and Japan"), 185 (n64)

Levine, James A., 40–41; ("The Other Working Parent"), 186 (n4)

Lichtblau, Eric ("Whistle-Blowing Said to Be Factor in F.B.I. Firing"), 195 (n28)

lifecycle, effects of gender throughout the, xiii

Lipton, Eric ("In Cold Numbers, a Census of the Sept. 11 Victims"), 202 (n37)

Loder, Asjylyn ("Female First Responders, Gays Push for 9-11 Equity"), 199 (n13)

Lorber, Judith (*Paradoxes of Gender*), 177
    (n2), 209 (n15), 211 (n26, n1); ("It's
    the 21st Century—Do You Know
    What Gender You Are?"), 177 (n3);
    ("Using Gender to Undo Gender: A
    Feminist Degendering Movement"),
    177 (n3), 180 (n19); ("Crossing Bor-
    ders and Erasing Boundaries: Para-
    doxes of Identity Politics"), 177 (n3);
    ("Beyond the Binaries: Depolarizing
    the Categories of Sex, Sexuality, and
    Gender"), 177 (n2); ("Dismantling
    Noah's Ark"), 178 (n5), 209 (n12);
    ("Guarding the Gates: The Micro-
    politics of Gender"), 195 (n25)
Lorber, Judith, and Lisa Jean Moore
    (*Gender and the Social Construction
    of Illness*), 182 (n37), 186
    (n73)
love in a world without genders, 166–67
Lundgren, Lena M., Jennifer Fleischer-
    Cooperman, Robert Schneider, and
    Therese Fitzgerald ("Work, Family,
    and Gender in Medicine: How Do
    Dual-Earners Decide Who Should
    Work Less?"), 193 (n5)
Lynch, Pfc. Jessica, 110–11, 112

McAdam, Doug ("Gender as a Mediator of
    the Activist Experience: The Case of
    Freedom Summer"), 205 (n15)
McAlister, Melani ("Abu Ghraib as Sym-
    bol"), 201 (n21)
McCall, Leslie, 160; (*Complex Inequality:
    Gender, Class, and Race in the New
    Economy*), 177 (n6), 179 (n9), 210
    (n17, n19)
McClary, Susan (*Feminine Endings: Music,
    Gender, and Sexuality*) 178 (n9)
McCloskey, Deirdre, 27; (*Crossing: A Mem-
    oir*), 183 (n50)
McDowell, Linda (*Capital Culture: Gender
    at Work in the City*), 195 (n25)
MacDonald, Eileen (*Shoot the Women First*),
    200 (n18)
MacFarlane, Alex, 29

MacKinnon, Catherine A. (*Toward a Femi-
    nist Theory of the State*), 209 (n15)
mainstreaming, 8–9, 142, 157, 163
    degendering distinguished from, xiv
Majors, Richard, and Janet Mancini Bill-
    son (*Cool Pose: The Dilemmas of Black
    Manhood in America*), 210 (n17)
Malone, Kareen, and Rose Cleary
    ("(De)Sexing the Family: Theorizing
    the Social Science of Lesbian Fami-
    lies"), 190 (n40)
Mansbridge, Jane, and Katherine Flaster
    ("The Cultural Politics of Everyday
    Discourse: The Case of 'Male Chau-
    vinism' "), 185 (n67)
Maria Theresa, 18
marital status, degendered, 174
Markowitz, Lisa, and Karen W. Tice
    ("Paradoxes of Professionalization:
    Parallel Dilemmas in Women's Or-
    ganizations in the Americas"), 207
    (n35)
Marriott, Michel ("For Venus and Mars, a
    Midpoint Design"), 180 (n 24)
Martin, Patricia Yancey, 69; ("Gender
    as Social Institution"), 180 (n16);
    (" 'Mobilizing Masculinities': Women's
    Experiences of Men at Work"), 195
    (25); (" 'Said and Done' versus 'Say-
    ing and Doing': Gendering Practices,
    Practicing Gender at Work"), 180
    (n19), 192 (n1), 195 (n22)
Martin, Patricia Yancey, and Shirley
    Harkreader ("Multiple Gender Con-
    texts and Employee Rewards), 195
    (n24)
Marx, Karl, 165
marxist feminists theories, 43–44, 158
Masculinities (Connell), 118
masculinity, post-September 11 uses of,
    112–16
maternity leave, 74, 76, 97
matrices of dominance, xii, 143
media after September 11, gender por-
    trayed by, *see* September 11, gender
    after

Melucci, Alberto, (*Nomads of the Present: Social Movements and Individual Needs in Contemporary Society*), 204 (n4)

Mennino, Sue Falter, and April Brayfield ("Job-Family Trade-offs: The Multidimensional Effects of Gender"), 193 (n13)

menopause, 23

menstruation, 23

mentoring, 72, 83

Mernissi, Fatima (*Beyond the Veil: Male-Female Dynamics in Modern Muslim Society*), 203 (n49); (*The Veil and the Male Elite: A Feminist Interpretation of Women's Rights in Islam*), 203 (n49)

Middle Eastern men, statuses of, 119–21

Middle Eastern women, *see* Islamic women

Mies, Maria (*The Lace Makers of Narsapur: Indian Housewives Produce for the World Market*), 196 (n39)

Mies, Maria, Veronika Bennholdt-Thomsen, and Claudia von Werlhof (*Women: The Last Colony*), 209 (n9)

Miller, John C. (" 'My Daddy Loves Your Daddy': A Gay Father Encounters a Social Movement"), 190 (n39)

Mindry, Deborah ("Nongovernmental Organizations, 'Grassroots,' and the Politics of Virtue"), 207 (n44)

misogynist views of women, 162

Mitchell, Juliet (*Psychoanalysis and Feminism*), 210 (n15)

Modood, Tariq ("Muslims and the Politics of Multiculturalism in Britain"), 202 (n41)

Moen, Phyllis ("Integrative Careers: Time In, Time Out, and Second Acts"), 193 (n10); (*It's about Time: Couples and Careers*), 193 (n6)

Moen, Phyllis, and Shin-Kap Han ("Gendered Careers: A Life-Course Perspective"), 193 (n10)

Moen, Phyllis, Ronit Waismel-Manor, and Stephen Sweet ("Success"), 197 (n52)

Moghadam, Valentine M., 146; ("Islamic Feminism and Its Discontents: Towards a Resolution of the Debate"), 203 (49); (*Patriarchy and Development: Women's Positions at the End of the Twentieth Century*), 209 (n9); ("Revolution, Religion, and Gender Politics: Iran and Afghanistan Compared"), 202 (n46); ("Transnational Feminist Networks: Collective Action in an Era of Globalization"), 207 (n40)

Mohanty, Chandra Talpade, 130; (*Feminism without Borders: Decolonizing Theory, Practicing Solidarity*), 204 (n1)

Molotch, Harvey ("The Restroom and Equal Opportunity"), 185 (n71)

"mommy tax," 42

Morgan, David, 56

Morris, Jan (*Conundrum*), 183 (n50)

Morrow, Betty Hearn, 107

motherhood
    degendering parenting, *see* parenting, degendering
    expectations in Western societies, 45
    used to delimit women's opportunities, 36, 42
    see also parenting, degendering

Ms. magazine, 156

Muhammad, Ozier, 110

mullahs of Iran, 119

multicultural feminism, 133–34, 159

multidimensional research methods, 30–33

multiple identities, 7–8, 12, 131–33, 138, 148, 155, 165, 174

multitasking, 96

Mulvey, Laura (*Visual and Other Pleasures*), 178 (n9)

Murray, Stephen O., and Will Roscoe (*Boy-Wives and Female Husbands: Studies of African Homosexualitites*), 180 (n20)

Muschamp, Herbert ("In the Land of the Free, Who Wears the Skirts?"), 208 (n2)

Myers, Steven Lee ("From Dismal Chechnya, Women Turn to Bombs"), 200 (17)

Myre, Greg ("Gaza Mother, 22, Kills Four Israelis in Suicide Bombing"), 200 (n17)

Namaste, Ki, 13; ("'Tragic Misreadings': Queer Theory's Erasure of Transgender Subjectivity"), 179 (n14)
Naples, Nancy A. (*Grassroots Warriors: Activist Mothering, Community Work, and the War on Poverty*), 207 (n33)
Naples, Nancy A., and Manisha Desai (*Women's Activism and Globalization: Linking Local Struggles and Transnational Politics*), 207 (n34)
National Organization for Women, 105
National Survey of Families and Households, 61–62
Nentwich, Julia C. ("Doing Difference and Equality in a Swiss Organization"), 186 (n4)
Netherlands, gender equality efforts in, 149
Network of East-West Women, 146–47
Newman, Andrew ("Back on the Beat in Her Hoboken and Identity Later"), 183 (n50)
New York City Fire Department, 117
New Yorker, 115
New York Times, 11, 70, 104, 105, 106, 109, 112, 115, 119; ("About Town: Skirts for Men"), 208 (n2); ("Facing Combat"), 200 (n19); ("A Fire Captain's Eulogy"), 201 (n26); ("The Road to Gay Marriage," editorial), 192 (n54); "Policewoman's Remains Found at Trade Center"), 198 (n8)
NGOs (nongovernmental organizations), feminist politics and, 45, 144, 147
Nieves, Evelyn ("Passenger on Jet: Gay Hero or Hero Who Was Gay"), 201 (29)
Nicholas, Justine ("Changing Gender without Changing Jobs"), 183 (n40)
night work, 90
9/11 Commission, 107

Nochlin, Linda (*Women, Art, and Power and Other Essays*), 178 (n9)
Norway
  breastfeeding in, 49
  gender equality in, 164
nurturance and bonding, 41, 161
  belief in gender differences in, 21, 46, 47, 48, 55

Oakley, Ann (*Gender on Planet Earth*), 178 (n2)
Obermeyer, Carla Mahklouf ("Female Genital Surgeries: The Known, the Unknown, and the Unknowable"), 206 (n27)
off-site work, 94
Okin, Susan Moller, 62; (*Justice, Gender, and the Family*), 191 (n48), 192 (n57), 210 (n19)
Oláh, Livia Sz., Eva M. Bernhardt, and Frances K. Goldscheider ("Coresidential Paternal Roles in Industrialized Countries: Sweden, Hungary, and the United States"), 189 (n36)
organizational/activational theory, 46
organizational citizenship, 73
Orloff, Ann Shola, and Renée Monson ("Citizens, Workers, or Fathers? Men in the History of U.S. Social Policy"), 189 (n36)
Orrange, Robert M., Francille M. Firebaugh, and Ramona K. Z. Heck ("Managing Households"), 196 (n31)
Oudshoorn, Nelly (*Beyond the Natural Body: An Archeology of Sex Hormones*), 181 (n32)
oxytocin, 47
Oyěwúmí, Oyèrónké, 24; (*The Invention of Women: Making an African Sense of Western Gender Discourses*), 180 (n23), 182 (n41), 211 (n28); ("Deconfounding Gender: Feminist Theorizing and Western Culture, a Comment on Hawkesworth's 'Confounding Gender' "), 182 (n40)

Paige, Karen Ericksen, and Jeffrey M.
Paige (*The Politics of Reproductive Ritual*), 189 (n29)
Palestinian women suicide bombers,
108–9
Paley, Grace, 39
Paley, Grace ("Fathers"), 186 (n1)
Paradoxes of Gender (Lorber), xi, 5, 165–
66, 171
paradoxes of gender identity, 139–43
parental leave, 42
parenting, degendering, 39–68
    to achieve gender equality, 41–45
    assumptions about gendered division of
        labor, 39–40, 43, 71, 77, 98
    biological hurdles to, 45–48
    breast-feeding and shared parenting,
        48–50
    burnout, 73
    career demands and, 40, 72–78, 85–
        88, 99–101
    cash-versus-care dimensions of father-
        hood, 56
    child care as women's unpaid work, 6–
        7, 19
    children's response to, 62–64
    language of, 40–41
    men's turn to parent, 52–57
    psychological hindrances to, 51–52, 55
    shared parenting, 39, 40, 41, 44, 48–
        50, 53, 57–62, 73–74, 161
    skills of parenting, on-the-job learning
        of, 54–55
    stay-at-home fathers, 40
    structuring degendered households for
        equality, 64–68
parity, 9–10, 166
part-time work, 42, 45, 94
Pashtun men, 115
Patai, Raphael (*The Hebrew Goddess*), 211
    (n29)
paternal leave, 76, 97
paternity, state policies on, 56
patriarchal privilege and dominance, xii,
    159, 164
    historically, 18

loop-back effect of gendered family
    structure and, 43–44
pensions, 42
Pentagon bombing of September 11, part-
    ners of lesbians and gay men killed
    in, 107
personalities, degendered, 173, 175
Philologos ("On Language: Those Are the
    Breaks"), 178 (n4)
Pitts, Leonard, Jr., 55; (*Becoming Dad:
    Black Men and the Journey to Father-
    hood*), 189 (n31, n34)
Pitt-Catsouphes, Marcie, and Bradley K.
    Googins (*The Evolving World of Work
    and Family: New Stakeholders, New
    Voices*), 193 (n6)
Polgreen, Lydia ("Families Savor Their
    Victory over Grief and a Reluctant
    Government"), 199 (n12)
police as heroes after September 11, 104–6
politics, women in, 18, 19, 146
population policies, 153, 155
Poster, Winifred R. ("Dangerous Places
    and Nimble Fingers: Discourses
    of Gender Discrimination and
    Rights in Global Corporations"),
    194 (n18), 196 (n40); ("Globaliza-
    tion, Gender, and the Workplace:
    Women and Men in an American
    Multinational Corporation in India"),
    196 (n40)
postmodern feminists, xii
Potuchek, Jean L. (*Who Supports the Fam-
    ily? Gender and Breadwinning in
    Dual-Earner Marriages*), 187 (n8)
pregnancy, 23
"pre-op transsexuals," 12
Preves, Sharon E. (*Intersex and Identity:
    The Contested Self*), 184 (n56)
procreative choices
    in degendered society, 174
    restrictions on women's, 19, 36, 153
promotion practices, 42, 80
property ownership, rules of, 18
psychoanalytic theory, 158, 160, 162
    gendered parenting and, 51–52, 55

Purkayastha, Bandana, and Rosalie Torres Stone ("Ethnicity, Gender, Place, and Earnings: The Case of Asian Indian, Filipino, and White Women"), 205 (n13)

Purnick, Joyce ("A Whistle Still Ringing in Wall St. Ears"), 195 (n28)

queers, 26–29

race, *see* multiple identities

Rahman, Momin, and Anne Witz ("What Really Matters: The Elusive Quality of the Material in Feminist Thought"), 182 (n36)

Rantalaiho, Lisa, and T. Heiskanen (*Gendered Practices in Working Life*), 193 (n12)

Raymond, Janice G., 27; (*The Transsexual Empire: The Making of the She-male*), 183 (n52)

Read, Jen'nan Ghazal, and John P. Bartkowski ("To Veil or Not to Veil? A Case Study of Identity Negotiation among Muslim Women in Austin, Texas"), 203 (n52)

Reinharz, Shulamit (*Feminist Methods in Social Research*), 184 (n61)

religion
  gender and, 34
  in a world without gender, 168

reproductive choices, restrictions on women's, 19, 36, 153

research methods, multidimensional, 30–33

Reskin, Barbara F. ("Bringing the Men Back In: Sex Differences and the Devaluation of Women's Work"), 181 (n30)

Reskin, Barbara F., and Patricia A. Roos (*Job Queues: Explaining Women's Inroads into Male Occupations*), 209 (n8)

Reskin, Barbara F., and Catherine Ross ("Jobs, Authority, and Earnings among Managers: The Continuing Significance of Sex"), 194 (n18)

Revolutionary Association of the Women of Afghanistan (RAWA), 124

Reynolds, Jeremy ("When Too Much Is Not Enough: Actual and Preferred Work Hours in the United States and Abroad"), 196 (n36)

Rhode, Deborah L. (*Theoretical Perspectives on Sexual Difference*), 209 (n15)

Rich, Adrienne ("Compulsory Heterosexuality and Lesbian Existence"), 188 (n26)

Rich, Frank, 102, 111–12; ("How Kerry Became a Girlie-Man"), 197 (n1); ("Pfc. Jessica Lynch Isn't Rambo Anymore"), 201 (n21); ("Saving Private England"), 201 (n21)

Richards, Renée (Second Serve), 183 (n50)

Ridgeway, Cecilia, 81–82; ("Interaction and the Conservations of Gender Inequality: Considering Employment"), 194 (n18), 195 (n24)

Ridgeway, Cecilia, and Shelley J. Correll ("Unpacking the Gender System: A Theoretical Perspective on Gender Beliefs and Social Relations"), 195 (n25)

Riley, Denise (*Am I That Name? Feminism and the Category of Women in History*), 180 (n23)

Risman, Barbara J., 55, 60, 62–63; ("Gender as Social Structure"), 180 (n19); (*Gender Vertigo: American Families in Transition*), 190 (n38), 191 (n44, n49); ("Intimate Relationships from a Microstructural Perspective: Men Who Mother"), 189 (n33)

Risman, Barbara J., Maxine P. Atkinson, and Stephen P. Blackwelder ("Understanding the Juggling Act: Gendered Preferences and Social Structural Constraints"), 193 (n12)

Roberts, Celia (" 'A Matter of Embodied Fact': Sex Hormones and the History of Bodies"), 181 (n32)

Roehling, Patricia V., Phyllis Moen, and Rosemary Batt ("Spillover"), 197 (n52) role models for fathers, 55

Rosenfeld, Sarah, 32

Rossi, Alice, 45–46; ("A Biosocial Perspective on Parenting"), 187 (n12); ("Equality between the Sexes: An Immodest Proposal"), 187 (n12); ("Gender and Parenthood"), 187 (n12)

Rothman, Barbara Katz, 50, 131; ("Existential Orphanhood and Identity Politics: On Jews, Dwarfs, and Gays"), 204 (n3); (*Recreating Motherhood: Ideology and Technology in a Patriarchal Society*), 188 (n23)

Roughgarden, Joan (*Evolution's Rainbow: Diversity, Gender, and Sexuality in Nature and People*), 181 (n32)

routinizing the radical, 99–101

Rowley, Coleen, 84–85

Rubin, Gayle ("Thinking Sex: Notes for a Radical Theory of the Politics of Sexuality"), 182 (n45)

Ruddick, Sara (*Maternal Thinking: Toward a Politics of Peace*), 186 (n1)

Rupp, Leila J., 133

Rupp, Leila J., and Verta Taylor (Drag Queens at the 801 Cabaret), 183 (n47); ("Forging Feminist Identity in an International Movement: A Collective Identity Approach to Twentieth-Century Feminism"), 204 (n9)

Rust, Paula C. Rodríguez (*Bisexuality in the United States*), 182 (n42)

Rwanda, 19

Sanchez, Laura, and Elizabeth Thomson ("Becoming Mothers and Fathers: Parenthood, Gender, and the Division of Labor"), 191 (n47)

Sanderson, Susan, and Verta L. Sanders Thompson ("Factor Associated with Perceived Paternal Involvement in Childrearing"), 191 (n47)

Sapolsky, Robert M., and Lisa J. Share ("A Pacific Culture among Wild Baboons: Its Emergence and Transmission"), 187 (n14)

Sasson-Levy, Orna, and Sarit Amram ("Gender Chaos in the Officer Training School"), 179 (n7)

Saudi Arabia, 164

Schachet, Carol ("Talking Politics with Barbara Smith"), 204 (n 7)

Schacht, Steven P. ("Lesbian Drag Kings and the Feminine Embodiment of the Masculine"), 183 (n47); ("Four Renditions of Doing Female Drag: Feminine Appearing Conceptual Variations of a Masculine Theme"), 183 (n47)

Schell, Jonathan, 165; ("No More into the Breach"), 211 (n24)

Scholem, Gershon (*On the Kabbalah and Its Symbolism*), 178 (n4)

Sciolino, Elaine ("A Prize, Laureate Says, 'Good for Democracy'"), 202 (n47)

Scott, Joan Wallach, 139, 152, 159; ("Deconstructing Equality-versus-Difference: Or, the Uses of Post-Structuralist Theory for Feminism"), 208 (4), 210 (n18); (*Gender and the Politics of History*), 180 (n23); (*Only Paradoxes to Offer: French Feminists and the Rights of Man*), 206 (n23)

Scott, Melissa (*Shadow Man*), 184 (n57)

Second Shift, The (Hochschild), 32

second wave of feminism, 132

Seidman, Gay W. ("Gendered Citizenship: South Africa's Democratic Transition and the Construction of a Gendered State"), 207 (n38)

self-employed, 90

self-identification, multiple identities and, 7–8, 12, 131–33, 138, 148, 155, 165, 174

Sen, Amartya ("Rational Fools: A Critique of the Behavioral Foundation of Economic Theory"), 192 (n4)

Sen, Gita, Asha George, and Priosko Ostlin (*Engendering International Health: The Challenge of Equity*), 186 (n72)

sense of self, 23
  gender and, xiii
September 11, gender and, 102–29
  American men's statuses, 116–19
  heroes, 104–106, 127
  Islamic women's statuses, 121–24
  "maidens in distress," 111, 127
  Middle Eastern men's statuses, 119–21
  the new normal, 127–29
  uses of homosexuality, 114–16
  uses of masculinity, 112–16
  widows, 106–8, 127
  women warriors, 108–12, 127
September 11th Victim Compensation
    Fund, 107
Sevenhuijsen, Selma ("The Place of Care:
    The Relevance of the Feminist Ethic
    of Care for Social Policy"), 177 (n8),
    193 (n7)
sexual harassment, 83, 153
sexuality
  denial of binary nature of, 22, 25
  gender scripts for, 25
  in a world without genders, 166–67
sexual orientations, degendered, 175
sexual scripts, degendered, 172
Shaheed, Farida, 126; ("Controlled or Au-
    tonomous: Identity and the Experi-
    ence of the Network, Women Living
    under Muslim Laws"), 203 (n51)
shared parenting, see parenting, degendering
shari'ah, 102
Sharoni, Simone ("Gender in Conflict: The
    Palestinian-Israeli Conflict through
    Feminist Lenses"), 204 (n5)
Showalter, Elaine (The New Feminist Criti-
    cism: Essays on Women, Literature, and
    Theory), 178 (n9)
sick leave, 97
Signs ("Roundtable: Gender and Septem-
    ber 11"), 198 (n2); ("Roundtable:
    September 11 and Its Aftermath:
    Voices from Australia, Canada, and
    Africa"), 198 (n2); ("Forum: The
    Events of 11 September 2001 and
    Beyond"), 198 (n2)

single mothers, 78
  in socialist societies, 44
  state support in U.S. for, 56
Silver, Catherine B. ("Gendered Identities
    in Old Age: Toward (De)gender-
    ing?"), 182 (n38)
Slade, Margo ("Have Pump, Will Travel:
    Combining Breast-Feeding and a Ca-
    reer"), 188 (n22)
Smith, Barbara, 131–32
Smith, Calvin D. (" 'Men Don't Do This
    Sort of Thing': A Case Study of the
    Social Isolation of Househusbands"),
    186 (n3)
Smith, Craig S. ("In Speech, Nobel Win-
    ner Rebukes the U.S."), 202 (n47)
Smith, Jackie ("Bridging Global Divides?
    Strategic Framing and Solidarity in
    Transnational Social Movement Or-
    ganizations"), 207 (n36)
Smith, Moira Ann, 105
social construction gender theory, 15, 20,
    21, 23–24, 130
  doing gender and creating structure,
    16–20
social control, xiii
  degendered, 173
social institution, gender as, xi, 4, 5
  changes in a degendered society, 171–
    74
  importance of dismantling, 13–16
socialist economies, 44
Solomon, Deborah ("Life after Whistle-
    Blowing"), 195 (n28)
South Africa, constitution of, 146
Spakes, Patricia ("Women, Work, and Ba-
    bies: Family-Labor Market Policies
    in Three European Countries"), 193
    (n7)
Spalter-Roth, Roberta ("ASA Issues Offi-
    cial Statement on Importance of Col-
    lecting Data on Race"), 184 (n59)
Sparr, Pamela (Mortgaging Women's Lives:
    Feminist Critiques of Structural Adjust-
    ment), 209 (n9)
Spelman, Elizabeth (Inessential Woman:

Problems of Exclusion in Feminist Thought), 179 (n13)

Sperling, Valerie, Myra Marx Ferree, and Barbara Risman ("Constructing Global Feminism: Transnational Advocacy Networks and Russian Women's Activism"), 207 (n36)

Spivak, Gayatri Chakravorty (*In Other Worlds: Essays in Cultural Politics*), 210 (n17)

sports in a world without gender, 168

Squires, Judith ("Representing Groups, Deconstructing Identities"), 204 (n8)

Stacey, Judith, 63, 64–65; (*Brave New Families: Stories of Domestic Upheaval in Late-Twentieth-Century America*), 188 (n18); (*In the Name of the Family: Rethinking Family Values in the Postmodern Age*), 191 (n53)

Stacey, Judith, and Timothy Biblarz ("(How) Does the Sexual Orientation of Parents Matter?"), 191 (n50)

standpoint feminism, 134–36, 158–59, 160–61

Stanley, Alessandra ("In Hoopla over a P.O.W., a Mirror of U.S. Society"), 201 (n21)

Stone, Sandy, 27–28; ("The *Empire* Strikes Back: A Posttranssexual Manifesto"), 183 (n52)

Storr, Mel (*Bisexuality: A Critical Reader*), 182 (n42)

Straus, Anselm L., and Juliet Corbin (*Basics of Qualitative Research: Grounded Theory Procedures and Techniques*), 184 (n61)

stress response, 46–47

structural inequality, xii

structure of feminist politics, 144–48

subordinated men, 116–19

subordination, xii, 15, 34, 166
    multiple systems of, 133–34

Sullivan, Maureen ("Alma Mater: Family 'Outings' and the Making of the Modern Other Mother (MOM)"), 190 (n39)

Sullivan, Oriel ("Changing Gender Practices within the Household"), 196 (n43)

Sum, Andrew, Neeta Fogg, and Paul Harrington (*The Growing Gender Gaps in College Enrollment and Degree Attainment in the U.S. and Their Potential Economic and Social Consequences*), 181 (n25), 205 (n17)

surgical transformation of the body to change gender, 26–27

Sweden, 88, 149, 164
    dual-earner couples in, 87
    paternal care, programs to foster, 56–57, 97
    support for women as workers in, 97
    women in politics in, 19
    work-week flexibility in, 94

Taliban, 115, 123, 143

Taylor, Shelley, et al. ("Biobehavioral Responses to Stress in Females: Tend-and-Befriend, Not Fight or Flight"), 187 (n15)

Taylor, Verta, 133

Taylor, Verta, and Leila Rupp ("Women's Culture and Lesbian Feminist Activism: A Reconsideration of Cultural Feminism"), 210 (n15)

Taylor, Verta, and Nancy Whittier ("Gender and Social Movements"), 181 (n29)

testosterone, 22, 47

Tewksbury, Richard ("Conformity Pressures and Gender Resistance among Transgendered Individuals"), 183 (n48)

theocracies, 34

Thompson, Becky ("Multiracial Feminism: Recasting the Chronology of Second Wave Feminism"), 179 (n13)

Time, 84, 85

Tobin, Terri, 105

Toren, Nine, and Dahlia Moore ("Family and Work Go Well Together: Changes in the Perceptions and Pref-

Toren, Nine, and Dahlia Moore (*cont.*) erences of Working Women in Israel"), 194 (n14)

transgendering, 26–29
  factions within the transgender community, 140

transnational feminism, 146–48
  divisions within, 141–42

Transsexual Empire, The (Raymond), 27

transsexuals, 26, 27
  "pre-op," 12
  transitioning, 13

transversal politics, 145

transvestism, 26

Trinh, T. Minh-ha (*Women, Native, Other: Writing Postcolonialty and Feminism*), 210 (n17)

Tronto, Joan ("Time's Place"), 177 (n8), 196 (n38)

Turner, Heather A., Robert B. Hays, and Thomas J. Coates ("Determinants of Social Support among Gay Men: The Context of AIDS"), 211 (n20)

Turner, Stephanie S. ("Intersex Identities: Locating New Intersections of Sex and Gender"), 184 (n56)

Uchitelle, Louis ("A Transsexual Economist's 2d Transition: She Says Gender Determines One's Approach to Her Field"), 183 (n51)

undoing gender, xiii, 8–10

Undoing Gender (Butler), 157

unions, 76

United Kingdom, dual-earner couples in, 87

United Nations conferences, 147
  Beijing Conference on Women, 146

United Nations Development Fund for Women, 149

U.S. Congress, women in the, 19

U.S. Department of Labor, Bureau of Labor Statistics, Report 972; ("Highlights of Women's Earnings in 2002"), 194 (n19)

U.S. National Study of the Changing Workforce, 88

universities
  academics, time demands on, 90
  affirmative action in, 11
  transgender students at, demands of, 28

Vaid, Urvashi, 142; (*Virtual Equality: The Mainstreaming of Gay and Lesbian Liberation*), 206 (n30)

Valentine, David (" 'I Went to Bed with My Own Kind Once': The Erasure of Desire in the Nature of Identity"), 185 (n65); ("We're 'Not about Gender': The Uses of Transgender"), 185 (n65)

Valian, Virginia (*Why So Slow? The Advancement of Women*), 208 (n7)

Van den Wijngaard, Marianne (*Reinventing the Sexes: The Biomedical Construction of Femininity and Masculinity*), 181 (n32)

Vidal-Ortiz, Salvador ("Queering Sexuality and Doing Gender: Transgender Men's Identification with Gender and Sexuality"), 185 (n65)

virtual equality, 142

Vogel, Lise (*Mothers on the Job: Maternity Policy in the United States*), 194 (n16)

Wadud, Amina (*Qur'an and Women: Rereading the Sacred Text from a Women's Perspective*), 203 (n49)

Waite, Linda J., and Mark Nielsen ("The Rise of the Dual-Earner Family, 1963–1997"), 195 (n30)

Wajcman, Judy (*Managing Like a Man: Women and Men in Corporate Management*), 195 (n25)

Walby, Sylvia, 137; ("Beyond the Politics of Location: The Power of Argument in a Global Era"), 205 (n18)

Wald, Priscilla, 138

Wallerstein, Immanuel, and Joan Smith ("Households as an Institution of the World Economy"), 188 (n18)

Walters, Suzanna Danuta, 142–43; (*All the Rage: The Story of Gay Visibility in America*), 206 (n30); ("Sex, Text, and Context: (In) between Feminism and Cultural Studies"), 178 (n9)

Walzer, Michael (*Spheres of Justice: A Defense of Pluralism and Equality*), 179 (n9)

Ward, Jane, 143; (" 'Not All Differences Are Created Equal': Multiple Jeopardy in a Gendered Organization"), 206 (n30)

Washington Post, 111

Watkins, Sherron, 84–85

Weeks, Jeffrey, Catherine Donovan, and Brian Heaphy (*Same Sex Intimacies: Families of Choice and Other Life Experiments*), 187 (n11), 191 (n54)

Weinberg, Martin S., Colin J. Williams, and Douglas W. Pryor (*Dual Attraction: Understanding Bisexuality*), 182 (n42, n43)

Wendell, Susan (*The Rejected Body: Feminist Philosophical Reflections on Disability*), 182 (n44)

West, Candace, and Don Zimmerman ("Doing Gender"), 180 (n19)

wet nurses, 49

whistle-blowers, corporate, 84–85

Whittle, Stephen (*Respect and Equality: Transsexual and Transgender Rights*), 184 (n57)

Wickman, Jan, 140; (*Transgender Politics: The Construction and Deconstruction of Binary Gender in the Finnish Transgender Community*), 206 (n25)

Widows of September 11, 106–8, 127

Wilgroren, Jodi ("A New War Brings New Role for Women"), 200 (n20)

Williams, Christine L. ("The Glass Escalator: Hidden Advantages for Men in the 'Female' Professions"), 195 (n26)

Williams, Joan, 94–96; (*Unbending Gender: Why Family and Work Conflict and What to Do about It*), 193 (n6), 197 (n49, n50)

Williams, Sonya, and Shin-Kap Han ("Career Clocks: Forked Roads"), 193 (n10)

Williams, Walter L. (*The Spirit and the Flesh: Sexual Diversity in American Indian Culture*), 180 (n20)

Winters, Sgt. Jeanette L., 108–12

Wittig, Monique, 156; ("The Straight Mind"), 209 (n12)

Wizemann, Theresa M., and Mary-Lou Pardue (*Exploring the Biological Contributions to Human Health: Does Sex Matter?*), 186 (n72)

"Woman's Place, A," 110

Women at Ground Zero: Stories of Courage and Compassion (Hagen and Carouba), 105–6

Women Living under Muslim Laws (WLUML), 126, 147

work and workplace, xiii, 69–101
  actual and desired work hours, 88–89
  affirmative action in, 11, 83
  balance with family demands, 40, 72–78, 85–88, 99–101
  burnout, 73
  career demands and degendered parenting, *see* parenting, degendering, career demands and
  clash between changed families and unchanged organization of, 86–89
  common arrangements of dual-career families, 76–77
  compensation, gender and, 6, 19, 20, 42, 43–44, 57, 79–80, 82, 154, 167
  degendering the discourse about workers, 96–99
  division of labor in, gendered, 20, 71, 74, 78, 153, 154–55, 171–72
  double workload of women, 20, 153
  emotional needs and, 70, 71
  family caretaking as work, 72–73
  flextime, *see* flextime
  gendered organization of, 78–82
  gendered workers, 82–86
  gender segregation and stratification, 78, 82, 154

work and workplace (*cont.*)
  glass ceiling, 154
  global economy, gendered divisions of
    work in, 154–55
  hiring practices, *see* hiring practices
  housework, *see* housework
  ideal worker from management's per-
    spective, 75, 76
  informal organization of, 82–83
  insiders and outsiders, 83–85
  part-time, *see* part-time work
  promotion practices, *see* promotion
    practices
  second shift, recognizing the, 71
  sexual harassment policies, 83
  similarities in behavior of men and
    women in the, 82
  societal pressures on couples' career de-
    cisions, 70–71
  strategies for restructuring, 92–96
  the third shift, 71–72, 73
  time as valued resource, 89–92
  work, family, and citizenship, 72–78
  in a world without gender, 167
WorldCom, 84
World Health Organization ("Women's
  Health: Improve Our Health, Improve the World"), 209 (n9)
Wyatt, Edward ("Victims' Families Sense
  Influence on Ground Zero Plans is
  Waning"), 199 (n12)

"X: A Fabulous Child's Story," 156

Yanay, Niza, 114; ("Understanding Col-
  lective Hatred"), 201 (n28)
Yoon, Carol Kaesuk ("Scientist at Work:
  Joan Roughgarden; A Theorist with
  Personal Experience of the Divide
  between the Sexes"), 183 (n50)
Yorùbá society, precolonial, 24
Young, Iris Marion, 131, 163; ("Gender as
  Seriality: Thinking about Women as
  a Social Collective"), 204 (n6); (*Jus-
  tice and the Politics of Difference*), 205
  (n22), 210 (n19), 211 (n23); ("The
  Logic of Masculinist Protection: Re-
  flections on the Current Security
  State"), 198 (n2)
Yuval-Davis, Nita, 131, 145; (*Gender &
  Nation*), 207 (n37); ("The 'Multi-
  Layered Citizen': Citizenship in the
  Age of 'Glocalization' "), 204 (2)

Zihlman, Adrienne ("The Paleolithic
  Glass Ceiling: Women in Human
  Evolution"), 188 (n17)
Zinn, Maxine Baca ("Family, Feminism,
  and Race in America"), 206 (n24)
Zinn, Maxine Baca, and Bonnie Thornton
  Dill ("Theorizing Difference from
  Multiracial Feminism"), 204 (n10),
  210 (n17)